Japan, China, and
the modern world economy

Japan, China, and the modern world economy

Toward a reinterpretation of East Asian development ca. 1600 to ca. 1918

FRANCES V. MOULDER

Assistant Professor of Sociology
Rutgers University, Livingston College

CAMBRIDGE UNIVERSITY PRESS

CAMBRIDGE

LONDON   NEW YORK   MELBOURNE

Published by the Syndics of the Cambridge University Press
The Pitt Building, Trumpington Street, Cambridge CB2 1RP
Bentley House, 200 Euston Road, London NW1 2DB
32 East 57th Street, New York, NY 10022, USA
296 Beaconsfield Parade, Middle Park, Melbourne 3206, Australia

First published 1977
First paperback edition 1979

Printed in the United States of America
Typeset by Vail-Ballou Press, Inc., Binghamton, NY
Printed and bound by Hamilton Printing Company, Rensselear, NY

Library of Congress Cataloging in Publication Data

Moulder, Frances V
Japan, China and the modern world economy.
1.   Japan – Economic conditions – To 1868.   2.   Japan –
Economic conditions – 1868–1918.   3.   China – Economic
conditions – To 1644.   4.   China – Economic conditions –
1644–1912.   5.   Economic development – Social aspects.
6.   Industrialization. I.   Title.
HC462.M64 1976   330.9′51   76-2230
ISBN 0 521 21174 3

Contents

Preface

Japan is the only non-Western country to have become a major industrial capitalist nation. Why? The explanation is usually found in Japan's unique sociocultural traditions. Japan, alone among non-Western nations, allegedly possessed traditional institutions or values that promoted, rather than blocked, modern economic growth. When the Western powers arrived in "feudal" Japan in the 1850s, they confronted a society already ripe with change, ready to transform along capitalist lines.

Such explanations, however, overlook the international context of Japan's development. This study argues that the paramount influence in the rise of industrial capitalism in Japan was not Japan's unique "traditional society." Rather, Japan, unlike most of the other non-Western nations, occupied a position of relative autonomy within the nineteenth-century world political economy. For a variety of reasons, other societies were more strongly incorporated as economic and political satellites of one or more of the Western capitalist powers, which thwarted their ability to industrialize. In contrast, Japan, from the time it was "opened" in the 1850s, occupied a more autonomous position, which permitted an advance into industrialization within the capitalist system.

I have based my conclusions on a comparison of Japan with Imperial China. Japan has been frequently compared to China by advocates of the sociocultural explanation. "Traditional China" has been seen as a bureaucratic monolith, capable of containing all change. When the Western powers arrived in China in the late eighteenth and early nineteenth centuries, they supposedly met a society organized in opposition to capitalist development. This study concludes, in contrast, that China's location in the world political economy, dominated by the Western capitalist nations, must be considered of prime importance in China's failure to develop industrial capitalism during the nineteenth and early twentieth centuries. China was more strongly "incorporated" than Japan, and thus lacked the autonomy to develop the same way.

The introduction to this study considers the treatment of Japan and China by theorists of economic development, noting some of the problems in comparative studies done from both the socio-cultural and the world-economy perspective.

The study is divided into three parts. Part I is a comparison of Japan and China prior to the expansion of Western hegemony into East Asia (Ch'ing China, from the early seventeenth century to ca. 1820; Tokugawa Japan, from the early seventeenth century to ca. 1850). I argue that sociocultural or "traditional society" theorists have exaggerated the differences between Ch'ing China and Tokugawa Japan and I emphasize similarities between the two societies, in contrast to the societies of Western Europe during the decline of feudalism and the rise of capitalism.

Part II contrasts the degree to which Japan and China were incorporated into the world political economy during the nineteenth and early twentieth centuries and traces how and why China was more strongly incorporated than Japan.

Part III analyzes the impact of differing degrees of incorporation on the rise of industrial capitalism during the same period. In particular, I trace the consequences of the differing degrees of incorporation for two elements that have been important in capitalist industrialization: the growth of a centralized state and the ability of the state to carry out policies promoting national industrial development.

In the effort to compare "external" relationships and their consequences systematically, some may feel that I have unduly neglected important differences in traditional Japanese and Chinese values, ethics, religions, and economic, political, and social structures. If this be the case, it is not due to a conviction on my part that such differences among non-Western societies are irrelevant to understanding their transformation under the Western impact. However, the burden of this study is that these differences are perhaps not as decisive as has been claimed and that the positions of non-Western societies within the world economy are far more decisive for their transformation than has been assumed.

Although this study focuses on nineteenth- and early twentieth-century Japan and China, it has broader implications. I have argued that Japan could industrialize along capitalist lines primarily because it enjoyed a favorable situation in relation to nineteenth-century imperialism. China, not so situated, has begun to industrialize rapidly only since the Communist Revolution decisively broke the ties that chained China to the imperialist system.

Most nations of Asia, Africa, and Latin America have never stood in Japan's shoes. Like pre-1949 China, they have been firmly tied into a world system that disproportionately benefits others. And many of them have been locked into this system since the sixteenth century, far longer than China. The lessons of Japan and China for these nations would seem to be that if national industrialization is to occur, revolutionary Communist movements will be necessary to bring it about.

May those readers who deplore this conclusion bear in mind that the people of Japan may not have gotten such a good deal. Although we are often told that Japan and the other industrial capitalist nations are *developed*, this term obfuscates the reality for millions in the industrialized capitalist world: an inferior, deteriorating, and ever insecure living standard and a legal-political framework that hinders efforts of the people to organize for fundamental improvement. Which is more "developed" today, the People's Republic of China or Japan?

This study has certain strengths and weaknesses, stemming from its methodology, that should be stressed at the outset. This is a *sociological* study, not a work of history. My concern has been to analyze Japan and China for the light they shed on the sociological theory of economic change. My approach has been broadly comparative and historical. Based mainly on secondary sources and covering a period of several centuries, the study undoubtedly contains errors, omissions, and misinterpretations of data (although, hopefully, not too many). This is the potential weakness of comparative and historical sociology. The strength of the sociological method lies in the possibility of seeing old data in new ways.

I believe that the study of Asian development has too long suffered from a one-sided emphasis on sociocultural explanations. I hope this reinterpretation, stressing the significance of location within the capitalist world economy, will serve to orient future studies along more fruitful lines.

Acknowledgments

Many people have encouraged me in writing this study and aided me with their insights. I am especially grateful to Morton Fried, who introduced me to the critical study of Chinese institutions and was a source of encouragement and inspiration. I am also especially indebted to Terence K. Hopkins and Immanuel Waller-stein, who supervised the study when it was my doctoral disserta-tion at Columbia University and whose work on the comparative and historical development of national societies suggested the theoretical framework for the study. I am grateful to Koya Azumi, John C. Leggett, Dale L. Johnson, William J. Goode, James Nakamura, Kay Trimberger, Theda Skocpol, and Herbert Passin for going over the manuscript in its dissertation form and offering their comments, valuable suggestions, and encourage-ment. An earlier draft was read by Robert Hartwell, Fred-erick W. Henssler, Irving Louis Horowitz, John T. Moffett, and my father, W. J. Moulder. I am indebted to them for their com-ments and advice.

F. V. M.

Introduction

Japan and China in theories of development and underdevelopment

One cannot but be struck by the great differences among the various countries of East Asia in the speed and nature of their responses to the West in the past century. . . . These variations in response must be attributed mainly to the differences in the traditional societies of the countries of East Asia. Only such differences can explain why a basically similar impact could have brought such varied initial results . . . why relatively small Japan, for example, soon became a world power, while China sunk to the status of an international problem.

(Reischauer and Fairbank, *East Asia: The Great Tradition*, p. 670)

What was it that enabled Japan to take a course so radically different from that of all the other countries in the now underdeveloped world? . . . The answer to this question . . . comes down to the fact that Japan is the only country in Asia (and in Africa and in Latin America) that escaped being turned into a colony or dependency of Western European or American capitalism, that had a chance of independent national development.

(Baran, *The Political Economy of Growth*, p. 158)

Japan in theories of underdevelopment: "the exception that proves the rule"

The case of Japan is of great importance to theories of economic change. Japan was the first non-Western nation to become a major industrial power. Japan's industrialization also occurred early; it began in the latter part of the nineteenth century and was well under way by World War I. Thus Japan's industrialization occurred only somewhat later than that of more advanced Western nations, such as the United States, Germany, or France.

Today, over half a century later, Japan is *still* the only non-Western advanced industrial power. Although considerable economic progress has been made in several other non-Western nations since World War II (for instance, in the capitalist world, Brazil, and in the socialist world North Korea and China), none is highly industrialized and only China can be regarded as a world power, playing a significant, independent role in international power politics.

Japan was also the first "Third World" nation to become a major industrial power.[1] The term *Third World* refers to those countries of Asia, Africa, and Latin America that have been economically and politically dominated by the industrial capitalist nations. It is often forgotten (as least outside Japan) that Japan was partially controlled by the Western capitalist nations during the nineteenth century. Although Japan never became a formal colony, the country was forced to trade with the capitalist nations under a set of treaties that reduced national autonomy and set up obstacles to industrial development. Western observers during the nineteenth century were just as confident of their sway over Japan as over the other areas of Asia, Africa, and Latin America. "The Japanese are a happy race, and being content with little, are not likely to achieve much," wrote the *Japan Herald* in 1881.[2]

What accounts for Japan's unique transformation? Why do the other nations of the Third World remain underdeveloped? These two questions are intimately linked, and there is little agreement on the answers. There are currently two major theories of Third World underdevelopment, which I will term *traditional society* theories and *world economy* theories. These theories are contradictory, and the case of Japan has been utilized by theorists in each camp as "the exception that proves the rule."

Since World War II, the study of economic development in America and Western Europe has been dominated by a concern with how "traditional" social, cultural, and personality factors influence economic development or underdevelopment. Traditional society theories stem from the concerns established by Max Weber in his famous comparative studies of the "ethics" of the Chinese, Indian, Hebrew, and Protestant civilizations. Poverty in the Third World countries is attributed primarily to their social characteristics rather than to their relations with imperialist powers. To traditional society theorists, Japan is the exception – the only Third World nation that had a change-promoting indigenous social system.

Traditional society theories of Third World underdevelopment have been challenged in recent years by a perspective that emphasizes the relationship of Third World societies to the world political economy. World economy theories, which stem from the studies of Marx, Engels, and Lenin, attribute underdevelopment to the "satellite" or "dependent" position of the Third World nations in a world economy that is constructed to benefit the Western industrial nations. To world economy theorists, Japan is again the exception that proves the rule – the only Third World nation that escaped becoming a satellite of the Western powers.

Let us examine the traditional society and world economy theories more closely.

Traditional society theories

In traditional society theories, the influence of the industrial nations on the nonindustrial nations is seen as basically development promoting, and underdevelopment is analyzed as a function of native social, cultural, and personality factors that block development. The argument of such theories could be summarized as follows:

The industrial nations have historically provided a "stimulus" to economic growth in the non-Western world. First, they have supplied *economic* preconditions for development that were absent or insufficiently present in the Third World prior to contact with the industrial world. For instance, the "diffusion" of capital and modern technology from the West, the creation of new markets for traditional products, and the establishment of an "infrastructure" of economic development, such as railroads, public utilities, and modern banking, have created a potential for development that was hitherto lacking.[3]

Second, the industrial nations have supplied *social* preconditions for industrialization. For example, Eisenstadt speaks of "modernizing elites" that emerge to promote development in imitation of Western entrepreneurs and statesmen.[4] Rostow speaks of a "reactive nationalism," appearing under the threat of control by the more advanced nations, that leads political and military elites to "take the steps necessary to unhinge and transform the traditional society in such ways as to permit growth to become its normal condition."[5]

Underdevelopment persists despite all this because Third World societies are unable, due to their very nature, to "respond" adequately to the "stimulus" to industrialization. This is because they are basically "traditional"; they fail to encourage change and innovation. For example, they lack such value orientations and qualities of personality which promote industrialization as "universalism," "specificity," "achievement motivation," and the capacity to "empathize."[6]

Aspects of their social structures also block economic development. For example, caste, clan, guild, or village loyalties may hamper economic growth by restricting the efficient utilization of labor and blocking geographic and social mobility. Or powerful and corrupt official bureaucracies may hamper the operation of business enterprise by their irrational and unpredictable administrative policies and by heavy taxes on commerce.[7] In Rostow's words, traditional societies lack "the existence or quick emergence of a political, social and institutional framework which exploits the impulses to expansion in the modern sector."[8]

In sum, traditional society theories argue that Third World societies are by their very nature insufficiently "open" to the development-promoting world economy created by the industrial nations.

World economy theories make precisely the opposite argument. They see underdevelopment as a result of a too-great openness to the world economy.

World economy theories

In world economy theories, the influence of the industrial capitalist nations on the nonindustrial nations is seen as basically development blocking, not development promoting. Underdevelopment is analyzed as a function of the subordinate or satellite position of the underdeveloped nations in a world economy that provides disproportionate benefits to the industrial nations. The argument of such theories[9] might be summarized as follows:

The Western nations have forcibly turned the non-Western nations into their economic dependencies. In the earliest stages of this process the non-Western nations became primary-producing satellites, outposts supplying the industrial nations with raw materials and consuming the output of their industries. The industrial countries failed to promote industrial development in their satellites, which would have seriously competed with metropolitan industry: foreign investment concentrated in primary production – agricultural and mineral produce for export – rather than in industry.

At the same time, the industrial countries set up obstacles to indigenous efforts to promote industrialization. Native handicraft industries were ruined and the development of modern industries was hampered by the competition of manufactures from the metropole. This was accomplished through the elimination of tariff barriers in the satellites on imports from the metropole and through the establishment of tariff barriers in the metropole on manufactured imports from the satellites.[10] Industrialization was also hampered by the consequences of the economy's becoming "skewed" toward production of one or a few primary products for export. The fluctuation of prices of primary products on the world market deprives the satellite countries of a steady flow of funds for industrial development. The nation also becomes subject to *declining terms of trade,* that is, the trend toward declining prices of raw materials relative to manufactures, which makes it more and more difficult for the satellite countries to purchase necessary producers' goods.[11]

According to world economy theorists, the infrastructures that were established in satellite nations did not promote industrialization but merely furthered the development of the export-oriented primary-producing sector. For instance, railway systems were constructed to link primary-producing areas to the seaports, rather than to form a national network that would promote the development of a national market. Banking systems were created to provide short-term credit for agricultural export purchases, not long-term loans that would have been suitable for industrial development. And so forth.[12]

In the later stages of the process, metropolitan capitalists also invested in modern industry in the satellite countries and native capitalists and/or governments succeeded in establishing modern industries, particularly during periods when imperialist controls were weakened, as during and between the two world wars. However, it is argued that this has not led to full-scale industrialization but is simply a "new dependency."[13] For example, a large part of the profits from foreign-owned industrial enterprises is repatriated to the metropoles rather than invested in the expansion of industry within the satellite. Capital must also be exported to the metropoles to pay for access to modern technology, which is controlled through patents. A large part of the necessary supplies for the enterprises is also imported from the metropole, rather than sought within the satellite economy. Many industrial enterprises in Third World countries consist of processing plants' putting together commodities whose parts have been manufactured elsewhere and utilizing machinery (often obsolete) imported from abroad; thus development-promoting "backward and forward linkages" to the rest of the economy are prevented. Moreover, the types of industries established are often not geared to the needs of the local masses; rather, they supply luxuries and durable consumer goods for an affluent minority.

Thus world economy theorists regard satellite nations as essentially depleted and impoverished. Although some industrialization occurs, it is inevitably a backward, externally oriented industrialization that remains many steps behind, and dependent upon, the advanced metropolitan countries and that fails to advance the living standard of the masses of the population. "Economic growth," for the majority of the population, is a step backward. Agricultural output grows, in the form of commercial crops exported to the metropolitan nations, yet the local population lives under threat of starvation. Industrial output also grows, yet millions live in urban slums without employment or the means to buy the output of industry.

The society of this kind of depleted satellite nation cannot be thought of as traditional, according to world economy theorists. The very notion of "traditional society," they argue, must be criticized on two counts.[14] First, it conceives of the satellite society as an entity in and of itself, rather than as a unit that is an integral part of a worldwide system or totality. Second, it conceives of the satellite society as a static, ahistorical phenomenon, rather than a society that is constantly changing within the world system. For example, traditional society theorists overlook major changes that have occurred in societies of the Third World due to the process of satellitization. New political structures, ranging from direct colonization to indirect rule through native-led regimes, have been created to serve Western interests. New classes have arisen (bourgeois classes, participating in the export sector and dependent industrialization), and new regimes have risen to power, while others have lost. If these new classes and new regimes hamper industrialization, it is not because they are "traditional" but because their fate is linked to the new, dependent economy, which can develop only if full-scale national industrialization is prevented. At their most radical, the best the new classes and elites can do is "negotiate the conditions of dependence."[15]

Changes in the direction of greater inequality are also overlooked. With satellitization, the class structure grows increasingly unequal. Peasants and urban workers are increasingly impoverished relative to the unprecedentedly affluent urban and rural bourgeoisie.[16] Again, if the new upper class consumes or invests its profits in ways detrimental to national industrialization, or in the face of mass hunger and unemployment, it is not because it is "traditional" but because it is constrained within a worldwide system, which can develop only if national industrialization in the satellites is avoided.

As noted above, both world economy and traditional society

theorists regard Japan as the exception that proves the rule. In the logic of traditional society theories, if Japan industrialized it must be because Japan is the only Third World nation that had a culture and social structure favorable (rather than unfavorable) to economic development. For instance, Marion Levy remarks in his comparison of "traditional" China and Japan: "It was not differences in the new forces introduced to China and Japan that accounted for their different experiences in industrialization. It was rather differences in the social structures into which the new forces were introduced."[17]

In the logic of world economy theories, if Japan industrialized it must be because Japan is the only Third World nation that remained relatively insulated from pressures to become a satellite within the world system. For instance, Paul Baran remarks in a comparison of India, Japan, and China:

It should not be overlooked that India, if left to herself, might have found in the course of time a shorter and surely less torturous road toward a better and richer society. . . . It would have been . . . an entirely different India (and an entirely different world) had she been allowed – as some more fortunate countries were – to realize her destiny in her own way, to employ her resources for her own benefit, and to harness her energies and abilities for the advancement of her own people. This is speculation to be sure, but a legitimate one. For the alternative to the massive removal of their accumulated wealth and current output, to the ruthless suppression and distortion of all indigenous economic growth, to the systematic corruption of their social, political, and cultural life that were inflicted by Western capitalism upon all of the now underdeveloped countries is by no means purely hypothetical. This can be clearly seen in the history of the only Asian country that succeeded in escaping its neighbors' fate and attaining a relatively high degree of economic advancement. For in the period under consideration – when Western capitalism was ruining India, establishing its grip over Africa, subjugating Latin America, and opening up China – conditions in Japan were as conducive, or rather as unfavorable, to economic development as anywhere else in Asia.[18]

Japan is thus a critical case for demonstrating the validity of either of these two major theories of underdevelopment. Their contradictory propositions about Japan's development, and about underdevelopment elsewhere in the Third World, need to be tested through comparative study. Unfortunately, there is not a body of empirical studies that has compared Japan systematically to one or several other non-Western societies. The only exception is a number of studies that compared Japan with Imperial China.[19] Do the results demonstrate the validity of either interpretation of underdevelopment? The answer, I will conclude in the following pages, is no. Although considerable attention has been directed to Japan and China, the studies must be regarded as inconclusive.

Comparing Japan and China: world economy theories

There are very few comparisons of Japan and China by world economy theorists. I will take Paul Baran's statement in *The Political Economy of Growth* as an example, since it has probably been most widely read in the West.[20] Baran argued that Japan's industrialization was possible because Japan was the only Third World nation to escape becoming a "colony" of the capitalist industrial nations. Why did Japan escape?

There are essentially two reasons, according to Baran. First, during the early nineteenth century, when merchants from the capitalist countries first appeared in East Asia, they became preoccupied with exploiting China, India, and other areas. By the time they got to Japan, the European nations had become burdened with intra-European wars. They were therefore not in a position to turn their full attention to Japan. Second, by the time Japan came under Western influence, after the 1850s, fierce competition had developed among the Western nations in Asia. Because of this, Japan escaped becoming a colony of any single power, as had India, and China during the greater part of the nineteenth century (China having relations predominantly with Great Britain).

Because Japan did not become a colony, Baran argued, this permitted the establishment of a capitalist-dominated regime that promoted the interests of industrialization. The country's economic surplus remained in Japanese hands and was utilized by the state and the capitalists to industrialize the country. Moreover, there was no large influx of Western traders, adventurers, and missionaries, and the Japanese were not stirred to xenophobic reactions against everything Western, which might have hampered industrialization, as were the Chinese and other peoples.

Baran indicated the possibility of differences in the internal social structures of China and Japan, but denied their analytic significance. His argument is made within the context of a Marxist stage theory of the development of societies from feudalism to capitalism. Baran argued that all preindustrial societies, both Western and non-Western, were feudal and all were undergoing, more or less rapidly, a series of transformations in the direction of capitalism. These transformations included increases in agricultural output, deepening class divisions in the country-side, the emergence of a potential industrial labor force made up of the poorest peasants, the growth of towns and a class of mer-chants and artisans, and the accumulation of capital by wealthy merchants and rich peasants. The structure of feudalism was not everywhere the same, however. There were "far-reaching diver-gences" between the different feudal systems; feudal Japan was quite different from feudal China, India, and other places. The significant difference between Japan and the other nations, how-ever, was not Japan's special social structure but its greater inde-pendence from nineteenth-century imperialism. The lesson of Japan is that development can occur only if a nation is able to escape colonial status.

This interpretation raises several problems. First, though Japan was not a colony, neither, of course, was China, if by *colony* we mean a country that is under the full and direct political control of another country. Mao Tse-tung has characterized China before 1949 as a "semi-colony," that is, not directly and completely ruled by an outside power, yet lacking political and economic auton-omy. Was not Japan in a similar situation? For example, as tra-ditional society theorists have pointed out, both Japan and China were subjected to the "treaty port system." Under this system, a number of ports were opened to Western trade and residence; import and export tariffs were set in such a way as to benefit Western trade; "extraterritoriality" was established, removing Westerners from the jurisdiction of native courts; and Western diplomatic corps were installed in the capitals and major ports. Did this not put Japan and China in a similar position with re-gard to the industrial capitalist countries?

Second, the traditional society studies have amassed consider-able evidence that Japan and China were in fact quite dissimilar. In the face of this, is it appropriate to characterize both systems as feudal? And if the social systems were divergent, are we to believe that this had little impact on how the two countries changed as they were integrated into the world system?

Comparing Japan and China: traditional society theories

The most striking characteristic of comparative studies within the traditional society perspective is that they simply exclude the question whether there might be differences in the relationship of China and Japan to the world political economy. For some authors, such as Moore, Holt and Turner, Jacobs, and Sheldon, the exclusion is a matter of emphasis. Others have excluded the question explicitly; for instance, Marion Levy: "In both China and Japan *the external sources were virtually identical. They were the factors involved in modern industrialization.*" (emphasis added)[21] Or Reischauer and Fairbank, in the statement also cited at the beginning of this chapter:

One cannot but be struck by the great differences among the various countries of East Asia in the speed and nature of their responses to the West in the past century. . . . These variations in response *must be* attributed mainly to the differences in the traditional societies of the countries of East Asia. Only such differences can explain why *a basically similar impact* could have brought such varied initial results . . . why relatively small Japan, for example, soon became a world power, while China sunk to the status of an international problem.[22]

Just as Baran pointed out differences between Japan and other Third World societies, yet denied their analytic significance, traditional society authors occasionally point out that the Western impact on Japan was much smaller that that on China, but deny that this has any analytic significance. To Fairbank, Reischauer, and Craig, for example, it is a "startling paradox" that Japan's "greater response" followed a "less violent impact" than in China:

As compared with the Chinese experience, the initial impact of the West on Japan in the middle of the 19th century was gentle. No wars were fought, no smuggling trade developed, no territory was forfeited. . . . And yet, Japan's response was far quicker and greater than that of China. . . . This startling paradox – that Japan's greater response followed a less violent impact than in China – has posed difficult questions of historical interpretation. What forces at work in Japan produced so great a ferment? Obviously, Japan in the mid-nineteenth century, even though it had derived a large part of its higher culture from China, was a very different country, capable of very different responses to the Western challenge.[23]

Alvan Obelsky has translated this approach into a Parsonian framework. He proposes three sets of "conditions" for economic development: "necessary," "initial," and "sufficient." Necessary conditions are "cultural" conditions (in the Parsonian sense of the term) that provide the most general, but latent, conditions for development. They do not themselves initiate development, yet are necessary for its ultimate emergence. Initial conditions are *social-structural* conditions, such as political and economic institutions. The sufficient conditions "activate the potential implied in the first two sets of conditions . . . they are the effective 'challenge'" that unleashes development. Obelsky suggests that these conditions are interrelated in the following way. "Given the minimum *necessary* conditions for development, the outcome will depend on the strengths of the remaining two sets of conditions. The more favorable the *initial* conditions, in this case, the *less insistent* need be the *external stimulus* in order to qualify as the *sufficient* condition." This, of course, stands the world economy thesis on its head.[24]

The traditional society studies of Chinese and Japanese development may be divided into two categories, which I will term *factor theories* and *ideal-type theories*.[25]

Factor theories are "particularistic," as Koya Azumi has put it; they search out and describe any and all differences between the two societies, and make little effort to analyze the consequences of the various factors in terms of a general theory of social change.[26] The assumption seems to be that *any* aspect of Japan's social structure, geography, population, or culture that differed from China's is relevant to an analysis of why Japan was able to industrialize.

For example, Fairbank, Reischauer, and Craig attribute Japan's development, versus China's underdevelopment, to the following miscellaneous factors: insularity; feudal loyalty, religion, "goal-orientation," "diversity and pragmatism of thought"; the military character of the ruling class; the small size of the country; diversity of the social structure; nationalism; relative advancement of the traditional economy; breakdown of traditional class structure; and the existence of an "imperial institution."[27] Another factor theorist, Jacobs, has attributed Japan's development, compared to China's, to differences in their traditional institutions of exchange and property, authority, occupation, stratification, kinship and descent, religion, and "integration and stability."[28]

The factor theorists are especially responsible for strewing confusion in the study of Japan and China. Because a theoretical focus is lacking, factors that have been singled out as the causes of development in Japan are often identified as the causes of underdevelopment in China or elsewhere, sometimes even by the same author. Thus Fairbank, Reischauer, and Craig see Japan's "imperial institution" as a factor in development, while simultaneously arguing that China's imperial government was an obstacle to development.[29] Or Japan's industrialization is sometimes inexplicably attributed to a set of factors that are completely divergent from those identified by other authors to explain industrialization elsewhere. For example (as noted above), Fairbank, Reischauer, and Craig have proposed that Japan's development was related to the small size of the country, its insularity, and so on, whereas China's underdevelopment was related to its larger size, continentality, etc. Theorists of United States development, in contrast, have often attributed America's growth to the large size of the country, the possibility of continental expansion, and so forth.

Ideal type theories make a greater effort to relate the comparisons of China and Japan to a general theory of development. They link several contrasting features of the "traditional societies" into two societal "types," then analyze the consequences of these typical features for industrialization and underdevelopment. A theory of industrialization is implied in the construction of the ideal types and in the analysis of their consequences.

No two "traditional society" ideal-type conceptions of China and Japan are exactly alike. Various theoretical perspectives have been utilized, ranging from the Parsonian AGIL scheme (Holt and Turner) to Weber (e.g., Jacobs) and/or Marx (e.g., Wittfogel, Moore). However, there is a convergence around one theme, which recurs in almost every study. This is a theory of industrialization that I will term the *class theory*. The class theory of industrialization is a simplistic argument that reduces the rise of industrial capitalism – whether in Japan, China, Europe, or elsewhere – to the growth of commerce and the rise of a bourgeois class. This theory is widely popular, and has deep roots in Western intellectual history. Thus it is worth devoting some attention to it.

The simplistic class theory of industrialization

A synthesis of this theme, as presented in the various traditional society comparisons of Japan and China, might be as follows.[30] Japan developed during the nineteenth century because it had a "feudal" tradition similar to the societies of Europe. China remained underdeveloped because it had a "bureaucratic" (or "centralized" or "despotic" or "Asiatic") tradition, radically different from the Western or Japanese experience.

Japan was a feudal state, a conglomerate of domains ruled by a warrior nobility, or *daimyo,* and hegemony was exercised by the most powerful *Tokugawa* domain. Under the daimyo were the *samurai,* an upper class of warriors who were dependent for their livelihood on stipends of rice allocated by the daimyo. Below the daimyo and samurai were the merchant, artisan, and peasant classes. The importance of the feudal state is that it is weak vis-à-vis the nobility and bourgeoisie. The Tokugawa rulers were unable to prevent the rise of commerce and the development of an increasingly powerful and wealthy bourgeois class in town and countryside. "Commercialization" began to erode the feudal social order in several important ways.

First, as the new bourgeoisie increased in wealth, it was increasingly discontent with restraints placed on commerce by the Tokugawa rulers and with the general subordination of merchants and rich peasants to the samurai and daimyo. Second, commercialization created a fiscal crisis within the domains, to which the daimyo responded by cutting the stipends of lower-ranking samurai, causing their deep disaffection with the feudal order. Third, the loose hegemony exercised by the Tokugawa over the other domains began to collapse as commercial development enabled the latter to increase their wealth relative to the Tokugawa. After Japan was significantly affected by the arrival of the Europeans, the two disaffected classes (bourgeoisie and lower-ranking samurai) in several of the wealthier domains united to overthrow the Tokugawa government and establish a new state (the Meiji Restoration).

The new Meiji government abolished Tokugawa restraints on commerce and industry and undertook many reforms that furthered industrialization. Although the new Meiji rulers were from the old samurai class, they acted in the interests of industrialization because they were allied with the rising bourgeoisie.

In contrast, the Chinese imperial state was a strong or bureaucratic state. China was ruled by the Manchu conquerors through a centralized officialdom. This officialdom was drawn from the Chinese landed upper class, but power in China was based on officeholding rather than (as in Japan) domain ownership. The Chinese bureaucracy was opposed to the rise of commerce, and because the state was strong it was able to contain the rise of commerce and the growth of a powerful bourgeoisie. Because there was no bourgeoisie in China with which a segment of the ruling class might ally, China's rulers remained conservative; no Chinese equivalent of the Meiji Restoration could occur after the arrival of the Europeans. China was thus compelled to remain underdeveloped.

Note the assumptions behind the class theory. First, industrialization is primarily the inevitable result of the appearance of a class that supports it. In capitalist industrialization, this is normally the bourgeoisie (the large mercantile bourgeoisie and/or bourgeois newcomers arising from the ranks of artisans or small farmers), which has appeared within the feudal society with the growth of commerce.

Second, a state policy of promoting industrialization is also necessary. Such state policies appear only after the state apparatus has come under control of the rising bourgeoisie.

The class theory of industrialization has its origins in nineteenth-century European social thought. It rose and flourished during the industrial revolution, and was invoked to explain the enormous transformations in Europe at the time and to justify (or criticize) the establishment of bourgeois rule. Europe's social and economic progress became equated with industrialization and the "rise of the bourgeoisie."

The class theory of European industrialization was frequently buttressed by comparing Europe with China, which was just undergoing its spectacular decline into subordination and underdevelopment. (Japan was hardly noticed in the literature of the time.) Prior to the nineteenth century, China had not been regarded as a bureaucratic state that was dedicated to the smashing of commerce and the suppression of all change. China was regarded as *different* from Europe, but frequently in a favorable light, and even as a model to which Europe might aspire. The Physiocrats, for example, wrote approvingly of the beneficial effects of Chinese economic policy on agriculture. All this changed in the nineteenth century.[31] If European progress was the work of the bourgeoisie, it followed that Chinese backwardness must have been due to the absence of a bourgeoisie.

As noted above, many traditional society theorists of China and Japan have been influenced by Karl Marx and Max Weber. Both of these major nineteenth-century social theorists of European modernization used China (also India and other Eastern societies) as a foil, against which they displayed their conceptions of Western social and economic progress. And although Marx and Weber interpreted the nature of Western progress differently, both touched on certain class-theory arguments about the nature of Europe versus China.

Marx and Engels, at various points in their work, elaborated the conception of a special *"asiatic" mode of production* that diverged from that of feudalism. This concept, which Marx and Engels never fully integrated into a systematic statement on comparative history, has greatly influenced subsequent theorists, who have utilized it in a simplistic way that I doubt Marx and Engels intended.

Marx and Engels mentioned five characteristics that distinguished "asiatic" societies from "feudal" Europe:

1 Agriculture, because of geographic and climatic conditions, was based on large-scale irrigation and flood-control works that were managed by the state. Marx wrote in the *New York Daily Tribune* in 1853:

> Climate and territorial conditions, especially the vast tracts of desert extending from the Sahara, through Arabia, Persia, India and Tartary, to the most elevated Asiatic highlands, constituted artificial irrigation by canals and waterworks the basis of Oriental agriculture. . . . This prime necessity of an economical and common use of water, which in the Occident drove private enterprise to voluntary association, as in Flanders and Italy, necessitated in the Orient where civilization was too low and the territorial extent too vast to call into life voluntary association, the interference of the centralizing power of government.[32]

2 Unlike feudal Europe, property was undeveloped in Asia. There was no nobility, no bourgeoisie. On the one hand, the state was the "real landlord," that is, all property was legally owned by the state; village communities possessed land only as a grant from the state. This constituted the rationale for tribute or labor services extracted from the villagers by the state. On the other hand, land was in fact the communal or common property of the villagers who tilled it.[33]

3 Unlike feudal Europe, the division of labor was little developed in Asia. Production was organized through a multitude of tiny, similar, self-sufficient village communities. Cities were not autonomous centers of industry and commerce but administrative outposts of the state, superimposed on the fundamental, village economic structure.

The village communities united agriculture and domestic manufacturing, "that peculiar combination of hand-weaving, hand-spinning and hand-tilling agriculture which gave them self-supporting power."[34] That is, the villagers owned the means of production and produced for their own use; thus both the market and the laborers for capitalist production were lacking.[35]

4 The combination of centralized control over the water supply and the isolation of peasants within self-sufficient villages provided a solid foundation for a highly despotic form of government, "asiatic" or "oriental despotism."[36]

5 Finally, as a result of the above, "asiatic" society was "stagnant" or "stationary." Marx commented on India: "India has no history at all, at least no known history. What we call its history, is but the history of the successive intruders who founded their empires on the passive basis of that unresisting and unchanging society."[37] It was only with the extension of capitalism to Asia by the British and others that real social and economic change began to occur:

English interference, having placed the spinner in Lancashire and the weaver in Bengal, or sweeping away both Hindoo spinner and weaver, dissolved these small, semi-barbarian, semi-civilized communities by blowing up their economical basis and thus produced the greatest, and to speak the truth, the only *social* revolution ever heard of in Asia. . . . England, it is true, in causing a social revolution in Hindostan, was actuated by the vilest interests, and was stupid in her manner of enforcing them. But that is not the question. The question is, can mankind fulfill its destiny without a fundamental revolution in the social state of Asia? If not, whatever may have been the crimes of England, she was the unconscious tool of history in bringing about the revolution.[38]

Thus the concept of the asiatic mode of production emphasizes the absence of a property-owning class in Asia that might have furnished an impetus to economic transformation. The economy was controlled by the state, on the one hand, and by isolated peasant villages on the other. No bourgeoisie existed to develop the productive forces to a higher level.

To Weber, the content of modern progress also was closely connected with the rise of the bourgeoisie. Weber also noted the function of the Chinese state in the management of water-control works, the administrative character of Chinese cities, and the lack of development of private property.[39] However, the emphasis of his argument lies elsewhere. He was less interested in the processes of capital accumulation, the division of labor, and industrial investment than in the extension of "rationality" into social life. Industrial capitalism, Weber argued, depended on the development of a class with a "rational" spirit, which in turn has extraeconomic origins.

Weber argued that "from a purely economic point of view, a genuinely bourgeois, industrial capitalism might have developed from . . . petty capitalist beginnings" in China.[40] The reason why it did not was, in part, the nature of the Chinese state and in part the nature of the Chinese ethic. The state, which he characterized as a "patrimonial" or "prebendal bureaucracy," failed to create a rational, calculable structure of law and administration within which a class of capitalists might be motivated to operate. Justice was substantive, not formal; arbitrary, not consistent. Private property was not "guaranteed." There were no civil liberties. "Capital investment in industry is far too sensitive to such irrational rule and too dependent upon the possibility of calculating the steady and rational operation of the state machinery to emerge under an administration of this type."[41]

Above all, however, the failure to develop industrial capitalism stemmed from the Confucian ethic of the "literati" stratum that staffed the Chinese patrimonial bureaucracy. The literati failed to promote industrial capitalism, or to encourage other classes to do so, because of the goals emphasized in Confucianism. Confucianism contrasted sharply with the Puritan or Protestant ethic of the Western European countries, which Weber regarded as significant in the rise of capitalism in the West. The Confucian ethic stresses the prime goal of self-perfection through a literary education. Confucian training rejected practical and specialized expertise in worldly affairs; the Confucian gentleman possessed the "ways of thought suitable to a cultural man" and was "thoroughly steeped in literature."[42] Proof of one's status as an educated gentleman was passing the state's official examinations. "The typical Confucian used his own and his family's savings to acquire a literary education." The Puritan ethic, in contrast, stressed personal salvation through hard work, sobriety, and thriftiness. "The typical Puritan earned plenty, spent little, and reinvested his income as capital in rational capitalist enterprise out of an aesceticist compulsion to save."[43]

Thus, Weber argued, capitalism failed to emerge originally in China, as in Europe, because the dominant class in China pursued the goal of education and officeholding rather than the rational accumulation of capital.

In this century, major China scholars have continued to support a class theory to explain why industrial capitalism emerged first in Europe, rather than in China. Etienne Balasz, for example, has popularized a view of China as the "mirror image in reverse" of Europe, drawing on many points mentioned by Weber and Marx.[44] The geographic and climatic foundations of "oriental" governments and the power of the "bureaucracy" to smash private property have been greatly elaborated in the works of Karl Wittfogel.

Wittfogel's main contribution to the discussion was to extend the concept of the asiatic mode of production (Wittfogel's term is *"hydraulic" economy* or *society*) to account for something that Marx and Engels omitted: the widespread existence of private property in land, commerce, and industry in China and other Asian societies. Wittfogel argued that although there were large amounts of private property in China and elsewhere, it was kept "weak" by the powerful despotic or bureaucratic state. The state prevented private property owners from building enough private wealth and from organizing politically on a national level in such a way as seriously to challenge state power. The state had decisive "acquisitive power" over private wealth in (1) heavy taxation of landlord, merchant, and industrial profits, (2) outright confiscation of private wealth, and (3) "fragmenting" inheritance laws (i.e., inheritance laws that dispersed property among all heirs rather than concentrated it in the hands of one). The state also possessed decisive "organizational power" over private property owners, especially through a national postal and intelligence network, and the ability to mobilize and supply vast masses of peasants for military service or other central purposes. These methods led to a "state stronger than society," a state that thoroughly controlled and stifled all opposition, all class conflict, and all change.[45]

It is probably safe to say that a rough class theory is still *the* theory of why European development diverged from the development pattern in other parts of the world. Versions of it appear everywhere. Lichtheim's formulation, in his *Imperialism,* is typical:

A fairly typical alignment during the Medieval epoch enlisted the urban agglomeration, the *bourg,* on the king's side against rebellious nobles. Alternatively, the city fought for freedom from feudal and monarchical oppression. These medieval class conflicts gave rise to the city-state, perhaps Europe's most distinctive contribution to political history. The East never saw anything like it, for there theocratic monarchies strangled civic autonomy along with security of private property. For the same reason, the Orient never developed a genuine capitalism.[46]

Traditional society theorists have simply adopted this theory (designed to explain why capitalism developed originally in Europe, not in China) and used it to explain why industrial capitalism developed in Japan, but not in China, *during the nineteenth century.* Another quote from Lichtheim shows the logic of the jump from the original question to the situation in the nineteenth century:

This statement (as to the failure of capitalism to develop in the Orient) applies to India and to the Islamic world with greater exactitude than to China and Japan, *the last mentioned country at least having developed a genuine feudalism and the notion of private property in land that commonly goes with it.* In China, and still more in India and the Middle East, this development was strangled at birth by the system of government usually described as Oriental Despotism. *The realization that capitalism could sprout from feudalism in Europe (and subsequently in Japan) forms the connecting link between Marx's and Max Weber's theorizing.*[47]

It is probably a mistake to attribute such thinking either to Max Weber or to Karl Marx. Although Weber believed that the pre-European rise of industrial capitalism was hampered in China by the Chinese state and the Confucian ethic, it is unclear, as far as I can tell, what view he held of the Tokugawa state. Moreover, he did not transfer this theory wholesale to the nineteenth century; otherwise it would be hard to understand the comment he made in his work on China: "The Chinese in all probability would be quite capable, probably more capable than the Japanese of assimilating capitalism which has technically and economically been fully developed in the modern culture area."[48]

It seems abundantly clear that Marx regarded *imperialism* as a primary factor in China's nineteenth-century underdevelopment, rather than the asiatic mode of production.[49] What Marx and Engels intended to say on why industrial capitalism emerged *originally* in Europe, rather than in Asia, may be more open to debate. Did Marx and Engels, as Mandel claims, intend the contrast between the asiatic mode of production and feudalism to be an explanation of this question? This seems doubtful to me.[50]

Marx and Engels did not write a systematic historical and comparative study attempting to answer the question of why industrial capitalism originally emerged in Western Europe rather than elsewhere. Marx's major concern appears to have been to understand the nature of the capitalist mode of production, with a view, above all, toward understanding its contradictions and eventual revolutionary transformation toward socialism. He seems to have been concerned with noncapitalist modes of production primarily in order to describe how they *differed* from the capitalist and as a method of understanding the latter. His theories were oriented toward influencing practical action in his time, and a pedantic concern with the origins of industrial capitalism has been left to his followers.

Much of what Marx wrote on the asiatic mode of production is contained in the *Grundrisse*, which was prepared in 1857–1858 for the subsequently published *Critique of Political Economy and Capital*. (The *Grundrisse* was not published in Marx and Engels' lifetimes.) It is difficult to believe that what Marx wrote in the *Grundrisse* was intended to be such a comparative historical study. As Hobsbawm has pointed out, Marx's discussion of various "pre-capitalist" modes of production in the *Grundrisse* (asiatic, ancient, feudal) is "not 'history' in the strict sense."[51] For example, the propertyless society with an undeveloped division of labor, described under the asiatic mode of production in the *Grundrisse*, is not that of complex eighteenth- or nineteenth-

(or even twelfth-) century China. Marx surely had more information on the real, historical China than is evidenced in the *Grundrisse*, yet it was not used.[52]

What Marx and Engels deemed worthy of publication contains little about the asiatic mode of production. Engels, in *Origins of the Family, Private Property and the State*, the latest and most developed historical work, omitted the asiatic mode of production altogether. The *Critique* says little about it, commenting (in passing) in the Preface: "In broad outlines we can designate the asiatic, the ancient, the feudal and the modern bourgeois modes of production as so many epochs in the progress of the economic formation of society."

In *Capital*, comments on asiatic societies are not introduced in the context of asking why capitalism originated in Europe rather than Asia. Rather, they are used as cursory illustrations for basic concepts and arguments. For example, in volume I Asian public works projects are used as examples of "simple cooperation"; the undeveloped division of labor within Indian communities, *along with the European medieval guild system*, are used as examples of hindrances to the establishment of the division of labor within capitalist workshops.[53] In Volume III, Asian forms of agricultural production and land tenure are used, along with the "ancient world" and feudal Europe, as examples of precapitalist forms, in the context of analysis of the structure and dynamics of capitalist agriculture. Moreover, what Marx *does* say in *Capital* about the rise of capitalism in Europe suggests a far more complex argument than the "asiatic" versus "feudal" contrast. Marx saw the rise of capitalism in Europe in terms of a twofold process: the accumulation of capital in the hands of a bourgeoisie and its investment in the means of industrial production, and the emergence of a "free" proletariat, dispossessed of means of production and forced to work for the bourgeoisie in return for wages.

Marx did not see the emergence of these two contradictory classes as a simple outcome of the "rise of commerce"; rather, it involved a variety of forces, including, for example, European colonial expansion, the establishment of state debts, national policies of protectionism, the impact of rising wool prices on enclosures of farmland, and repressive labor legislation.[54] (The contradiction is "overdetermined," in Louis Althusser's terms. See *For Marx* [New York, 1970], pp. 200ff.) This suggests that had Marx or Engels in fact written a systematic comparative historical study of why industrial capitalism originally emerged in Europe, they would not have stopped with a contrast between asiatic and feudal modes of production.

A number of facts about European, Chinese, and Japanese history are not consistent with a simple class theory of industrialization.

First, there does not seem to have been a straight line leading from the autonomous towns and the "rise of commerce" in medieval Europe to the capitalist industrialization that occurred in the eighteenth and nineteenth centuries. Medieval England had the least-independent towns, yet England was the first European nation to industrialize. Medieval Germany had some of the most powerful, autonomous towns in Europe, yet nineteenth-century Germany was a latecomer to industrialization. The same is of course true of Italy, which experienced urban progress in the Middle Ages, followed by relative industrial backwardness in the nineteenth century. Poland had many flourishing towns in the Middle Ages, yet moved to agrarian status after the sixteenth century.[55] In some cases the very commercial success of a nation seems to have contributed to its failure to industrialize rapidly. For example, in Holland, a powerful commercial bourgeoisie successfully opposed the institution of protective tariffs that elsewhere encouraged industrialization.[56]

Second, the commercial bourgeoisie has repeatedly shown itself reluctant to invest in modern industry without government prodding and encouragement. In Japan after the Restoration, there was little interest by bourgeois investors in investing in large-scale modern industry. Industrial investment was forthcoming only after vigorous state efforts to prove its potential profitability and to eliminate risk. It appears that Japan's bourgeoisie would have remained commercially oriented in the absence of government intervention and would have doomed the nation to industrial backwardness.[57] This is true, however, not only of nondemocratic, industrial latecomers but also of states with the most impeccable bourgeois democratic credentials. For example, the U.S. bourgeoisie invested in railway development only when it was encouraged by large state subsidies in the form of land giveaways.[58]

Third, there does not seem to have been a simple relationship between bourgeois control of the state in Europe and state policies that furthered capitalist industrial development. Many Western European rulers, prior to bourgeois control of the state, and in pursuit of their own goals (such as increasing state power vis-à-vis other European states), engaged in policies that promoted national commerce and industry, such as colonial expansion, subsidies to industry, and unification of tolls and tariffs.[59] Policies were probably more systematically carried out and more successful once the state was strongly influenced by the bourgeoisie, but this active character of the European governments, I believe, distinguishes them from both the Chinese and the Japanese governments prior to the Western impact.

Finally, the class theory does not explain why declining feudalism in one place (Europe) gave way to original industrialization, whereas declining feudalism elsewhere (Japan) did not, until the latter was "stimulated" by external factors. The view that feudalism per se promotes the rise of commerce, and eventually industry, founders on the massive facts of slow economic growth during Tokugawa times in Japan, compared to early modern Europe. No one seriously contends that Tokugawa Japan was undergoing a commercial or industrial revolution comparable to what happened in Europe. Yet the class theory of industrialization does not account systematically for why this was not so.

The problem

The comparative studies of Japan and China are thus not very conclusive. The world economy studies suggest differences between the social structures of Japan and China but deny that these differences were of consequence for Japan's nineteenth-century development and China's underdevelopment. The traditional society studies point out differences in the relationship of Japan and China to the Western industrial powers but deny that they were of consequence. And many of the traditional society studies make highly problematic assumptions about the relationships among feudalism, bureaucracy, commercialization, and industrialization.

The purpose of this study is to reexplore the cases of Japan and China with the aim of clarifying the several questions that have been raised by the comparative studies but not adequately answered:

1 What was the nature of Japanese society, compared to Chinese society, "on the eve of the Western impact"? Were they really radically different? Do the terms *feudal* and *bureaucratic* adequately characterize the two societies? Can Tokugawa Japan be usefully compared with the nations of Europe? Why had industrial capitalism failed to emerge in *both* Japan and China by the time of the European expansion into Asia?

2 Did different relations evolve during the nineteenth century between the industrial powers and China and between these powers and Japan? Did Japan enjoy substantially greater autonomy in its relationship to the industrial capitalist nations than China? Or was

the nature of the "Western impact" on the two countries basically similar?

3 If differences existed – if Japan enjoyed greater autonomy – did these differences affect the two countries' internal political-economic structures and processes, so that Japan had achieved "development" or "national industrialization" by the early twentieth century whereas China was "underdeveloped"?

The first group of questions will be considered in part I, the second in part II, and the third in part III.

Part I

Economy and society in Ch'ing China and Tokugawa Japan

What was the nature of Chinese and Japanese society on the eve of nineteenth-century Western capitalist intrusion into Asia? This section argues that traditional society theorists have exaggerated the differences between Ch'ing China and Tokugawa Japan on the one hand and the similarities between Tokugawa Japan and the societies of early modern Europe on the other. Although there were certain similarities in *political* structure between Japan and early modern Europe ("feudalism"), the process of Japan's political-economic-social development, taken as a whole, was more similar to that of China than that of Europe.

European industrialization occurred within a different *total* developmental context from that of China and Japan. In Europe there was an ever greater centralization of state power; European governments developed from feudal to what I call "imperial," into centralized, "national" states. National economic policies of mercantilism emerged aimed at strengthening, unifying, and expanding the national economy, and contributed to the industrialization and "intense" commercialization of Europe during the eighteenth and nineteenth centuries. Accelerating military expenditures and growth of the state apparatus led to the establishment of large national debts in Europe, which greatly furthered capital accumulation and thus contributed to industrialization.

In neither China nor Japan was there a comparable trend toward ever greater centralization of state power. Japan remained feudal, China remained imperial, and neither showed signs of developing toward a centralized national state. In neither China nor Japan did governments have a comparably active mercantilist relationship to the national economy which would have strongly encouraged national industrialization and "intensive" commercialization. In neither country did accelerating military expenditures and a rapidly growing state apparatus, on a scale comparable to Europe's, give impetus to capital accumulation. Whatever differences there were between feudal Japan and Imperial China were encompassed within a dynamic of development that was distinct from the dynamic of development in Europe.

In consequence, on the eve of the Western intrusion, as Baran put it, "conditions in Japan were as conducive, or rather as unfavorable, to economic development as anywhere in Asia."

1

Economy and social classes in
Ch'ing China and Tokugawa Japan

Similarities in agricultural and industrial foundations

Traditional society theorists have overlooked enormous similarities in the economic foundations of Ch'ing China and Tokugawa Japan in their rush to find traditional institutional divergences that might have caused China and Japan to take different paths during the nineteenth century. Above all, both China and Japan were fundamentally agrarian. Agriculture accounted for about 70 percent of the national income in each country.[1] The vast majority of the population, perhaps 80 to 85 percent, in both countries were peasants, working directly in agricultural production.[2] Moreover, although economic growth was occurring in both Japan and China, the rate of growth was quite slow compared with that of developing countries today.[3]

Peasants in Ch'ing China and Tokugawa Japan produced largely the same things and by largely the same methods. Food production was paramount, and grain, especially rice, constituted the bulk of agricultural production. (Even in 1877, after the Meiji Restoration, rice still accounted for 60 percent of all farm products in the Kinai, one of Japan's most advanced areas.)[4] In addition to grain and lesser food crops, peasants in China and Japan cultivated a variety of similar crops that went into handicraft industry, for example, silkworm eggs and cocoons, mulberry leaves, cotton, and tea.

Both China and Japan were, of course, "pre-industrial": draft animals, and especially human beings, provided the energy for planting, harvesting, and transporting crops. Similar kinds of agricultural technology prevailed in both countries. Intensive rice cultivation, based on the construction of irrigation, drainage, and flood-control works, was a key feature of both economies. Other basic farming techniques, practiced in both countries, included multiple cropping, seed selection, and the use of commercial fertilizers, such as night soil, mud from sewers and ponds, oil cake, or dried fish. A wide variety of farm implements was used in China and Japan during the Ch'ing and Tokugawa periods (e.g., hoes, water pumps, and plows), yet few new mechanical implements were developed in either society.[5]

Peasants and urban artisans carried on flourishing industries in both countries. The textile industry (cotton and silk) was perhaps the most important industry in both countries. Other major industries included tea processing, oil pressing, grain milling, pottery, rice wine production, paper and ink. Industry, however, remained on a handicraft basis in both Ch'ing China and Tokugawa Japan. Needham has argued that China's and Europe's industrial technologies were at a roughly similar level up to 1450, after which Europe moved ahead. Japan's seems to have remained close to China's.[6]

Processes of change

Although change was occurring slowly, neither the Chinese nor the Japanese economy was standing still, and both, in general, were changing in the same ways. Several important economic and social transformations in both societies prior to the nineteenth century will be considered here: growing agricultural productivity; increasing population; improvements in transportation; a process that will be termed *"extensive" commercialization;* expansion, then relative closure, to foreign trade; and social changes accompanying commercialization, including the monetization of tax structures, the growth of an increasingly broad-based and powerful merchant class, and changes in rural stratification from "status" to "class."

The major difference between China and Japan seems to be that these changes began much *later* and occurred more *rapidly* in Japan. Traditional society theorists may have confused this greater rapidity of change in Japan with a higher level of development. Another difference is that certain processes of growth seem to have halted or slowed markedly in Japan during the eighteenth century, but not in China. (In this chapter I will simply take note of these differences. Their causes will be taken up in chapter 3, after discussion of the relationship of state and economy in China and Japan.)

It must first be noted that it is highly artificial to draw a line at the Ch'ing period in a discussion of changes in Chinese economy and society. As Mark Elvin recently emphasized, China underwent a process of marked economic growth during the eighth to thirteenth centuries (T'ang and Sung dynasties), a process that, although broken during the subsequent Mongol or Yüan dynasty and slowed in its intensity, continued into the following Ming and Ch'ing times.[7] From the eighth to the thirteenth century, Elvin argues, China underwent what amounted to an "economic revolution." Agricultural productivity increased notably as the population shifted from the dry North to the Southern irrigated rice areas; land transport was improved and a nationwide water transport network was established; credit devices were developed and the amount of money in circulation increased; commercialization occurred, and a network of urban centers was established that reached from tiny rural periodic markets to the largest cities; foreign trade flourished; the urban population grew, as did the proportion of the urban population in the largest cities; and there were technological innovations in the textile and other industries as well as progress in mathematics and medicine. After the thirteenth century, however, according to Elvin, technological innovation halted and foreign trade was curtailed. However, economic growth continued at a slower pace and social transformations continued, for example, in class relations and in the organization of the urban marketing network. The Ch'ing period constituted no sharp break in this process of slow-paced growth.

The Tokugawa period seems to mark a more distinct period in Japan's economic history than does the Ch'ing in China's. Although some of the transformations (to be considered below) had begun earlier in Japan – such as the growth of commerce and the formation of an urban network[8] – it seems that they reached their fullest development only after 1600. For these reasons it will be possible to limit the discussion of Japan primarily to the Tokugawa period, but it will be necessary to reach further back into Chinese history.

Population was growing in both China and Japan. Both countries had a very high population density compared to the nations of Europe. China's population had reached the 100 million mark in the eleventh century, during the Sung dynasty. The rise and fall of the Mongol dynasty was accompanied by great loss of life through killings, disease, and starvation caused by crop destruction. However, population began to grow thereafter, rising more or less steadily from an estimated 65 to 80 million around 1400 to 120 to 200 million in 1600, to about 270 million in 1770 and about 400 million during the nineteenth century.[9] Japan's population also grew, by about 50 percent from 1600 to 1721; thereafter, however, it grew at a slower rate, and by the mid-1700s growth had halted, in contrast to the continued expansion in China.[10] (China, of course, was much larger in terms of population, about ten times the size of Japan; in fact, China had about 30 percent of the world's population at the time.)[11]

As population grew, grain production increased in both China and Japan. Japan's rice production grew at a rapid rate, probably doubling during the years from 1600 to 1730.[12] The rate of growth seems to have slowed, however, beginning in the eighteenth century.[13] Grain production in China, as noted above, had increased markedly during the Sung period, and it continued to increase steadily during the Ming and Ch'ing periods, more or less keeping pace with population growth and slowing down only in the nineteenth century.[14]

Largely similar factors seem to account for rising grain production in China and Japan. First, there was an increase in the amount of land under cultivation.[15] Second, there was an increase in yields per unit of land. An important factor behind increasing yields in both countries was the expansion of acreage under high-yielding irrigated rice cultivation. Japanese peasants devoted increased efforts to irrigated rice cultivation during the Tokugawa period, both on new lands and by converting dry fields to paddies. The Chinese had been expanding their rice cultivation frontier for many centuries. As noted above, a major population movement from the North into the Southern rice-growing area had occurred from the eighth to the thirteenth centuries. During the Ming and Ch'ing dynasties, the peasants continued to move onto new lands and open them to rice cultivation. There was also an extension of rice cultivation northward and increased double cropping of rice with other grains.[16]

Other factors underlying increased yields in both China and Japan included the introduction of the techniques mentioned above: improved seeds, increased double cropping, and the application of purchased fertilizers. In China these techniques had been introduced prior to the Ch'ing period; in Japan they appear to have been introduced primarily during the Tokugawa period. Fertilizer use, for example, appears to have undergone three stages in both China and Japan.[17] In the first stage the fertilizers were grasses cut by the peasants. In the second stage, fertilizers were purchased, such as night soil and oil cake. The third stage is the use of modern chemical fertilizers, industrially produced. The Chinese peasants probably shifted from the first to the second stage during the Sung, Mongol, and Ming periods, whereas the Japanese made the shift during Tokugawa times.

Transport was greatly improved in China from the eighth to the thirteenth century.[18] There was a continual expansion of the main road networks, spurred by the government's desire for a nationwide postal network. Water transport, above all, was improved. "Ways were found to pass through or around previously unpassable difficult places in rivers" and river and canal shipping expanded as "a number of hitherto separate waterway systems were now linked into an integrated whole."[19] Sea transport also increased as ships were improved and safety was increased by use of the compass. The Grand Canal, linking North and South China, was built during the Sui dynasty (581–617) and was extended to the vicinity of Peking during the Mongol dynasty, becoming one of Ming-Ch'ing China's major shipping arteries. Elvin has argued that, by Ch'ing times, China's water transport system was probably as developed as it could have been without a major leap forward into the technology of steamships.[20] Transport in Japan was greatly improved during the Tokugawa period. Despite barriers to travel erected by the daimyo domains, five main roads, radiating from the capital, tied the nation together and imposed a hitherto lacking centralization on the road network. Because it was an island, more of Japan was accessible to water transport than China. China's dry North and Northwest were restricted to land transport, but all parts of Japanese territory, and most of the major cities, were linked by ocean routes during the Tokugawa period.[21]

Population increase, greater agricultural productivity, changing agricultural techniques, and improvements in transportation were accompanied in both countries by a growth in commerce and attendant changes in class structure. Was Japan's economy more "commercialized" than China's?

The question of "commercialization"

Commerce, commercialization, and related terms such as *national market,* which are frequently applied to the economic development of Europe, China, and Japan, are in great need of clarification.

Commercialization seems to have two aspects, as it is commonly used. First, it refers to a decline in *regional* self-sufficiency. That is, each region no longer produces all the food and manufactured goods it needs, but has begun to depend on other regions for some of its needs. Second, it refers to a decline in *local* self-sufficiency, or the growth of interchanges between town and countryside. That is, peasants no longer produce simply for their own consumption and no longer consume only what they have themselves produced; they are part of a trading network or hierarchy of urban centers, producing goods that are shipped "upward" to ever higher urban levels and consuming goods that are produced in or channeled through large urban centers.

The process of commercialization, in either of these two aspects, may be "extensive" or "intensive," depending on the extent to which self-sufficiency is lost and exchange relations come to dominate production. An increase in commerce occurs in an extensive way when increasing regions or people that had hitherto been self-sufficient become involved in exchange relationships, but only to a minor degree. It occurs in an intensive way when these regions or people begin to specialize in production of one or another commodity to such a degree that they are highly dependent on exchange relationships for their livelihood.

Extensive commercialization occurs, for instance, when region A, earlier self-sufficient, begins to consume the cotton produced in region B but remains self-sufficient in the production of other goods. Or, again, when peasant A, who had hitherto been self-sufficient, begins to sell beans and to purchase oil at market, but continues to produce his own grain, vegetables, yarn, cloth, and the like.

Intensive commercialization occurs when region A begins to specialize in producing cotton, sugar, silk, etc., and begins to depend on other places for most or all of the other necessary articles of livelihood. Or, again, when peasant A specializes in sugar or mulberry production and depends on the market for most or all other goods. That is, intensive commercialization implies the destruction of peasant industry primarily oriented toward producing items for the peasants' own consumption.[22]

The term *market* is frequently used in two ways, which are not synonymous. First, it refers to market*place:* a place or site where goods are exchanged. Second, it refers to a market: the situation in which the prices of goods being exchanged are influenced by the interaction of supply and demand.

On the one hand, goods may be sold and bought in a "marketplace" at prices determined by fiat, as by decision of a government authority – as well as by the interaction of supply and demand. On the other hand, "markets" for commodities may exist without being located in a specific place.[23]

In a *national market* the prices of goods are determined by the interaction of supply and demand on a nationwide scale (and thus the price that a commodity fetches in one city greatly affects its price in other urban centers in different regions of the nation). A *national marketplace,* on the other hand, is simply a central place into which goods are channeled for exchange, whether by means of barter, purchase, and sale at market prices or at prices determined by government or guild decree.

The conception of a national market assumes that regional and local self-sufficiency have broken down, that producers and distributors will channel goods where they will receive the highest price. This is not the case with a national marketplace, which may exist with the most extreme variations of prices in various regions, reflecting regional barriers to trade.

The economies of Western Europe passed through two phases in relation to commercialization and market formation. The first phase, which lasted until the late eighteenth and early nineteenth century, was one of extensive commercialization and the emergence of national marketplaces. After the decline of the Roman Empire, commerce again began to expand significantly in the tenth and eleventh centuries. Rural areas increasingly exchanged goods with the towns, the regions of Europe exchanged a variety of goods with one another, and European commerce with the rest of the world increased (especially, of course, after the sixteenth century).

During the first phase, the interaction of region and region and town and country was slight. In the eighteenth century, the situation in most of Europe was still similar to what an English observer reported of northern England: "Almost every article of dress worn by farmers, mechanics and labourers is manufactured at home, shoes and hats excepted. . . . There are many respectable persons at this day who never wore a bought pair of stockings, coat or waistcoat in their lives."[24] National marketplaces also appeared during this period: cities such as London and Paris came to be centers into which goods flowed from all over the country. However, national markets for most commodities hardly existed.

Intensive commercialization began only in the late eighteenth and early nineteenth centuries. It was associated with the industrial revolution – the enormous advances in output achieved through the use of mechanical energy – and with the revolution in transport: with the rapid expansion of canal and, especially, rail networks, which accelerated the circulation of goods from town to country and region to region. As Marx noted, "Modern industry alone, and finally, supplies in machinery the lasting basis of capitalistic agriculture, expropriates radically the enormous majority of the agricultural population, and completes the separation between agriculture and rural domestic industry."[25] And as the self-sufficiency of localities and regions dwindled rapidly, national markets for a wide variety of commodities began to emerge.

Was Japan more commercialized than China? It will be argued here that (1) *intensive* commercialization was not occurring in either Japan or China; (2) although both economies were becoming increasingly commercialized in an *extensive* way, the level of extensive commercialization was not greatly different in Japan and China during the Tokugawa and Ch'ing periods; and (3) a national market did not yet exist in either country.

Commerce and markets in China

Chinese peasants were hardly self-sufficient. Since the Sung dynasty, at least, many of them had come to purchase such goods as oil, fertilizers, and metals, which they did not themselves produce. They also produced goods beyond their personal needs, which were sold. These exchanges were made in local periodic marketplaces, which proliferated in China with the growth of population and the increasing numbers of people involved in exchange relations. These local marketplaces were linked into a hierarchy of urban places that functioned as centers for ever larger areas of exchange.[26]

Peasant dependence on the outside was not great, however. For most peasants, cash crops and handicraft items were sold to supplement their subsistence production. Only a small percentage of the peasantry was so specialized that it depended upon purchases for its survival. Only a small percentage of total farm production went into exchange. Perkins has estimated that perhaps 20 to 30 percent of China's farm produce was exchanged within local areas in the nineteenth century; 5 to 7 percent went into long-distance trade; and another 1 or 2 percent was marketed abroad. Balasz estimated that 20 to 30 percent of farm output was exchanged during the Sung period.[27] Thus China may have been no more intensively commercialized in the nineteenth century than during the Sung dynasty.

Nor were the regions of China self-sufficient. For centuries there had been a great deal of regional specialization in China. This was founded primarily on the unequal distribution of climatic and soil conditions necessary for producing certain goods. For example, sugar cane could best be grown in Kwangtung,

Fukien, Szechwan, and Taiwan. Tea and mulberry leaves for silkworm production could best be grown in Chekiang and southern Kiangsu. Cotton was most easily grown in the Kiangsu area and the North. Copper, which served as the basis of the empire's coinage, was found mainly in Yunnan. Manchuria and the Northwest supplied timber, wool, fur, and various products of the forests. All these goods were transported from their places of origin to the other regions of China. Regions that were favorably situated for producing raw materials usually came to specialize in the manufacture of goods made from them. Thus, for example, peasants of the Kiangnan area produced silk and cotton yarn and cloth, which were shipped throughout the empire.[28]

The interregional transactions in China can be regarded as taking place between more and less industrially developed areas. The provinces of Kiangsu, Chekiang, Anhwei, Kiangsi, Fukien, Kwangtung, Shansi, Chihli, and Honan produced manufactured goods and exported them to Manchuria, Shensi, Kansu, Hupei, Hunan, Kwangsi, Szechwan, Yunnan, Kweichow, Taiwan, Mongolia, Sinkiang, Tsinghai, and Tibet, from which they imported primary products.[29] As commerce and industry developed, even grain began to enter interregional commerce on a large scale. During the Ch'ing period the manufacturing provinces of Kiangsu and Chekiang imported rice from Anhwei, Hunan, Kiangsi, and even Szechwan.[30] Interestingly, there do not seem to have been insurmountable political or economic barriers preventing the more backward regions from "catching up." For example, Northern China, once dependent upon the Kiangnan region for cotton textiles, became a center for the production of such goods after the sixteenth century.[31]

Regional commercialization was not intensive in China, however. Only a small variety of goods entered interregional trade: primarily cotton and silk, tea, sugar, salt, drugs, and grain. These were usually goods that could be produced only in certain areas due to climatic conditions and/or luxury goods that were consumed by the upper classes and thus could bring high profits, despite the high transport costs in China's premodern economy.[32]

There were a number of important national marketplaces in China, such as Peking, Canton, Nanking, Wuban, Foochow, Chungking, Chengtu, Soochow, Hangchow, and Sian.[33] Did a true national market exist in Ch'ing times, prior to the Western expansion? Data 'are lacking, but it seems doubtful, due to the country's strong regional and local self-sufficiency and the importance of such factors as high transport costs.

Commerce and markets in Japan

Japanese peasants of the Tokugawa period were also losing their self-sufficiency – purchasing fertilizers and other commodities in exchange for food and handicraft items.[34] As in China, commercialization was accompanied by a proliferation of rural periodic markets that served the needs of the peasants and were linked into a network of ever larger urban centers. It might be noted that these rural markets spread throughout Japan despite efforts of the daimyo to curtail their growth in order to centralize all commerce in the domain capitals. Their rate of growth seems to have slowed after 1700, however, in contrast to China's, where local markets continued to multiply into the twentieth century.[35]

There was also a good deal of regional specialization and exchange in Japan. For example, cotton production was concentrated in the Kinai area and silkworm production and silk reeling in the three prefectures of Fukushima, Yamanashi, and Gumma. Certain domains produced more porcelain, lacquer, paper, silk, or wax than others. Satsuma produced sugar on a large scale and exported it throughout Japan. As in China, there were interchanges between more and less developed areas of the country, some of the domains exporting manufactured goods, others primarily agricultural products.[36]

The process of commercialization in Tokugawa Japan is frequently described as though it were intensive. Smith comments:

In the late Tokugawa period one still found villages with the characteristic subsistence pattern of cropping. But by the beginning of the nineteenth century, this stage was long past. Except in notably backward places – wild and remote valleys, isolated promontories, areas cut off by poor soil from the main stream of economic development – peasants by then typically grew what soil, climate and price favored, regardless of what they themselves happened to need. If a family were short of food or critical raw materials as a result, it made no difference since nearly anything was available in the local market, supplied with commodities from places scores, or even hundreds of miles away.[37]

And Crawcour:

In contrast to the subsistence agriculture of the Early Tokugawa period, by the 1860's agriculture over most of Japan was basically commercial agriculture, that is to say that the bulk of farm produce was grown for a market rather than for consumption by the cultivator.[38]

However, when such authors begin to cite figures the extensive character is striking, and the figures are not very different from those cited by authors on commercialization in China. As noted above, Perkins estimates that perhaps 20 to 30 percent of the farm output in China went into local trade, 5 to 7 percent into interregional trade, and another 1 or 2 percent into foreign trade. Smith cites figures from a work by Furushima on the percentage of "total agricultural production" in Japan that was accounted for by "cash crops" in several regions. They vary from 10 to 27 percent, the median being 12 percent.[39] Unfortunately, Smith does not say exactly what is meant by "cash crops." However, if these figures are at all comparable, the difference between China and Japan was not very great.

The conceptions of commerce and market, as used in this context, must also be clarified. Crawcour later qualifies the comment (quoted above) that in Japan the "bulk of farm produce was grown for a market" by saying that "in the part of agricultural produce grown for a market we must include the significant proportion of staple crops used to pay taxes in kind and marketed by the federal (i.e., the domain) authorities."[40] (Domain taxes, mainly rice, were largely collected in kind; perhaps one-third of what was collected was shipped to the city for sale.) According to Rozman, grain taxes marketed in the city constituted 2 million koku, or about 10 percent of the total rice output of the domains, compared to around 7 million koku, or some 30 percent of the rice output, that was marketed directly by peasants or other private persons.[41] It is this 30 percent figure that should be compared to Perkins' estimate for China, because estimates of marketed grain in China do not normally include grain taken in taxes by state authorities. (Grain taxes taken in kind in China, however, amounted to less than 1 percent of farm output, according to Perkins [*Agricultural Development in China*, p. 150].)

It is frequently stated that a national market was emerging in Tokugawa Japan. It seems to me that this results from a confusion between *market* and *marketplace*. It is true that there were two cities with strong central or national marketplace functions: the cities of Osaka and Edo. However, was there a true national market in Tokugawa Japan? The price of rice thoughout the land is said to have been strongly affected by prices prevailing at Osaka.[42] But was this true of most other commodities? Again, it seems doubtful, given the high level of local and regional self-sufficiency in Japan.

Foreign commerce

Consideration should also be given to foreign trade in a discussion of commerce. Both Ch'ing China and Tokugawa Japan conducted a slowly growing commerce with other nations. Yet in both countries this commerce contracted after an earlier period of expansion. China had long traded with other parts of the Asian world. Prior to the Sung period, this trade was generally carried by Southeast Asian, Persian, and Arab ships. During and after the Sung period, however, Chinese ships became involved, and both Chinese merchants and the government undertook lengthy trading expeditions to Southern Asia, the Arab world, and even East Africa. This trade was generally controlled by the government, but to varying degrees: the policies of the earlier dynasties were less restrictive than those of the later dynasties.[43]

For example, during Sung times there was a government monopoly in specified import goods, but private merchants could trade in them after the government's business was done. The government also taxed imports, and licensed Chinese merchants who wanted to go overseas, but did not prohibit other Chinese from going abroad or foreigners from coming to China. China's coastal cities in that period came to be filled with foreign residents. The Ming dynasty witnessed the famous official trading expeditions led by the eunuch admiral, Cheng Ho. However, these expeditions were soon halted and increasing restrictions were placed on foreign trade. Chinese were prohibited from going abroad and ships from abroad were allowed to trade only as part of an official "tributary mission" from another state to the Chinese government. The ban on Chinese going overseas had a checkered career, being lifted in the 1560s, reimposed in the last years of the Ming and the early years of the Ch'ing dynasties, then lifted in 1684 and reimposed in 1717.

The Ch'ing period generally continued the restrictive Ming policies. Chinese were prohibited from going overseas, with the exception of an officially approved copper trade with Japan. Foreign traders were restricted to the frontiers of the country – for example, to the seaports of Canton and Macao and the "land-ports" of Kiakhta and Nerchinsk on the Russian frontiers. Only Chinese merchants who had official approval were permitted to trade with them. The institution of the tributary mission also was maintained, with a certain amount of trade accompanying missions to Peking and such ports as Foochow.

In Japan, the Tokugawa period marked a retreat from earlier, less restrictive policies. Prior to this period, the Japanese had engaged in a flourishing trade with other parts of Asia, and numerous foreign merchants came to Japan. However, during the early seventeenth century the Tokugawa rulers forbade Japanese to go abroad and drove foreigners out of the country, with the exception of a certain number of Dutch and Chinese traders. The Dutch and Chinese were restricted to a particular number of ships per year and, while in Japan, were not permitted to leave the town of Nagasaki. (This trade was essentially an exchange of Japanese and Chinese goods, with the Dutch and Chinese acting as middlemen; there was little trade between Japan and Holland.) There was also some trade with China, carried on by the Satsuma domain through the Ryukyu Islands.[44]

The Ryukyu Islands trade provides a fascinating glimpse into Asian interstate relations. The Ryukyus, like a number of other small Asian kingdoms, were involved in a tributary relationship with Ch'ing China. In 1609, however, the Ryukyus had been conquired by Satsuma, reduced to a dependency, and deprived of fiscal and military autonomy. However, the Satsuma daimyo permitted the Ryukyu king to retain his title and continue to receive investiture from the Chinese throne as he had in the past, so that tribute missions might continue to be sent from the Ryukyus to China. These missions, carefully controlled by Satsuma, came to be vehicles of a regular Japanese-Chinese commerce.

Social transformations

The development of commerce in Japan and China was accompanied by major yet, again, quite parallel changes in class structure and political structure. First, relations between peasants and local overlords changed from "status" relations to monetized "class" relations. Second, taxes came to be paid in money rather than in kind. Third, merchants grew wealthy and increased in power vis-à-vis those who controlled the land.

The upper-class population in both China and Japan was composed of merchants, on the one hand, and a leisure class of those whose position was primarily based on ownership or control of the land and its surplus. The controllers of the land were divided into two levels in each country, which I will term the *tax-dependent* and the *mercantile* strata. The upper level, or tax dependents, was the stratum of the population that lived off taxes or tribute extracted from the peasants by the coercive and/or ideological powers of the state. The lower-level stratum enjoyed what Eric Wolf calls a "mercantile" relationship to the peasantry: income was derived from ownership of alienable private property.[45]

The upper level of the landed class in Ch'ing China consisted of several groups, amounting to no more than 1 or 2 percent of the population. The first group comprised members of the conquering Manchu nobility and their troops (the bannermen) – some 200,000 households, or around a million people – who lived on tax-derived stipends or state-granted lands that were worked by peasant tenants.[46] The second group was some 27,000 Manchu and Chinese civil and military officials and their families (altogether some 135,000 people), who were paid tax-derived stipends or salaries. The third group was made up of some million Chinese "quasi-official activists" and their families (altogether about 5.5 million people); the vast bulk were men who had passed only the lowest level of civil service examinations, thus held only the lowest academic title, and were not eligible to hold office. These activists utilized state connections to extract income from the peasantry, charging the peasants for services rendered in organizing water-control projects, local or clan charity operations, crop preservation associations, teaching, and the like.[47]

The lower level of the landed upper class in China was the Chinese "landlords." By the Ch'ing period they were a highly urbanized group of absentees who often used bursars to collect the rents from their noncontiguous and far-flung landholdings. Landlords also profited from lending money to the peasants and engaging in commerce and industry.[48] (The Chinese landlords and the tax dependents must not be regarded as two completely distinct groups since, in fact, the landlords, together with the merchants, provided most of the candidates for the official examinations. Although the majority of landlords probably were not officials or quasi-official activists, many of the officials and activists were landlords.)[49]

The daimyo and the samurai constituted the upper level of Japan's landed upper class, amounting to 5.5 to 7.5 percent of the population.[50] Japan was divided into some 200 domains, or han, ruled by hereditary daimyo to whom the samurai owed allegiance. The Tokugawa house, essentially the largest domain, exercised hegemony over the rest of the daimyo. The daimyo and the Tokugawa rulers collected taxes from the peasants and paid stipends to the samurai. The lower level of the landed upper class was an emerging stratum of landlords. They were an upper level of the rural peasantry who, like the Chinese landlords, lived off rents, moneylending, and profits from commerce and industry.[51]

The development of commerce in China was accompanied by a transformation in the way taxes were collected, from taxes in kind to money payments. During the late sixteenth and early seventeenth centuries the so-called single-whip reform was extended throughout the land. Before this, land taxes had been owed in kind and in the form of labor services, and they were assessed primarily in terms of the households (i.e., people) in rural areas rather than in terms of land. The single-whip reform merged these taxes into a single tax (thus "single whip") that fell primarily on land, rather than on people, and commuted them into a money payment. Thus China's tax dependents came to stand in an increasingly monetary relationship to the peasantry.[52]

A similar process occurred in Japan. In most domains in Tokugawa Japan, only about one-third of the land tax had been commuted. However, in the Tokugawa realm the share of money payments came to average 45 percent of the total toward the end of the period.[53]

The mercantile lower stratum of the landed upper class also developed an increasingly monetary relationship to the peasants. Chinese peasants of the Sung period had lived on manors and were bound in serflike fashion to manorial lords, to whom they had labor obligations. During the next centuries, and with the growth of exchange, these lords transformed themselves from a rural status group, living off the peasants' obligatory labor, into the urban landlord class described above. They moved into the towns and cities and lived off rents extracted from peasant tenants, interest on loans they made to the peasants and others, profits from commerce and industry, and income from office-holding or quasi-official services.[54]

At the beginning of the Tokugawa period most of the Japanese peasants had also been bound to local overlords in various ways.[55] These overlords were also categorized as peasants, and were subordinate to the ruling samurai class, but were raised above the rest of the peasantry by their control of the village offices, through which the domain tax collectors communicated with the peasants, and by various status privileges given them by the daimyo. For example, they had the power to allocate the tax burden among the villagers (which the tax collectors imposed on the village as a unit) and they were sometimes permitted to wear swords, a privilege normally confined to the samurai. The peasants performed services for these lords and were dependent upon them for farm animals and tools. The peasants and lords were often bound by kinship ties as well, the lords being the "main family" of the extended family and the peasants the "branch families."

As the Tokugawa period progressed, these local overlords began to transform themselves into a landlord class, renting out the land they claimed instead of asking for labor services. They also began to lend money to peasants at interest and to engage in commerce and industry. Thus, as in China, relationships in the countryside changed from status to class relationships.

The merchant population also changed in China and Japan with the growth of commerce. In both societies it became an increasingly broad-based group and gained in power vis-à-vis the landed sector of the upper class. The broadening of the merchant class in China is evidenced by the proliferation of merchant associations, the *hui-kuan*. These associations were formed by merchants in one region or locality in order to further their economic interests when they were trading far from home. In 1560 there were hui-kuan only in the capital city. By the late sixteenth and early seventeenth century there were hui-kuan in most major cities. By the late Ch'ing period there were 400 hui-kuan in Peking alone, and others in all provincial capitals, major and minor ports, and in some smaller towns.[56]

Commercialization in China also increased the merchants' wealth, prestige, and power. In the early dynasties Chinese merchants had been restricted by various sumptuary laws. They were also prohibited from holding office and were the objects of government persecution. Although these restraints were often evaded in practice, they were nonetheless there, a social fact to be contended with. However, by the Ming period the merchants had become sufficiently forceful to get the government to permit them to take the civil service examinations and enter the officialdom. Sumptuary laws were dropped and, as will be discussed in chapter 2, persecutions became rare. Thus the Chinese upper class became a highly fluid group: landlords and officials engaged in commerce and merchants bought land, obtained degrees, and became officials.[57] Although social distinctions still remained, dividing the upper class in China into a landed and a commercial sector, these distinctions were increasingly eradicated with the growth of commerce, and it would be a mistake to depict the interests of China's tax dependents and landlords as inexorably opposed to those of merchants.

The same is true of Japan, albeit to a lesser extent, because the changes occurred later. As in China, Japanese merchants began to make their influence increasingly felt vis-à-vis the landed upper class. For example, they began to purchase samurai rank from impoverished samurai families. However, they had yet to cast aside as many barriers as in China. Japanese merchants were still largely excluded from holding political office, which was reserved for members of samurai families. Thus the Japanese upper class remained divided into two sectors with more distinct interests.

One major difference between China and Japan has been emphasized here: the lateness and rapidity with which change occurred in Japan. Japan came late to many changes that occurred earlier in China. Transformations that began centuries earlier in China began in Japan during the Tokugawa period. Yet once they began, they happened quickly, so that Japan was rapidly "catching up" with China. China's extensive commercialization pattern had been established centuries prior to the Ch'ing period; in Japan it was completed during the Tokugawa period. Chinese peasants had been using purchased fertilizers at least since the Ming dynasty, Japanese peasants primarily since the Tokugawa. Relations between Chinese peasants and their mercantile overlords had changed from those of status to increasingly monetary class relations long before the Ch'ing period; this transformation began in Japan primarily during the Tokugawa. Chinese taxes were commuted to money payments prior to the Ch'ing; this was under way in Japan during the Tokugawa period. Much earlier, Chinese merchants had become powerful enough to break the barriers between themselves and the landholding class, whereas Japanese merchants began this process only during the Tokugawa period.

Another major difference is that some of these changes appear to have halted or slowed in Japan, but not in China. For example, population growth ceased in Japan after a certain point but it continued in China; the growth rate of agricultural production appears to have declined earlier in Japan than in China; the rate of addition of local periodic markets slowed in Japan but not in China.

Why did changes occur more rapidly in Japan than in China? Why did some of them slow, or halt? Was the pattern of change in Japan a manifestation of a different kind of social order, similar to the societies of early modern Europe? Is it likely that the kind of change in Tokugawa Japan would have led to industrialization? And, in contrast, is it likely that such a transformation was inevitably stifled in China? I will return to these questions after considering the structure and development of the Ch'ing and Tokugawa states.

2

State and economy in Ch'ing China

Heaven is high and the emperor is far away.

(Chinese proverb)

Feudal, imperial, and national states

Was the Ch'ing state strong, centralized, bureaucratic? Was the Tokugawa state similar to the feudal states of Western Europe?

The simplistic class theory fails to make a distinction among three types of state structures, which I shall term *feudal, imperial,* and *national.* In particular, it equates national and imperial states, lumping both together as "bureaucratic." These three types of state structures may be distinguished in terms of the degree to which control over the population is exercised by central as opposed to local rulers.

In the *feudal* state, military, financial, and judicial powers are concentrated in the hands of local nobility. The powers of state are indistinguishable from, or derive from, private property in land. If there is a monarch or emperor, he is merely *primus inter pares* and his power is based, like that of the other nobles, primarily on the size and wealth of his domains.

In the *imperial* state, military, financial, and judicial powers are no longer the prerogatives of private property; they have been removed to a central government, which exercises its powers through a staff of local officials.

In the *national* state there is also a central government that rules through local administrators. The national state differs from the imperial state primarily in that the national state is *stronger.* In the national state the central government exercises greater control over its officialdom and, therefore, over the surplus of the producing classes.

The central government in a national state exercises greater control over its officialdom because the officialdom is *bureaucratic.* What does it mean to say that an organization is bureaucratic?[1]

The first major characteristic of a bureaucratic organization is that the officials are dependent for their livelihood on salaries, which are dispensed from the center. In the national state the central government dispenses salaries to the official staff, and because the masses of the officials tend to be drawn from the ranks of the propertyless middle stratum or the working class, they have no sources of income apart from their salaries. In the imperial state, officials tend to have direct control over sources of revenue rather than obtain their salaries from the central government, and they tend to be drawn from the landed or commercial upper classes and thus are not wholly dependent on their official position for their livelihood. Because the officials of an imperial state are not dependent – not "bureaucratic" – they are far less amenable to central control and supervision of their activities than the officials of a national state.

The second characteristic of a bureaucratic organization is that it operates on the basis of a corpus of rules and regulations that are enforced by a hierarchy of officials. In the national state, a large proportion of the activities and the personnel of the administrative system are subjected to rules and regulations and to a hierarchy of supervision. In the imperial state, rules and regulations and an official hierarchy may exist, but the activities of the officials and the proportion of personnel to which they apply are smaller than in a national state.

The central government in a bureaucratic, national state exercises greater control over the resources of society in general than does the imperial state, in large part because the officialdom is bureaucratic. For example, in a national state local tax-collectors rarely pocket a large proportion of the tax revenues because most of what is collected is gathered in accord with regulations and audited by supervisors and because the officials are dependent and thus more amenable to central control. In an imperial state the percentage of revenues appropriated by the local collectors is far larger because the central government lacks such mechanisms of control.[2]

Because imperial governments have more limited control over their officials and because the officials have a grasp on a large percentage of the surplus, the imperial state tends (unlike the national state) to collapse into a feudal form. This can happen in one of the following ways.

First, local officials may gradually appropriate the powers of the state to such an extent that they become the effective owners of the territories they administer. Second, the local upper classes may extend their influence over the local officials so that the latter no longer respond to the imperatives of the central government. For example, in the mechanism frequently described by theorists of a Chinese "dynastic cycle" the property of the upper classes may become increasingly tax exempt whereas that of the peasantry is not. If landlords buy increasing amounts of land and install an increasingly large proportion of the peasantry as their tenants, they will steadily gain, and the central government steadily lose, revenue.

The result of these processes may be either a complete collapse into feudalism or, as has frequently been the case in Chinese history, a reestablishment of imperial rule after a period of warfare.

Much of the confusion surrounding comparisons of Ch'ing China and Tokugawa Japan is related to the tendency to equate imperial and national states and to project characteristics of national states back onto the Chinese imperial structure. It is assumed that because the Chinese state was not feudal that it was *therefore* a bureaucratic, strong, or centralized structure. These seem to be characteristics of national states, however, not of the Chinese structure, which was imperial. It will be argued below that the Chinese central government enjoyed a very restricted capacity to control its officialdom. In this it was little different from the Tokugawa state.

Confusion also stems from an assumption that there is an inevitable progression from feudal to national state. Such a progression *did* occur in Europe. Feudalism was overcome after the sixteenth century; imperial states were established and the process of centralization continued until national states were created.

The European monarchs first fought feudalism by establishing imperial states. They created central governments with executive departments; they established provincial and local offices under central control; they created independent armies and independent financial support for their rule. The independent power of the landed nobility was steadily reduced. However, the offices were at first often held by members of the landed upper classes and officials appropriated a large share of the tax revenues.

However, the European monarchs then went on to transform this structure into a national structure. They expropriated privileges that had first been alienated to the upper classes, replacing the imperial armies and civil administrations with national, bureaucratic structures, and they launched an attack on the economic privileges of the landed and commercial classes in an effort to increase state revenues.[3] European modern history is the history of continual struggle and conflict between the government and the upper classes, nobility, and bourgeoisie and between the government and its officials. The outcome was the establishment of national state structures far stronger than what had existed before.

Because the societies of Western Europe after 1600 developed from feudal to national states, it is assumed that wherever feudalism exists but is declining, national states must be emerging. Such a progression need not be inevitable, however. If changes were occurring in feudal Tokugawa Japan, they need not have culminated in the establishment of a national state. For millennia, feudal states have declined, to be replaced by imperial states, without further progression in the direction of national development. For example, as Mosca notes: "It must not be forgotten that the history of ancient Egypt covers about 30 centuries, a period long enough, in spite of the alleged immobility of the East, for a society to pass back and forth between feudalism and bureaucracy [by this he means an imperial structure] any number of times."[4]

Was Japan, like the societies of Western Europe, to be an exception to this rule? I will argue that this would have been rather unlikely in the absence of certain economic and political circumstances that were present in Europe. Changes in Japan would have been more likely to have ended in the creation of an imperial state, either stopping there or recollapsing into feudalism.

Provisioning and mercantilist economic policies

The class theory of industrialization also fails to distinguish between different types of state economic policies, which shall be termed *provisioning* and *mercantilist* (following Heckscher).[5] Provisioning policies are typical of feudal or imperial states that are not moving in the direction of greater centralization. The aim of government policy is above all to acquire revenues and supplies for a static or relatively slowly expanding state civil and military apparatus and to ensure an adequate supply of food and other necessities to the rural and urban populations in order to forestall riots and rebellions against the upper classes. The state that has a provisioning policy plays a relatively passive role in the economy. Provisioning policies generally neither suppress commerce, industry, and private capital accumulation nor especially encourage their development.

Mercantilist policies were characteristic of the European regimes as they moved toward greater centralization, and are the policies of the regimes of industrial capitalist states in present times. The key element of mercantilism is the conception of the economy as a national economy whose wealth and strength can be increased in part through government action. A history of mercantilist policies has given support and encouragement to private capital accumulation and industrial development in the now advanced industrial capitalist nations. Mercantilist economic policies have functioned in the following ways.

1 They have encouraged the development of modern national industries and an industrial infrastructure (railways, shipping, public utilities, etc.) by policies related to
  a *Capital accumulation:* policies that had the effect of dragging capital out of the usual channels of hoarding or investment in commerce or landholding and into industrial investment. These policies included subsidies to industry, ranging from the use of tax funds to provide outright monetary grants to tax exemptions, low-cost loans, and the like; government-sponsored industrial pilot projects; the establishment of national banking systems that funded industrial investment, and so forth. Important here was the establishment of the national debt, which, in Marx's words, "as with the strike of an enchanter's wand . . . endows barren money with the power of breeding and thus turns it into capital, without the necessity of its exposing itself to the troubles and risks inseparable from its employment in industry or even in usury" (*Capital*, I: 827).
  b *Protectionism:* protecting national industries from foreign competition. The major weapon was perhaps tariff policy but other mechanisms were also important, such as government purchase policies that favored national over foreign industries and policies such as the English Navigation Laws (which prevented foreign ships from moving in and out of British ports).
  c *Expansion:* the pursuit of colonial policies that created a worldwide division of labor between industrial metropoles and dependent, primary-producing satellites. This division of labor enabled national industries to expand their output significantly, further and faster than the initial narrowness of the home market permitted; to control sources of industrial raw materials that were not available, or available in insufficient quantities, at home; and it provided the colonizing powers with windfall gains from plunder, taxation, and indemnities that could be utilized for industrial investment in the homeland.
  d *Diffusion of technology:* efforts to import advanced technology and technicians (if not available at home), creation of native

technical schools, sending students abroad, and the purchase or pirating of inventions, as well as the reverse: preventing important technological innovations from leaving the country or restricting the emigration of skilled technicians.

2 Mercantilist policies have also encouraged the development of a national market, on the negative side, by the elimination of obstacles to the creation of a national market, including the abolition of internal tariffs and tolls and the unification of currency, weights, and measures, and, on the positive side, by the improvement of internal transport and communications – the infrastructure of railways, roads, shipping, and telephone and telegraph service.

3 They have promoted development of an industrial proletariat by state efforts that enforced labor discipline, such as antivagrancy laws and the creation of welfare systems that made relief a fate worse than factory work, and by the repression of labor unions, state complicity in the dispossession of the peasantry from the land, legislation to force wages down and lengthen the working days, and the creation of compulsory educational systems and military conscription, both of which facilitated the establishment of factory discipline.

It will also be argued that Tokugawa Japan's economic policies, despite superficial similarities to the states of early modern Europe, were more like China's than otherwise. Both were essentially provisioning rather than mercantilist policies.

The state in Ch'ing China

It should again be noted that it is artificial to draw a dividing line at the Ch'ing period. The imperial state is yet another structure that had been developed in an earlier period. It had been perfected during the preceding Ming dynasty, and the Ch'ing brought few important innovations.

The Ch'ing dynasty was a "conquest dynasty" established by the Manchus, a Northern people who were once nomads but had become settled agriculturalists under Chinese influence. The Manchus established imperial rule over China only after overcoming an almost feudal situation that had arisen from their efforts to overthrow the Ming imperial state.

The Manchus had been able to conquer China and the Ming dynasty only with the help of Chinese generals who had defected, and several of these generals became territorial rulers in the process. After the remainder of China had been brought under Manchu imperial rule, the Southern provinces of Yunnan,

Kwangtung, and Fukien were known as the Three Feudatories and the three generals who ruled them as "princes." Hsü describes the situation:

Wu controlled an army of over 100,000 men, while the other two princes maintained forces of 20,000 each. The military forces of the Three Feudatories cost the Ch'ing court some 20 million taels annually by 1667 – more than half the total state expenditures – while at the same time they were virtually independent within their own realms. Wu built a palace for himself in Yunnan, collected taxes, increased trade with Tibet, imported thousands of horses annually from Mongolia, and established monopolies on salt wells and gold and copper mines. So powerful and independent was he that his expenditures were not subject to examination or auditing by the Board of Revenue in Peking. His selection of civil and military personnel for appointments in Yunnan as well as in other provinces . . . could not be rejected by the Board of Civil Office or the Board of War.[6]

After the Manchus had consolidated their rule in the North, they announced their determination to reduce the Three Feudatories to provinces. The Three Feudatories joined in revolt, and for a time it looked as if they would maintain their independence or perhaps even replace the Manchus with a new Chinese dynasty. After eight years of battle, however, the Three Feudatories were defeated and China became a unified empire under Manchu rule.[7] The Manchus established central, provincial, and local administrations modeled largely on the administrative system of their Ming predecessors.

The most important divisions of the central administration were the Grand Council, a group of men who were the emperor's closest advisers,[8] and six administrative departments that supervised provincial and local affairs: the departments of civil office, ceremonies, revenue, war, punishment, and public works. Other important divisions were the Court of Colonial Affairs, which controlled affairs related to the political and trade relations between China and the states of Tibet, Mongolia, Sinkiang (their governments were restricted in operations by the Manchus through a system of garrisons and resident advisers), and Russia, and the Censorate, which exercised surveillance over the officialdom and had the power of impeachment.[9]

The Ch'ing civil administration further consisted of provinces (18), circuits (92), prefectures (about 180), and districts (about 1,500). Provincial officials were appointed by the departments of the central government and were responsible to it. The most important provincial offices were those of the governor general, governor,[10] financial commissioner, judicial commissioner, and the salt, customs, and grain intendants.[11]

The circuits, presided over by intendants, were subprovincial administrative divisions that had control primarily in the collection of special taxes: salt, customs, grain.[12] The majority of these officials were centrally appointed but some were appointed by high provincial officials. For instance, about one-third of the customs intendants were appointed by the provincial governors in the late eighteenth century.[13]

The lowest level of administration was the district, which had, on the average, a population of about 200,000. The major – and in most districts the only – office was that of the district magistrate. The magistrate devoted most of his efforts to collecting the regular land tax, to judicial cases, and to the maintenance of law and order, but he was also responsible for innumerable other affairs, including flood and famine relief, census taking, educational matters, and communications.[14]

Ch'ing military organization was divided into two sections: a Manchu army and a Chinese army. Control over the Chinese army was exercised by the Department of War, by provincial commanders in chief, and by circuit military commissioners. In addition, the governor generals and the governors each had several thousand independent troops under their control.[15]

The Manchu rulers' efforts to control the administration and the Chinese population were concentrated in two areas. First, they attempted to ensure that the Manchus would not be displaced in government by the Chinese. Second, they attempted to prevent refeudalization, that is, to ensure that local power monopolies would not emerge in the provinces. In these efforts, they were largely successful for about two centuries. They did *not*, however, exercise a strong, bureaucratically centralized control over the officialdom.

A certain percentage of the high offices in the administration was reserved for Manchus. Half the members of the Grand Council, the six departments, and the Censorate, and the entire staff of the Court of Colonial Affairs were Manchus. The situation in provincial administration was similar; for example, from 1644 to 1850 Manchus accounted for almost 64 percent of the governor generalships and 57 percent of the governorships.[16] There is a tendency in sociological accounts of Ch'ing society to overlook the Manchus and to emphasize the native Chinese degree-holding "gentry". This is unfortunate, because the Manchu nobility and "banner" population not only constituted a considerable proportion of the upper class (as noted above, there were some 200,000 households of bannermen, over a million souls, compared to about a million households of imperial degree holders, or some 5 million people) but controlled a disproportionate number of government offices.

Efforts to ensure that the provinces would not turn into feudatories were twofold. First, the carrot of social mobility within the imperial structure was held out to ambitious men in the provinces. Apart from the positions reserved for Manchus, the Ch'ing officialdom was in theory, and to a surprising extent in practice, an open opportunity structure for China's upper classes of landlords and merchants. Any ambitious person with sufficient wealth to spend years in study might obtain a higher academic title through passing the imperial examinations and thus become eligible to hold office. A title or office could also be purchased. There were no regional restrictions on entrance into officialdom and mobility within it, and no restrictions on the basis of status or rank – unlike Tokugawa Japan (see "Structure and development of the state" in chapter 3).[17]

Regional barriers were broken by the establishment of state schools in every district of the country to equalize the opportunity to study. More important, quotas were set for each province of the number of participants in the official examinations, ensuring that men from the poorer, less populated provinces (as well as from the wealthier, more densely populated provinces) would be represented in officialdom.[18]

As noted above, merchants and artisans had once been prohibited from taking the government examinations and entering the officialdom. As they grew increasingly important in the economy, however, they began to work their way in, and during the Ming period discrimination against them was halted as a "belated recognition by the state of their increasing power." The Manchus continued the Ming policy.[19]

Along with the carrot went a stick: a complex system of controls on provincial officials designed to prevent their defection.[20] First, officials were not permitted to serve in their province of origin. This had the effect of setting a barrier between the official and the people he administered and also made it possible for the official's family to be used as hostages, should he try to usurp power.

Second, a "law of avoidance" prohibited members of the same patrilineal clan (and even maternal relatives) from serving in the same province.

Third, officials were rotated from place to place at intervals of about three years, intensifying the barrier between the official and the administered population.

Fourth, there was little specialization of office and few clear-cut lines of command. For instance, there was a large overlap among the functions performed by such provincial officers as the governor, governor general, financial commissioner, and intendants, and there was no hierarchy of command among them. Each knew what the other was doing and each reported separately to the central government, which was a barrier to anyone's attempting to aggrandize his power. For example, instead of a clear chain of command in the armed forces, officers were distributed in such a way that it was difficult for one officer to get control of others. As noted above, provincial governors, as well as the provincial military commanders, had control over army units.

Fifth, officials from the Censorate traveled around the country continuously, investigating suspicious activity and reporting it to the central government.

Efforts to prevent refeudalization were economic as well as political. The imperial structure, on one hand, created wide economic opportunities for the merchant population. There were no regional or local political barriers to trade – no "town economies" as is medieval Europe or "domain economies" as in Tokugawa Japan, in which local governments attempted to officially exclude outsiders from pursuing profit opportunities. Moreover, the Manchu government granted monopolies over several arenas of production and commerce – most important, the salt and foreign trade monopolies – to favored merchants. Such merchants accumulated enormous fortunes through participation in the imperial monopolies, which gave them leverage to expand into many other arenas of trade in many other areas of China.[21]

The central government also took steps to secure this imperial opportunity structure from local forces that worked against it. For instance, during the Ming dynasty, when groups of local wholesale merchants tried to set up monopolies, the central government established trading warehouses in various cities at which visiting merchants could sell goods to local retailers.[22] During the Ch'ing dynasty, the government attempted to prevent local grain monopolies from arising by forbidding members of the local gentry class[23] from becoming grain brokers. Licenses were issued (upon payment of a fee) only to rich nongentry merchants. This measure, however, was circumvented through a black market in licenses.[24]

Once an empirewide economy was established, with merchants from everywhere going everywhere, however, the imperial government did not need to enforce the structure as the merchants found it in their own interest to do so. The hui-kuan, which proliferated enormously during the Ming-Ch'ing period, were the agents of this process. As mentioned above, these *landsmannschaften*, consisting of merchants from one town or province who traded in a strange area, vigorously pushed the interests of their group against local resistance. Far from being particularistic, as many have argued, they were the agents of universalism in traditional Chinese commerce.[25]

These carrot-and-stick policies of the Manchu government were aimed at preventing refeudalization and at maintaining the imperial structure; the Manchus did not move on to establish a strongly centralized system. Contrary to the theorists of "asiatic society" or "oriental despotism," they did not move to bureaucratize the officialdom. Nor did the government make powerful inroads on the wealth of the upper classes of landlords and merchants.

Was the Ch'ing officialdom bureaucratic?

The organization of China's officialdom lacked several qualities of the bureaucratic organization: (1) salaries and (2) central control over a high proportion of official activities and the personnel of the system.

Chinese officials were not salaried and dependent. On the one hand, many of those who entered the officialdom were from the upper classes of landlords and merchants, and they retained sources of income separate from their official positions.[26] On the other hand, officials did not receive a salary in the bureaucratic sense. Chinese officials received what is often termed a salary from the central government; however, this sum was intended not only as a personal remuneration but also as a means of paying for the officials' staff and for the purchase and upkeep of necessary equipment and facilities. This sum was very small and, moreover, had been fixed in the early eighteenth century, so that with inflation it became worth less and less.

Officials tended to make up for this by adding surcharges to the taxes they collected. These surcharges were not audited or checked by higher authorities, and thus a major source of officials' income from their position was largely out of central control.

These two features of the official's situation worked in what, from the imperial point of view, was a vicious circle. The more the official added surcharges and increased his income relative to the central government, the more he could buy land, invest in commerce, and so forth, and thus increase his independent sources of income.

It is often said that the Chinese administrative system was bureaucratic because there were many rules and regulations and because the hierarchy of national to provincial to local officials was engaged in supervising, checking, and auditing the activities of their subordinates to see whether they were in accord with the rules and regulations. However, the character and function of the rules and hierarchy in Ch'ing China differed from those in a modern bureaucracy in two important respects.

First, a much smaller proportion of the *activities* of the officials was subjected to rules and regulations and checked by superior officers and, second, a smaller proportion of the entire *personnel* who operated the system was subjected to central rules and regulations.

Activities of the officials

Let us take the operation of the fiscal system as an example. This is a critical example because it was probably *the* concern of the imperial government, as all scholars of the Chinese administrative system note.

The bulk of government revenues, about 75 percent, was derived from the land during the Ch'ing dynasty prior to the nineteenth century, and the provincial and local officials tended to add surcharges (a major source of their income) to the land tax. Let us take a closer look at the way this worked.

Wang points out that the Ch'ing taxes must be divided into "statutory" and "non-statutory" categories. The former were that portion that was collected and utilized in accord with rules and regulations established by the central government; the latter were that portion collected and utilized in accord with local decision making.[27]

A formal rate for the collection of the land taxes had been fixed during the early eighteenth century by the Yung-cheng emperor, and the rate was not raised throughout the remainder of the dynasty. It was mainly the revenues that were collected in accord with this fixed rate that were reported from lower to the higher levels, and it was the officials' performance in collecting and utilizing these taxes that served as the basis for evaluation of their general performance by the higher authorities.

The district magistrates reported to the provincial finance commissioners on the amounts collected. Of this, a certain proportion was retained in the districts for the magistrates' salary, expenses of schools, post stations, and the like and the remainder was forwarded to the provincial treasury. The provincial finance commissioner and the governor submitted a report on what had been collected to the Board of Revenue for auditing. The Board of Revenue then instructed the provinces on what part of the revenues was to be shipped to the capital and what part they might retain for provincial expenses. (Sometimes a province would be instructed to send part of its revenues to a province that had run a deficit, due to flood or drought, perhaps.) The expenditures that the provinces made were also audited by the Board of Revenue in order to check whether they had been made in accordance with rules.[28]

However, in addition to the basic tax rate the district officials collected "non-statutory" surcharges, and these tended to increase as time passed, as the local officials tried to keep up with inflation, to aggrandize their personal incomes, and so forth. The revenues supplied by the surcharges were partly retained on the local level and partly passed on to provincial officials in a complicated web of gifts, forced contributions, and customary fees.

In the seventeenth and eighteenth centuries, one-fifth of the total revenues collected were nonstatutory. Since the surcharges were always flexible (upward), the central government made little effort to regulate them. By the nineteenth and early twentieth centuries, an even larger percentage of the revenues was out of central control. Wang estimates that the total land revenues in 1908 were 102,400,000 taels. In 1903, however, the central Board of Revenue reported a land tax revenue of only 35,360,000 taels.[29]

System personnel

The rules and hierarchy of the Chinese administrative system differed from those of a modern bureaucracy in that they did not apply to as large a proportion of the personnel. In a modern bureaucracy all the personnel of the system are enrolled in the formal hierarchy and perform their functions in accord with central rules and regulations. In the Chinese imperial structure, however, a large proportion of the personnel who carried out the daily activities of administration were not formally officials; they were not, that is, recruited by the examination system (or by purchase of a degree or office from the imperial government) and they were not subject to promotion, demotion, or dismissal on the basis of their performance.

Some were personal staff of the official, selected and paid by him and maintaining a loyalty to him rather than to his superiors. For instance, most officials, from governors down to district magistrates, had a staff of secretaries and advisers (some of the latter highly specialized) who traveled with them from post to post. Some of these people were even relatives of the official or neighbors from his home province. The central government made a feeble effort to prohibit the hiring of relatives, ordering provincial officials to submit yearly reports on whom they had hired as secretaries, but the effort was foiled when none of the provincial officials followed the order.[30]

On the local level, the district magistrate not only had his personal staff of advisers and secretaries but was supplied with a staff of unofficial tax collecters, policemen, and clerks who more or less "went with" the office and had to be supported from the official's salary and appropriations from the surcharges.

The magistrate was supposed to select these people when he arrived at his post, but in practice the local people selected themselves: positions often appear to have been hereditary, and were freely bought and sold as well. Not only did the magistrate not control the selection of this staff, he had little control over its activities. Clerks, for instance, often extorted extra taxes from the population to an extent unknown to the magistrate. And because they had been in the locality through numerous official administrations and had knowledge of the files, they frequently ended up in almost complete control of the administration. Controlling the clerks was one of the major problems of every magistrate and was never resolved.[31] As one official said: "If they [the clerks] are dealt with leniently, they will seek personal profit by every means; if they are dealt with strictly, they will submit a statement asking to resign. Since there are hundreds of things to be done daily, they can hardly be allowed to leave. This is the concealed problem of an official and it cannot be mentioned openly." [32]

Thus many operations of the Chinese officialdom were not performed in accord witih regulations and subjected to scrutiny by an official hierarchy, and many personnel who performed the operations were not even part of the official system. The result was a tendency for power to shift toward the provinces and for the center to lose control.

The Chinese administrative system had a curious quality of fakery about it. There was, on one hand, an elaborate structure of rules, regulations, procedures, punishments, rewards, and so on, but on the other hand it appears to have been often little attended to.

There are several interesting indicators of the "fake" character of the Chinese bureaucracy. Ch'ü points out that magistrates usually had very little knowledge of the body of regulations that they were supposed to follow. The imperial government was more assiduous in establishing rules and regulations than in enforcing them. Magistrates were able to perform their duties in ignorance of much of the body of existing law.[33]

Also, edicts and regulations were often repetitive. The imperial government issued a large number of edicts, which made for a great show of authority, but many of them were repetitive in nature, which indicates their ineffectiveness. The best known of these are the numerous antiopium edicts of the late eighteenth and early nineteenth centuries.[34]

Again, despite a complicated schedule of rewards for good performance and punishment for bad, most officials were neither rewarded nor punished. Every three years, there was a grand reckoning when superiors evaluated their subordinates, classifying them into one of three categories: those who were "outstanding and distinctive," those who were incompetent or corrupt (which fell into eight categories: avarice, cruelty, tardiness, impropriety, old age, infirmity, incompetence, and hastiness), and those who were neither one nor the other. Those in the first category were advanced in grade, those in the second were demoted or dismissed, and those in the third were left alone. Most officials fell into the third category.[35]

Not only was the Chinese officialdom not bureaucratic, it appears that no serious efforts were made to increase bureaucratization. In contrast to Europe, where the direction was clear cut, examples are hard to find of Chinese government efforts at bureaucratization, and such efforts as were made do not appear to have been cumulative. One example is the Yung-cheng emperor's attempt (early in the eighteenth century) to expand official salaries in order to cut down on the expansion of taxation that had passed out of central control. Magistrates were given an additional stipend, called "money to nourish honesty." Although the amount was insufficient to accomplish the purpose, there were apparently no further efforts to increase official salaries.[36] Another example is that one of Yung-cheng's successors in 1820 tried to extend central jurisdiction over local surcharges; however, when he met provincial opposition he quickly gave up.[37]

Moreover, the policies of the Chinese government seem frequently to have gone deliberately in the opposite direction of centralization. As mentioned, the Yung-cheng emperor announced the fixing of the land tax at its current level, and it would never be raised, he said. And it never was.

Because the central government made little effort to aggrandize itself, the atmosphere of struggle that pervaded European history was much less intense in China. I believe this is what Ch'ü is getting at in the following statement:

The action and interaction of all the groups we have studied in detail indicate that there were strains and tensions among them: between the magistrate and his superior officials, between the magistrate and his clerks, runners, and personal servants, between the officials and the local gentry, between the people and the officials and their subordinates, and between the people and the gentry. As strains and tensions are often stimuli to change, we naturally ask why they induced no noticeable change in the Chinese situation. A decisive factor, I suggest, is that all these groups, with the single exception of the common people, secured maximal returns under the existing system. Therefore, in spite of the tensions and conflicts among them, they were not interested in altering the status quo and we find stability and continuity in the social and political order.[38]

Was the Chinese state the "real landlord"? Did the state suppress commerce?

It is one of the basic tenets of Wittfogel's theory of "oriental despotism" that the state hampers the development of commerce and industry by cutting into the wealth of private property holders through such devices as heavy taxation, confiscation, and fragmenting inheritance laws. This does not seem to be true of Ch'ing China, however. In fact, landlords and merchants had a great deal of wealth and power relative to the imperial government, and the government did not use its official apparatus to smash either landlord or merchant wealth. It may be true that the government controlled a larger share of the surplus than any *single* member of the upper class or small number of them in combination; however; the bulk of the surplus was in the hands of Chinese landlords and merchants, not the state, and this shaped and limited state power in important ways.

The Chinese government was a "landlord's dream."[39] Perkins estimates that the landlords of Szechwan province alone controlled funds equal to the amount raised by the basic government land tax.[40] Landlords were, for all practical purposes, tax exempt in Ch'ing China. Although they were in theory subject to taxation, local officials, themselves often landlords, reduced their taxes and pushed the burden onto the peasants. When tax rates were to be raised, the magistrates frequently discussed it with the local landlords. Newly opened land was often kept off the land registers by officials under pressure from local magnates, and also because the officials had an interest in reducing the total area within their jurisdiction that was subject to taxation so that they would not have to work so hard to collect the revenues due under the basic rate.[41]

The Chinese system of equal inheritance undoubtedly tended to fragment property, compared to a system of primogeniture or ultimogeniture. However, the impact was not to diminish private wealth at the expense of the public but rather to increase the size of the upper class. Moreover, there is some indication that the system of inheritance simply functioned as a stimulus to upper-class families to diversify their holdings (e.g., into commercial and industrial property and urban real estate as well as rural landholding) and thus to strengthen a family's overall wealth and ability to survive.[42]

Rather than attacks on the wealth of landlords, the official and military apparatus of the state was continuously invoked to protect their privileges from the wrath of the general population. When peasants rioted in protest of high rents or prices, or refused to pay rent, the army was sent to reduce them to submission.[43] Wittfogel has characterized this phenomenon as "paralysis of class struggle by total power." He writes:

During the middle period of the Ch'ing dynasty in 1746, some Fukienese tenants joined together in requesting an adjustment of their rents. Apparently this was nothing but an argument between two groups of private persons, yet the local officials quickly intervened, arrested, and punished the leaders. A subsequent edict blamed the provincial officials for the fact that "stupid people assemble and violate the law."[44]

If class struggle was paralyzed at certain times in Ch'ing China, it was not stifled in the interests of a despotism removed from the class struggle. It was stifled because the state interfered on behalf of the landlords or merchants, who therefore usually won the struggle.

This is indicative, moreover, not of the total power of the state but of its lack of power. Had the Ch'ing government rested on a salaried and dependent officialdom rather than on candidates produced by the upper classes, it might have tried to force landlords to reduce their rents so as to prevent riots, rebellions, and revolutions that threatened their rule; that is, it might have forced them to look to their long-range interests. This is a basic difference between the Ch'ing imperial state and the more powerful governments of contemporary capitalist societies, which establish minimum wage laws, force corporations to reduce occupational health hazards, and so on, setting maximum limits to exploitation of the working class. The capitalist state today, that is, is strong enough to curb certain short-range interests of sectors of the upper class in order to see to the long-range interests of the class as a whole.

The result of this disproportionately local and class-based control of resources in China, according to Perkins, was that

if local gentry-landlord economic power could be mobilized and placed under unified control, it could meet the economic power of the central government on nearly even terms. If several major provinces combined, the authorities in Peking were powerless to prevent it unless they could mobilize gentry resources in areas loyal to the central government. The more remote the rebelling province, and the greater its natural defenses, the more difficult was the task of Peking. Further, as more provinces broke away from central control, the power of the center declined, since it was a simple matter for the rebelling province to end the remittance of local land-tax revenue to Peking.[45]

"The surprising fact," remarks Perkins, "is that China held together at all."

Did the Chinese government suppress commerce? Chinese government economic policy was primarily a provisioning policy, designed to support the government and population with vital needs. It had, I believe, three major functions, and the suppression of commerce and private capital accumulation was not one of them.

The first function was the acquisition of revenues to supply the needs of the state. The bulk of government revenues, about 75 percent, came from agriculture, not commerce. Commerce was taxed, but more lightly than agriculture. The philosophy behind the taxation of commerce was hardly ruthless exploitation. Thomas Metzger writes that Chinese government documents emphasized the necessity of allowing merchants a large profit margin since commercial prosperity was the basis of the great taxpaying capacity of the richer Yangtze provinces. Squeezing merchants too much would kill the goose that laid the golden egg.[46]

Confiscations of merchants' property during the Ch'ing dynasty were also uncommon. According to Ho Ping-ti, "cases of rich merchants rendered bankrupt by extortionate officials . . . are exceptional rather than normal."[47] If Chinese merchants did not accumulate capital on a scale comparable to European merchants, the causes must be sought not in the government's suppression of capital accumulation but in the government's failure to undertake economic policies that had the effect of encouraging capital accumulation.

Government revenues increased only slowly in China during the Ch'ing dynasty, from around 28 million taels of silver annually in the Shun-chih reign in the seventeenth century to 43–48 million in the Ch'ien-lung reign in the eighteenth century. Moreover, the imperial government generally had a surplus; Ch'ien-lung, for instance, left a surplus of 70 million taels at the end of his reign.[48] In Europe, in contrast, expenditures were always rocketing upward and revenues had to be found to meet them (see "State economic policy" in chapter 3). Due to a continually expanding government apparatus and accelerating military expenditures, the needed amount continually outstripped what could be taken from the peasants, nobles, and merchants and, as a result, European rulers vied with one another to borrow money from financiers. Large and increasing public debts were established, frequently relieved at first through repudiation but later honored and thereby providing enormous impetus to capital accumulation. Because the state apparatus and its activities did not grow continually and rapidly in China, the imperial government was able to live on its established tax sources. In fact, rather than borrow from merchants the Chinese government often lent money to them to earn interest![49]

A second function of Ch'ing economic policy was to ensure an adequate supply of the commodities needed by the civil and military apparatus. Balasz, Hucker, and others have argued that the Chinese imperial government restricted capital accumulation by refusing to purchase many of the goods it needed from private capitalists and, instead, organizing their production in government workshops:

The major factor in repressing the growth of business interests was . . . active government monopolization of the production and distribution of various commodities. . . . Manufactured goods that were consumed by the government itself were, generally speaking, produced by the government. Peking abounded with armories, textile factories, metalwork shops, leatherwork shops, saddlery shops, paint shops, apparel factories, wineries, and the like, all operated by the Ministry of Works or by eunuchs, to provide the court and the central government with their commodity needs. In addition, there were government-operated weaving and dying [sic] establishments at Nanking, Su-chou, Hang-chou and other great cities, and a famous pottery factory at Ching-te-chen in Kiangsi province. Since the government was by far the largest single consumer of many commodities, its reliance on its own producing agencies deprived private businessmen of one of their best opportunities for enrichment.[50]

This argument rests upon the assumption that the demand generated by the central government was highly significant in the overall economy. But was it? The central government may have been the largest consumer of metal for armaments and coins, but what about the demand for textiles, pottery, and other consumption items? The central government, or even the officialdom as a whole, was only a small percentage of the upper-class population that consumed such items.

Of about 20,000 civil officials in Ch'ing China, only half were employed in the central government. The broader stratum of degree holders who aspired to office numbered over a million. And affluent landlords and merchants must have been double or triple this, if not more. Altogether, the nonpeasant sector constituted at least 15 percent of the population. It would seem that there were many opportunities for enrichment through production for consumers outside the central government.

A third major function was to ensure an adequate supply of basic foodstuffs and other necessities to the rural and urban populations in order to prevent rebellion. Policies concerned with this included maintenance of irrigation and flood-control works; manipulation of the monetary supply so as to promote steady but minor inflation, which was believed to stimulate peasant production (see "China's incorporation and the Taiping Rebellion" in chapter 6); and efforts to prevent merchants from making profits from vital commodities at the expense of popular needs.

To this latter end (and also with revenue in mind), the imperial government had for centuries established monopolies in key commodities such as salt and iron and had created the system of "ever-normal granaries" under which grain was stored by provincial governments, to be released in times of dearth. Did such policies restrict capital accumulation and suppress commerce?

This, again, is not very plausible. As for monopolies, large and lucrative areas of commerce were *not* monopolies; the trade in tea, silk, sugar, cotton, tobacco, and so forth were all open. Moreover, as the experience of government regulation in contemporary capitalist countries and mercantilist England shows, where everything "from buttons to mousetraps" was a government monopoly, government monopolies are hardly inconsistent with higher levels of capital accumulation than prevailed in Ch'ing China.

As for the "ever-normal granaries," their amount of grain was not significant in terms of the economy as a whole. During the eighteenth century, for instance, it probably constituted only 3 to 4 percent of the country's total grain output. It was never sufficient to alleviate more than the most minor crop failure.[51]

The Chinese government's foreign trade policies have often been attacked as an obstacle to commercial expansion. Heavy taxes and the restriction of Western trade to Macao and Canton, where it was monopolized by a dozen-odd merchant firms, are said to have significantly hampered trade and thus capital accumulation and the rise of the bourgeoisie. As we have seen, the Ming and Ch'ing governments' policies toward foreign trade were more restrictive than in previous dynasties. However, I would argue that the "suppressive" effects of these policies have been exaggerated.

The government appears to have had two major concerns about foreign trade, the first of which was the provisioning concern with regard to vital goods. Like many of the towns and principalities of medieval Europe, the aim was to ensure that people and government were well supplied with foodstuffs and other commodities they needed. The export of vital commodities was regarded as threatening the supply at home, not as a means of increasing the overall demand for them and thereby stimulating their production on a larger scale at home. Thus the Chinese government forbade the export of grain, iron, and a variety of other goods and, in general, may have taxed exports more heavily than imports.

This policy cannot be regarded as having suppressed commerce with the West, however. The items that were most highly sought by European traders (such as silk, tea, and porcelain) were exported in large quantities.

The second major concern was revenue. Like domestic commerce, foreign commerce was regarded as a source of revenue but, again, was not to be taxed so heavily as to retard its growth.

The basic tariff rates for imports in the late eighteenth and early nineteenth centuries, according to Wright, were about 4 percent of the value of the goods, and about 16 percent, for exports; surcharges and "squeeze" raised them by perhaps four times. Western merchants in China complained that these tariff rates (from 16 to 64 percent) were extraordinarily high, and their complaints have been generally regarded as justified by Western scholars.

Were these rates really high? It is instructive to compare them with rates prevailing in Western Europe at the same time, for instance, with the British tariffs on tea. The import rate on tea ranged from 76 to 128 percent ad valorem up to 1784, was reduced to 12.5 percent in that year, but crept up to 100 percent during the next twenty years, where it remained until 1833![52]

The major difference between the Chinese and the European old regimes seems to be not that the Chinese government was able to *suppress* commerce and industry, whereas the European governments were not, but that the Chinese simply failed to *promote* commerce and industry as the European governments did. Chinese policy *did* have certain mercantilist elements. For example, the government carefully fostered key national industries, such as copper mining in Yunnan. The government also furthered the development of a national market by establishing the road network linking all of China's major regions and by promoting the construction and maintenance of the Grand Canal and other waterworks. Moreover, the imperial system of rule prohibited internal tax barriers to trade dictated by local interests. However, despite these elements, the policy as a whole was passive. The government neither greatly interfered with the economy nor greatly promoted its growth.

Contradictions in the imperial system

It must be emphasized that although the pace of change in Ch'ing China was slow, China was hardly unchanging or without social conflict. Revolutions and rebellions occurred repeatedly in Chinese history. However, the imperial model of government was such an ingenious mechanism for maintaining stability and providing profit opportunities that revolutionary movements tended to establish a new imperial government under control of the revolutionaries rather than a "provincial secession" or restoration of feudalism.

Opposition in China had two major sources, which joined together in most revolts that truly threatened the existing dynasty:

an opposition from above, that is, from elements in the upper classes of landlords and merchants, and an opposition from below, that is, from the peasantry.

The upper classes as a source of opposition

A major flaw in the imperial structure was that its carrot of social mobility simply was not held out to enough members of the upper classes. The available merchant monopolies and official positions could accommodate only a small percentage of the candidates.

As noted above, there were only some 20,000 civil and 7,000 military offices. Competing for these offices were about 120,000 upper gentry – men who had won higher degrees by passing examinations or through purchase. Attempting to get into the higher gentry were about 980,000 lower gentry – men who had won lower degrees through examination or purchase. And besides them were countless others who aspired, but failed, to pass the examinations.

The most lucrative government monopolies – the salt monopoly and the Canton foreign trade monopoly – were granted to only a few merchants. In the Liang-huai salt area, for instance, "which easily outstripped all other areas in production, sale and revenue," about thirty merchants were in control of the production and 230 were in control of the distribution.[53] The Canton monopolists numbered around a dozen.[54] Moreover, these positions came to be disproportionately controlled by men from certain provinces: the salt monopoly by natives of Shansi, Shensi, and Anhwei; the Canton monopoly by natives of Kwangtung. And since the monopolies gave them a better chance than other merchants to accumulate capital, the natives of these areas came to figure prominently in the trade of other provinces.[55]

Under normal circumstances, the disadvantaged elements of the upper classes were "pacified" by competition to get into the system and by the imperial control structure that made organization difficult. However, peasant rebellions often broke out, and if disadvantaged upper-class elements could seize leadership of the rebellions, they were provided a base for seizing power.

Even in peaceful times, however, many upper-class people maintained ties to the peasants that were potentially revolutionary. They joined with peasants in the omnipresent Chinese secret societies, which "drew their members from disaffected gentry, from the peasantry, especially from dispossessed and marginal peasantry, and from artisans, petty merchants, smugglers, demobilized soldiers and bandits."[56] The situation is described in these lines about the ritual initiations of new members in a nineteenth-century secret society:

The happy ties of the brethren are with
  incense fire solemnized:

After burning the incense can there still
  be barriers between you and me?

Officials, scholars – all into the fold are
  received;

Yamen runners, servants, soldiers – none is barred![57]

The participation of people from the upper classes was critical in several ways if a peasant rebellion was to become a serious challenge to the dynasty, that is, if it was to become more than a local event, a revolution rather than a rebellion or revolt. They were helpful in formulating an ideology for the movement and, most important – unlike the peasants, whose horizons usually extended only as far as the nearest market town – they had supralocal contacts who were helpful in linking simultaneous local revolts into an empirewide movement. Merchants who engaged in commerce had contacts along the myriad trade routes of the empire. Men who had held office or participated in the official examinations could count on the loyalty of former classmates, examination mates, and colleagues scattered throughout the land.[58]

The peasantry as a source of opposition
The Ming dynasty was toppled by a peasant revolt in conjunction with the Manchu invasion; the Ch'ing dynasty was nearly toppled in the mid-nineteenth century by a peasant revolt in conjunction with the Western invasion. The imperial system contained contradictions within itself that bred increasing peasant opposition to the system, contradictions that have been summarized by Chinese historians in the "dynastic cycle" theory.[59]

The dynastic cycle theory is somewhat suspicious because it neatly legitimizes the overthrow of the corrupt old dynasty by a new one. Indeed, this is the function the theory has served in Chinese history writing, as the history of the old dynasty in China has usually been written by members of the new one. Nevertheless, the theory helps make sense out of Chinese history.

The imperial system, as we have seen, rested on the ability of landlords and merchants to siphon off a disproportionate amount of the peasant surplus. Because local officials, searching for additional revenues to keep up with inflation and to add to their personal incomes, were confronted with the massive resistance of landlords and merchants, they could make inroads only on the income of "independent" peasants, that is, peasants who did not till land that was owned by others whose power was sufficient to ward off increased taxation.

In the early years of a dynasty, according to the theory, the amount of land held by landlords tended to be minimal because the insurgents murdered many of them, the peasants seized the land of those who had taken flight, and the new rulers confiscated the land of their enemies. Taxes tended to be lighter, in part because the new dynasty was trying to pacify the country and in part because the new central government had sufficient control over local officials to prevent them from adding surcharges.

As time passed, however, new landlords emerged and old landlords added to their holdings, as a consequence of wealth accumulated through officeholding or the profits of commerce. Taxes on the independent peasants increased as local officials raised surcharges. And as independent peasants came to be burdened with heavier and heavier taxes, they began to sell their land to landlords, thus accelerating the vicious circle.

During the Ch'ing dynasty, though peasant revolts had occurred from the earliest times, these revolts occurred with increasing frequency and on an increasingly large scale beginning in the late eighteenth century. The great White Lotus rebellion (1796–1804) was the culmination of several decades of growing revolt. This rebellion covered large parts of several provinces and was put down by the government only with difficulty, after almost ten years of fighting.[60]

Dynasties have often maintained themselves in China, despite the operation of this "internal" cycle, until external events provoked a sudden and large tax increase that the peasants would no longer tolerate. Due to long periods of peace and government stagnation, taxes tended to rise slowly, and large increases came as a shock to the entire system. For instance, in the latter years of the Ming dynasty taxes increased suddenly and greatly, primarily due to sudden expenditures occasioned by the Manchu pressures. According to Wang,

For more than fifty years before the fall of the dynasty, the agricultural economy of China was being bled to exhaustion by special taxes levied on the peasantry and known by such names as "Liaotung supply", "expedition supply", and "training supply", which were supposed to finance and provision the armies fighting against the Manchus in South Manchuria.[61]

Again, in the Ch'ing dynasty, the peasantry's real threat to the dynasty came in the Taiping Rebellion of the 1850s, but only after the invasion of the Western powers and the increased expenditures for defense that this entailed:

By the middle of the nineteenth century . . . huge expenditures were necessary, but the only reward for the peasants was an increase in the demand for land tax, and for China the humiliating Treaty of Nanking, which destroyed national independence and legalized the import of opium, again increasing the burden of the people. The process of collapse was thus moved forward a stage, and in 1851 there began in the south, in Kuangsi, the Taiping Rebellion, followed a year or two later in the north by the rebellion of the Nien Min, in Shantung, together with a Moslem rebellion in Yunnan. . . . Then came the British and French occupation of Peking in 1860, when vast amounts of money had to be raised to meet war expenses and an indemnity of 18 million taels. In 1862 the Moslem rebellion spread to the northwest provinces, with the result that more than half of China was beyond the control of the central government.[62]

Dynastic cycle theorists usually relate *internal* and *external* in the following way. External invasions are the fault of internal decay and corruption. If officials had not increased taxes and if landlords had not accumulated land, the society would have remained strong enough to fight off outside invasions. Too little attention has been paid, in my opinion, to the other part of the cycle. A comparative study of the impact of external relations on internal events in the various historical empires and in the emerging national states of modern Europe would probably be very illuminating.

3

State and economy in Tokugawa Japan

Structure and development of the state

Unlike China, Japan remained a feudal state into the nineteenth century. However, this state had some intriguingly centralized features. In some respects, in fact, feudal Japan was more bureaucratic than China. To understand the development of the state during the Tokugawa period, it is necessary to recount Japan's earlier development.

In the eighth century an imperial state was established in Japan for the first time. The country was divided into provinces and districts and administered by officials recruited from the nobility. After a few centuries, however, the powers of the imperial officials had begun to be usurped by regional military commanders.

For several centuries the institutions of empire and those created by the military commanders continued to exist side by side. The most powerful commanders even legitimized their hegemony by obtaining the imperially bestowed title of *shogun* or general. But the power of the central government steadily waned, and by the fifteenth century the imperial structure had all but disappeared. Little was left but a powerless emperor and his court in Kyoto. Japan was divided into the 200-plus domains that were ruled by the military nobility (the daimyo) and their vassal samurai.

The fifteenth century is termed the Warring States Period by Japanese historians.[1] The century was one of incessant warfare among the domains, in which none was able to achieve a stable hegemony. Toward the end of the century, however, there appeared in succession three "great unifiers" (Hall). These men enlarged their domains at the expense of others, entered into alliances with some of the han that remained, and the alliances reduced the others to submission. The first two unifiers died before they could consolidate their conquests, but the third, Tokugawa Ieyasu, lived long enough to create a structure that pre-served the hegemony of his family for the next 200 years.[2]

The Ch'ing rulers, looking across the sea at Japan, must have regarded the Tokugawa unification as a miserable failure. Toku-gawa Ieyasu did not try to establish an imperial state. The im-perial court continued to exist at Kyoto – although lacking in any real power – and the Tokugawa rulers styled themselves shogun in the manner of their predecessors. Tokugawa Ieyasu and his successors contented themselves with living off their personal domains and maintaining a loose hegemony over the 200-odd other lords. The shogun sometimes exacted monetary contribu-tions or labor services from the han, but the latter were basically independent, compared with the provinces of an "empire." The daimyo retained their private armies and were in full control of local tax collection.[3]

The Tokugawa supremacy rested on three factors: the large size and wealth of the Tokugawa personal domains, compared to those of the other daimyo; the ability to dole out official positions in the Tokugawa administrative structure, or *bakufu*,[4] to some of the daimyo; and a complex structure of controls on the activities of the daimyo and the imperial court.

The Tokugawa domains at the beginning of the seventeenth century yielded about one-third of the agricultural output of the country. This was perhaps six or seven times larger than that of any other domain. Most of the other domains were small, how-ever, though some were quite large. The yield of the sixteen next-largest domains amounted to another one-third of the country's agricultural output.[5]

The wealth of the Tokugawa domains was more than agrarian. The shogun had gained control of most of the country's gold and silver mines. Moreover, the Tokugawa domains included Japan's largest and most important cities: Osaka, the center of Japan's domestic commerce; the new capital of Edo, which grew to a population of over a million and also became a commercial center; and Nagasaki, the center of foreign commerce. Control of the major commercial cities of the time meant control of an im-portant source of revenue.

The government of the Tokugawa domains was amazingly ex-tensive. There were about 17,000 civil and military offices; in an area far smaller than China there were almost as many offices.

The major government offices were the State Council, which advised the shogun; the Junior Council, which served the State Council; a Censorate, which watched over the other officials and the daimyo; another set of officials who watched over the court at Kyoto; the mayors and governors of the large cities; and a Finance Commission. For purposes of tax collection and local administration, the Tokugawa domain was divided into districts, presided over by forty to fifty intendants who, like the Chinese district magistrates, combined fiscal, police, and judicial functions. There were also numerous military units.[6]

In contrast to the open opportunity structure of the Chinese administration, access to positions in the Tokugawa officialdom was highly restricted. Most of the domain offices were occupied by the vassal samurai of the shogun. And the highest positions in the administration (numbering about sixty) were reserved for a select group of the daimyo.

In general, Tokugawa policy was to permit friendly daimyo to participate in the administration and to exclude the rest. The daimyo can be classified into categories in terms of

1 Their status as friends or enemies – whether they had been allied with Tokugawa Ieyasu before the decisive Battle of Sekigahara, after which he was recognized as shogun. Allies included the twenty-three *shimpan* or "related" daimyo, who were bound by kinship ties to the Tokugawa family, and the approximately 150 *fudai* or "inside" diamyo, who had formed alliances with the Tokugawa before Sekigahara. Enemies were the approximately 100 *tozama* or "outside" diamyo, who had been enemies before Sekigahara.

2 The status of their domains – whether their domains were large, contiguous, and defensible units. Many of the shimpan and tozama had domains that could serve as an independent military power base. However, only about twelve of the 150 domains of the fudai daimyo qualified. Most of the fudai domains were small and scattered, and many of the scattered sites were surrounded by land belonging to the Tokugawa.

3 Special considerations. The shimpan daimyo, even when their domains were small, were threats because they had special hereditary rights, such as the right to succeed to the shogunate if the Tokugawa main line died out.

The shimpan and the tozama daimyo were excluded from officeholding in the Tokugawa administration, as were the twelve largest fudai daimyo. This left about 140 of the fudai daimyo, who at any given time were competing for positions.[7]

Officeholding entailed a grant of land or a stipend, either of which was welcome to the fudai daimyo with small domains. Officeholding also brought other concrete benefits, such as easier access to credit and ability to influence bukufu economic policy to the benefit of one's land (e.g., if one's land was surrounded by land belonging to the bakufu and the bakufu planned to construct irrigation works, it was to one's benefit to be able to influence their planning).

There was a ladder or hierarchy of positions, and a young man had to work his way up to the top. The point at which he entered the hierarchy, however, depended upon his family's rank in the feudal hierarchy, that is, on the size of his family's domain relative to the others. Some of the positions, usually the lower, less desirable ones (most frequently military officers), were completely hereditary; others were competed for and awarded on the basis of contacts, nepotism, or ability. There was no formal selection procedure such as the Chinese examination system.[8]

Although access to the system was open only to the fudai daimyo, these few were well taken care of: at any given time, about 40 percent of the eligible fudai and other diamyo held office in the bukufu regime, and "most families could expect to reap the benefits of bakufu office at one time or another in almost every generation."[9] Compare this to the 120,000 upper gentry and 980,000 lower gentry, all aspiring to the 27,000 offices in China. By this method the loyalty of the fudai daimyo was guaranteed.

The third method by which the Tokugawa preserved their hegemony was a system of controls over the activities of the daimyo and the imperial court. The han were prohibited from forming marital alliances without the consent of the shogun, to make contact with the court, to build military fortifications without the consent of the shogun, to build oceangoing ships, and so forth. Censorial officials watched the han to ensure that these prohibitions were obeyed. In addition, the Tokugawa had placed loyal han in strategic positions around potential enemies, and thus one han watched the other. There were even special residents in some of the shimpan domains, reminiscent of the Manchu method of controlling Tibet and other outlying areas.

The most important control was the *sankin kotai* ("alternate attendance") system.[10] Under this system the daimyo were required to build residences in the capital, Edo, and to come to the capital regularly for attendance upon the shogun. The fudai daimyo usually came for a six-month period, went home for six months, returned for another six months, and so on. The tozama daimyo alternated in periods of one year. While the daimyo were away they were made to leave their wives and childen in the residences at Edo as hostages.

The sankin kotai system functioned as a control in two major ways. First, leaving hostages made revolt extremely unpleasant. Second, the expenses entailed by the establishment of two residences were very great and tended to weaken the finances of the daimyo vis-à-vis the shogun.

Despite all these factors, the Tokugawa hegemony was precarious. Theorists of Japanese feudalism are correct in arguing that this was not a very centralized structure. It was much more unstable than the Chinese imperial, let alone a national, structure.

Because the han retained essential powers of government, fiscal and military, there was no way to prevent them from eventually gathering sufficient strength to reopen the struggle. Over the two centuries of Tokugawa rule, economic power shifted in favor of the han. Agricultural productivity increased in the han, commerce increased, and the wealth of the han grew; yet the Tokugawa rulers had no systematic means of siphoning off the expanded wealth. In the early seventeenth century, as mentioned above, about one-third of the agricultural output of the country was produced by the bakufu domains; by the nineteenth century, however, their share had shrunk to about 23 percent.[11]

Unlike the Chinese structure, the Tokugawa provided few material benefits to local rulers. The annoyance of the controls was not counterbalanced by positive inducements for the largest and wealthiest han. The independence of the han, together with this lack of positive inducements, was the major weakness of the Japanese state compared to the Chinese.

Despite this, the Tokugawa rulers (as in China) did not make any effort to achieve a further centralization of power. They kept the system as it had been established in the early years of the regime. In the beginning of their period of rule, the Tokugawa had confiscated certain domains and shifted various daimyo around, rewarding some and punishing others. However, this was later halted; a status quo was established. And apparently there were never any attempts to abolish the han or end their fiscal autonomy.

Many scholars have characterized the Tokugawa situation as "centralized feudalism." As Bolitho points out, this concept is imprecise because it glosses over the *direction* of change:

[It suggests] a passive balance of forces which were in fact in constant tension and competition . . . one of the two warring elements has always predominated over the other. In France and England, the balance was overturned when the monarch began to destroy the feudal order around him, making himself stronger at the expense of his barons. In Japan, there was a similar rejection of passive balance but in the opposite direction, towards a diminution of central powers with increasing baronial independence.[12]

Although Japan as a whole was politically decentralized, this was not true of the internal structure of the domains of the daimyo and shogun.

There appears to be an inverse relationship in prenational states between the degree of centralization on the societywide or "national" level and the degree of centralization on the local level. Paradoxically, although the Tokugawa state was far less centralized societywide than the Chinese imperial state, the daimyo and shogun exercised much greater control over affairs in their domains than did Chinese provincial officials. Heckscher has pointed out a similar contrast between France and Germany in the seventeenth and eighteenth centuries: in France an imperial provincial structure coexisted with a high degree of independence of local tax-collectors, judges, etc., while in Germany the princes remained independent but exercised strict control over local administrations.[13]

The structures of state and society in the han and in the Tokugawa domain were very similar. Both were administered by a staff of officials and recruitment to office was determined by rank and connections. The samurai were ranked, as noted above, by the size of their fiefs or stipends; the higher the rank, the higher the office to which one might aspire.

The domains were more centralized than the Chinese provinces in two ways. First, the upper class had been removed from the land and turned into a group of dependent stipendiaries. Prior to the fifteenth century, the samurai had been landed nobility, smaller versions of the daimyo. During the Warring States Period, however, the samurai had generally moved off the land and into the fortified castle-towns of their lords. After the establishment of Tokugawa hegemony, this situation was imposed as a norm. The samurai became stipendiaries, living on grants of rice. Collection of the tax rice was made by the daimyo's official staff, the rice was stored in the castle-town in a warehouse, and was doled out to the stipendiaries. In some cases the value of the stipend was attached to the yield of specific pieces of land that the samurai had formerly held, but in others the stipend was fixed and came from the general yield of the domain land.

The removal of the samurai from the land gave the daimyo and the shogun vastly greater power over them than the

Chinese officials had over the landlords and gentry. Because the samurai were totally dependent on the state for their support, they could be pushed around much more easily. In a fiscal crisis, for example, the daimyo or shogun could simply slash the samurai stipends in order to cut expenditures. And because the state was in a fiscal crisis throughout the Tokugawa period, samurai stipends were steadily cut, pushing many of the samurai into debt, forcing them to take to trade, and so forth.

Second, the administration of the Tokugawa domain, and probably that of many of the other domains, developed from a decentralized situation like China's into an almost bureaucratic structure.

In the early Tokugawa period, intendants operated in much the same way as the Chinese district magistrates:

Imitating fief-holders, they built elaborate defensive walls around their official residences . . . giving themselves undue strength at the expense of both the local peasants and the bakufu. Tax rates and corvee labor duties were fixed by bakufu regulations, but Ieyasu's intendants tended arbitrarily to levy excessive corvee on local farmers for various private reasons, for example, to build and maintain their elegant private residences, to till their vegetable lots, to transport tax goods to Edo, to sustain the necessary post-horse messenger system, and to perform numerous ceremonial functions on the intendant's behalf. Moreover . . . the intendants were instructed to deduct their operating costs from tax receipts.[14]

However, the shoguns successively reduced the powers of their intendants:

By the mid-eighteenth century the intendants had completely lost their military character; they were unable to exploit the peasantry significantly; they had difficulty feathering their nest at bakufu expense; and they rarely found themselves able to make their position a hereditary sinecure . . . they had developed into effective representatives of the bakufu.[15]

According to Totman, only about 6 percent of the revenues collected by the intendants went into their pockets. This amount, he points out, compares favorably with what it costs contemporary governments to collect their taxes.[16]

The centralized character of domain administration must not be exaggerated, however. The samurai may have become dependent, and they were more easily dealt with than Chinese landlords, but they by no means gave up. They periodically pressured the bakufu and daimyo into seeing that their unpaid debts to merchants were repudiated and they demanded greater access to official positions in exchange for stipend cuts.[17]

In addition, as discussed in chapter 1, a local and rich peasant or landlord elite remained in the countryside. With the growth of commerce, many of this group became increasingly wealthy, wealthier in some cases than the stipendiaries. They began to purchase the right to bear swords from impoverished samurai families, to intermarry with the intendants, and to claim the right to become intendants. This class opposed higher land taxes and was doubtless beginning to see that taxes were transferred to the poorer peasants (as did the landlord class in China).

State economic policy

As in China, the economic policy of the bakufu and han was of a provisioning kind. The major function was to produce revenue to supply the stratum of tax dependents and to ensure an adequate supply of necessities to the government and to the rural and urban populations. If anything, the Tokugawa government probably did more to suppress merchants and landholders than did the Ch'ing. As noted above, in foreign commerce the Tokugawa rulers were more restrictive than the Chinese. And the bakufu and daimyo, as we have seen, constantly cut the stipends of the samurai.

Bakufu and han revenues in Japan were produced primarily through taxes on agriculture and commerce, monetary manipulations aimed at keeping the price of rice high, and loans raised from merchants. A major difference between China and Japan was the Japanese government's greater reliance on commerce as a source of revenue through a proliferation of bakufu and han commercial monopolies and licenses and through borrowing from merchants. This phenomenon is often taken as a sign of greater commercialization in Japan and as an indicator of similarities between Japan and the nations of Western Europe, assumptions that will be questioned below.

The Tokugawa and han rulers and the samurai class as a whole incessantly borrowed from the Japanese merchants, and just as incessantly repudiated their debts. There was also much greater interest in taxing the proceeds of commerce in Japan than in China. For instance, in China the revenue from commercial taxes amounted to only about one quarter of the total revenue in the eighteenth and early nineteenth centuries; in Japan it approached one-half in the bakufu domains by 1841.[18]

Or, though in China there were only a few monopolies, in Japan the bakufu and many of the han granted numerous monopolies to merchants in exchange for revenues.

These monopolies were a source of much conflict in Japan. The Tokugawa rulers were no more able to guarantee nation-wide economic opportunities to Japanese merchants than nation-wide political opportunities to all the daimyo. The bakufu granted monopolies over the distribution of many commodities, but the privileges of the monopoly merchants could be main-tained only within the shogun's jurisdiction, primarily within the shogunal and smaller fudai domains. The han maintained "do-main economies," granting monopolies over the sale of domain products inside and outside the domain to local merchants and excluding merchants from other areas of the country from trans-actions within the domain.[19] The result was dissatisfaction in all quarters: Tokugawa monopolists were pitted against han mo-nopolists and the monopolists of one han against those of another.

Many people have pointed out the parallel between govern-ment indebtedness and the reliance on commerce as a source of revenue in Japan and in early modern Europe and have con-trasted this with China. The similarities between Japan and Europe are usually attributed to the impact of commercialization, and the assumption is made that government indebtedness to merchants in Japan portended the rise of industrial capitalism. An argument is often presented that is reminiscent of Sombart's "luxury and capitalism":

In the beginning of the Tokugawa period the expenditures of Japan's rulers were in line with their revenues. Then they moved into the city and commercialization set in. An ever rising demand for luxury goods was engendered by the competitive status-seeking environment of Edo and encouraged by profit-seeking merchants. A discrepancy arose between the rulers' revenues, de-rived mainly from agricultural products, and the prices of manu-factured luxury items. Expenditures began to outstrip revenues, and Japan's rulers went increasingly into debt to the merchant class.

Is this an adequate explanation? At first glance it seems very plausible that such mechanisms might have been at work in Japan and not in China. The expenditures of shogun and daimyo appear to have been rising more rapidly in Japan than in China. For instance, the Choshu han debts rose by about four times between 1682 and 1840. As noted above, Chinese revenues did not even double from the seventeenth to the eighteenth century and the state did not resort to borrowing. However, was this difference due to Japan's far greater commercialization? Can it be compared to the phenomenon of indebtedness in the states of Europe?

First, the commercialization argument overlooks the far greater proportion of the population that the Japanese state undertook to support. It seems that the development of commerce in Japan probably intensified a problem that was present from the outset of the Tokugawa period: supporting a numerous unproductive stratum on a relatively poor agrarian base. For example, in the Tokugawa domain the crisis in finances seems to have set in early in the seventeenth century, prior to the greatest rise in commerce, or as soon as the rulers had used up the stores of treasure they had amassed during the earlier period of warfare (through conquest, foreign trade, and the seizure of silver mines). When the silver mines gave out and when the surpluses were exhausted in paying for normal expenses and some unusual disasters (such as repairs after a great fire in Edo in 1657), the support of the samurai became increasingly difficult, especially when natural disasters made for a poor harvest, as frequently happened.[20] The fiscal crisis also began in Choshu in the early seventeenth century, according to Craig.[21]

The samurai were a much larger stratum in relation to the population than were the Chinese tax dependents: the Manchu peoples, the Manchu and Chinese degree-holding officialdom, and the quasi-official degree-holding activists. In Japan as a whole, they were 6 to 7 percent of the population; and in some areas, such as Choshu, they were as much as 10 percent of the population. In contrast, the degree holders constituted only about 1.3 percent of the Chinese population, and the Manchu nobility and Bannermen an even smaller percent.[22] Moreover, as noted above, only a tiny percent of China's degree holders were directly state supported, that is, officeholders who received stipends directly from the state treasury. The bulk of the gentry lived on income from land, commerce, schoolteaching, and fees collected from peasants for various services. But the bulk of the samurai was *largely* supported by stipends and income from salaried positions. In the Tokugawa domains, for example, 89 percent of the samurai received stipends and 78 percent of the lower-ranking and 25 to 40 percent of the higher-ranking samurai were dependent on additional income from government jobs.[23] Have any other agrarian rulers in world history made such a lengthy experiment in providing for such a large upper class in this style?

Second, luxury created only part of the rising demand for revenues by European rulers. Another and major part was war (see Sombart's *Krieg und Kapitalismus,* the companion to *Luxus und Kapitalismus*). War expenditures have been one of the most important causes of rising state indebtedness in the West from the sixteenth century to the present. And war expenditures in the West were associated with mercantilist economic policies that promoted capitalist industrial development. Warfare promoted colonial expansion; warfare provided large markets for the armaments industries (iron and steel, textile and leather manufactures, etc.); warfare produced windfall gains that increased government revenues and provided funds to subsidize national industries; and so forth. In Tokugawa Japan, as well as in Ch'ing China before the nineteenth-century Western expansion, large military expenditures did not accumulate after the initial pacification in the seventeenth century. *Pax Tokugawa* and *Pax Ch'ing* created an entirely different world from the European one, which has steadily alternated between warfare and armed peace for centuries.

As a result, although Japanese revenues and debts rose more rapidly than the Chinese, they did not rise as rapidly as those of the European governments. For example, Choshu's debts rose by only about four times between 1682 and 1840. In contrast, the English national debt increased thirty-six-fold from 1697 to 1827 and the French debt twenty-seven-fold from 1678 to 1830.[24]

Thus the similarities between Tokugawa Japan and Europe seem to be superficial. The increased revenues of the bakufu and han were used primarily to support a large and increasing upper-class stratum in its accustomed, luxurious life-style. The increased profits of the moneylenders, in turn, were also going into personal luxury expenditures, as well as into the established agricultural, handicraft, and commercial activities.

I have been arguing that government economic policy in Japan was more similar to that of China than to the states of early modern Europe. If this is the case, what accounts for the greater rapidity with which Japan's economy was growing? Let us return to this question, which was raised at the end of the last chapter but not answered.

Political institutions and demand

A major source of rapid change in Japan seems to have been a rapid increase in demand, caused by the sudden and extensive urbanization of much of Japan's upper class at the outset of the Tokugawa regime. Such important increases in demand did not occur in China at this time. As we have seen, the pattern of Chinese urbanization had been set for centuries and city populations were expanding in a stable manner. And no other factors promoting a rapid increase in demand (such as a major breakthrough in transport technology or a rapid emergence of foreign markets) had appeared.

In the century prior to the establishment of Tokugawa rule, the samurai were dispersed about the country and there was incessant warfare among the domains. With the establishment of the Tokugawa hegemony, and with peace, all this changed. One of the major methods the Tokugawa used to control the daimyo was the sankin kotai system, which required the daimyo to install their families in residences at the capital and to divide their time between the capital and their domains. The daimyo, accompanied by large retinues of samurai, resided much of the time, therefore, in Edo, and much of the domain tax was sold and consumed in the capital.

Edo was transformed from a small town into a vast city with a population of over a million. Over half the population was composed of the families of the Tokugawa rulers, the daimyo, and their retainers; the remainder consisted of artisans and merchants.[25] The city of Osaka became a large commercial center that funneled goods into Edo. And with peace the urban samurai and merchants began to consume on a large scale.

The importance of the sheer size of Edo for Japan's economic transformation cannot be underestimated. As Spencer points out, it was a huge city by eighteenth-century world standards. Even China produced only one city as large (Peking). London's population was only 600,000 in 1750 and Paris's only 576,000 in 1755. Moreover, the European countries did not have secondary cities as large as Osaka or Kyoto, with populations of 380,000 and 526,000 in the late seventeenth and early eighteenth centuries. Perhaps 3 percent of Europe's population was living in cities or large towns in 1800, compared to over 10 percent of Japan's.[26] And most important, much of this urbanization had been remarkably sudden in Japan, occurring not quite overnight but certainly in a generation or two.

Support for the argument that the rapid increase in demand in Tokugawa Japan was responsible for Japan's more rapid economic growth, compared with Ch'ing China, can be found in several instances in China in which a similar rapid rise in demand *did* occur.

Evelyn Rawski has compared two prefectures in sixteenth-century Fukien.[27] One, Chien-ning, was in the interior and participated primarily in China's domestic commerce. The other, Chang-chou, was on the coast and participated in a rapidly expanding foreign trade. This rapid expansion of foreign trade in Chang-chou was due to two factors: Portuguese sailors were relocating in Fukien after being driven out of Canton and a new Fukienese trade with the Philippines was developing. Rawski shows how the new and high level of demand that was generated by this foreign trade led to marked economic changes in Chang-chou: a rise in agricultural productivity, expansion of production for the market, and the rapid growth of local periodic markets. In the inland prefecture of Chien-ning, in contrast, agricultural productivity did not change significantly, production for the market remained at a steady level, and periodic markets declined in number. Rawski emphasizes that it is the rapidity of expansion of commerce, not just its existence, that appears to lead to notable economic changes.

Chien-ning, however, was more typical of China as a whole than Chang-chou. "The case of Chien-ning," Rawski writes, "suggests that as a rule, domestic commerce grew too slowly to stimulate changes in areas which were already commercialized. Chien-ning had reached a plateau of development in Sung times, subsequent growth required increased levels of market activity which domestic commerce failed to generate."[28]

Other examples from Chinese history also indicate that rapid increases in demand could lead to rapid economic growth. During the Northern Sung dynasty, the establishment of the capital at K'ai-feng created a city of some 750,000 to 1 million population and led to a phenomenal growth in the scale and output of the coal and iron industries in the Honan-Hopei border areas, which was curtailed by the decimation of the capital in the Mongol period.[29] Finally, and more generally (following Elvin), it is probable that "economic revolution" in China from the eighth to the thirteenth century was influenced by rapid increases in demand due to a combination of the great improvements in transportation, the disproportionate growth of the population in the largest cities, and expansion of foreign trade. Economic growth subsequently slowed, when there was an increasing closure to foreign trade, when the spurt of growth in great cities stopped, and when water transport was so well developed that it could no longer be improved by premodern methods. Moreover, as we have seen, government policies, which might have provided a stimulus, remained passive and provisioning.

Additional support for the idea that it was the rapid rise in demand, occasioned by the establishment of the sankin kotai system, that led to the more rapid transformation of the Tokugawa economy might be found by looking at what happened in Japan *after* this initial spurt died down. As noted above, the Japanese population had grown at a rapid rate in the seventeenth century, then slowed, and ceased to grow in the eighteenth and nineteenth centuries. Grain production had also grown rapidly, but then the rate of growth slowed. Many local periodic markets had been added in the seventeenth century, but fewer new ones had appeared in the eighteenth. What accounts for this slowdown?

The slowdown is not always seen as a whole, and authors have attributed its various aspects to different factors. For example, Hanley and Yamamura emphasize the impact of eighteenth-century famines on slowing population growth.[30] Other authors have analyzed how Tokugawa institutions might have encouraged birth control, compared to the institutions of other traditional societies. Rozman suggests that local periodic markets ceased to proliferate because, with the growth of regional and local merchant groups, more direct procedures may have been established to sell local products to distant areas.[31]

It seems, however, that the phenomena are interrelated and constitute a unit that must be explained. And although it is admittedly speculation in the absence of further data, the development of the sankin kotai system seems to provide an explanation that is consistent with what is known about other places. The rapid expansion of demand associated with this reorganization led to the rapid extension of commerce over the country at large, to a rapid growth in agricultural output, to population expansion, and to the appearance of new local markets. The political system was soon stabilized, however. Urban demand did not continue to rise at the same rate. Government economic policies, which might have provided a stimulus, remained primarily of a provisioning nature. Thus the economic expansion leveled off after 1700. Population growth halted, rural markets ceased to multiply, and agricultural output grew more slowly.

Where was Japan headed?

Where was Japan headed? Might it have taken the European road in the near future? This seems unlikely. Although Japan was similar to Europe in its feudal political character, the overall dynamic of European political-economic development seems to have been different. Despite Japan's feudal form and China's imperial form, the dynamics of their development seem more similar than different, when compared to the development of the societies of Western Europe. I have emphasized what have seemed to me two important ways in which Europe differed from China and Japan: the steadily increasing state centralization in Europe and the development of mercantilist economic policies.

What accounts for these contrasts? This is an extraordinarily difficult question and an adequate answer is not possible within the confines of this work. There are several hypotheses. One, which seems plausible to me, was raised by Max Weber several times in *The Religions of China* and has been elaborated by John Moffett in "Bureaucracy and Social Control." This hypothesis suggests the importance of the international context of the European state compared to the Asian states. Weber, as we have seen, considered the "irrational" character of the Chinese state of major importance in the failure of industrial capitalism to emerge originally in China. He went on to ask: "*Why* did this administration . . . remain so irrational from a capitalist point of view? That is the decisive question." He answered:

Capitalism lacked . . . political prerequisites. To be sure, the feud was not lacking. On the contrary, the whole of Chinese history is replete with great and small feuds, including the numerous struggles of individual villages, associations, and sibs. Since the pacification of the world empire, however, there has been no rational warfare, and what is more important, no armed peace during which several competing autonomous states constantly prepare for war. Capitalist phenomena thus conditioned through war loans and commissions for war purposes did not appear. The particularized state authorities of the Occident had to compete for freely mobile capital in Antiquity [before the World Empire] as well as during the Middle Ages and modern times. As in the Roman Empire, political competition for capital disappeared following the unification of the Chinese Empire. . . . During the period of the Warring Kingdoms and their contest for political power, there was a capitalism of moneylenders and purveyors which was politically determined and apparently very significant. . . . When China was politically unified into a world empire like the *orbis ter-*

rarum of Imperial Rome, the result was an obvious retrogression of this capitalism, essentially linked to competition between states.[32]

Elaborating on Weber's suggestion, Moffett has argued that it was the *competitive state system* in Europe – and the frequent wars it produced – that gave rise to the continuous centralization of European administrative and military systems, to the economic policies of mercantilism, including colonial expansion, and to the rising state indebtedness that gave impetus to rising levels of capital accumulation in the hands of merchants and financiers.[33]

These arguments might as well be applied to Tokugawa Japan as to China. Japan, like China, was a "pacified" state. On the one hand, Japan, like China, was not involved in systematic competitive relations with other nations of equal power. On the other hand, the Tokugawa hegemony had mitigated internal conflict. *Pax Tokugawa* was not an armed peace; systematic and internal conflict among the han had been suppressed.

Another interesting hypothesis – a more plausible, updated version of the asiatic mode of production conception – has been suggested by Immanuel Wallerstein. Wallerstein's major concern is with explaining the origins of the capitalist world economy, or the worldwide division of labor that provided disproportionate benefits to the Western European metropoles, that he takes as the decisive characteristic of European development. He argues that a major factor behind the European expansion that created this world economy was the "extensive" nature of the European method of agricultural production, based on livestock and wheat, compared to the "intensive" nature of Asian rice agriculture. Although the surplus from rice cultivation can be expanded for a long time on the same amount of space through additional inputs of *labor* (e.g., construction of irrigation and flood-control works, double cropping, etc.), the surplus from livestock and wheat cultivation could be expanded only through expansion of the *territory* covered: "China had in fact been expanding, but internally, extending its rice production within its frontiers. Europe's 'internal Americas' in the 15th century were quickly exhausted, given an agronomy that depended on more space."[34] This gave a powerful impetus to the ruling classes of Europe to expand control over other areas of the world. Again, the same argument could be applied to Japan, with its agriculture based (like China's) on intensive rice cultivation.

Wallerstein also suggests that China's imperial structure was responsible in part for the failure to create a world economy.

Strong states in Europe, he argues, were one of the preconditions for expansion. The Chinese imperial structure militated against strengthening the state, in contrast to the feudal structures of Europe:

A prebendal land-controlling class can better resist the growth of a truly centralized monarchy than a feudal landowning class, because the feudal value system can be used by the king . . . to build a system of loyalty to himself which, once constructed, can simply shed the personal element and become loyalty to a nation of which the king is an incarnation. Prebendalism, being a far more truly contractual system than feudalism, can't be conned by such mystical ties. . . . To strengthen the center of an empire was a colossal job, one only begun in the twentieth century under the CCP. To create centralized units in smaller areas was impossible as long as the center maintained any coherence, which it did under the Ming, and then the successor Manchu dynasty; whereas creating centralized units in a feudal system was, as we know, feasible, if difficult.[35]

The problem with this argument, it seems to me, is that centralization did not occur in feudal Japan any more than in imperial China. It may be true that feudal structures lend themselves to centralization more than imperial ones, *once the impetus to centralization is there*, but the question seems to be *why* there was such a strong trend towards centralization in Europe and there was not such a trend in East Asia, whether in feudal or imperial societies. The state-system argument addresses this question more directly.

Where was Japan headed? A scenario
In the absence of an impetus to greater centralization, to colonial expansion, to the national economic development engendered in Europe by its special political-economic circumstances (such as the competitive state systems), and to the agronomy of livestock and wheat, it seems that contradictions in the Japanese feudal political economy would most likely have resolved themselves through the creation of an imperial structure on the Chinese model.

As in China, the Japanese system contained many contradictions, and two major currents of opposition: from "above" and from "below." In Japan, however, the two currents rarely joined.

A large number of peasant rebellions occurred during the Tokugawa period, perhaps as many as 1,600.[36] Their motivation was similar to that of the Chinese peasants: exorbitant taxation, grievances against officials, high rent, exploitation by merchants, and the like.[37] These uprisings increased in scale and violence over the centuries, especially after the beginning of the eighteenth century. This was probably due to the slowdown in the rate of economic expansion and to the increasingly inequitable distribution of wealth in the countryside that accompanied commercialization and the transformation of the local elite into a class.

Peasant discontent in Japan, in contrast to China, did not have national consequences. Large-scale rebellions went no further than the han level, with appeals to the local authorities for redress of grievances. We have seen that it was the fusion of upper- and lower-class discontent in China that created revolutionary movements aimed at creating a new dynasty, and it is precisely this fusion that was lacking in Tokugawa Japan.

The sources of the opposition from "above" have been mentioned at various points in this chapter: the rulers of the outside han resented their exclusion from participation in the Tokugawa administrative system, as well as the annoyances of the sankin kotai system. Lower-ranking samurai in han and bakufu domains were put in a steadily declining economic position due to the reduction of their stipends. Merchants were excluded from political power and their economic opportunities were limited to the horizons of the han or bakufu domain.

However, none of these groups sought to utilize peasant movements to their own ends because, despite opposition, the system was still viable: all strata of the upper class – merchants, samurai, newly rich peasants – were still oriented toward the political organization of the domain and toward maintaining or improving the domain's position in the Tokugawa framework, not toward building an empire to replace it. When upper-class movements to unify the country began after Japan was "opened" by the Western nations in the nineteenth century, the peasantry (as we shall see below) began to appear as actors on the national scene.

Where was Japan ultimately headed, had the Europeans not appeared on the scene? It seems that establishment of an imperial structure might have eventually been sought as a solution to the problems of almost all the powerful dissident groups in Japan:

First, the samurai. The establishment of a decentralized officialdom and an examination system to recruit officials from all classes, ranks, and regions would have eliminated the rancor of the samurai, especially those of lower status. It would have permitted them to compete for the positions they were excluded from in the Tokugawa structure and would have removed their hated dependence on the allocation of stipends. Moreover, in an imperial system the samurai would again have been permitted to own land and derive an income directly from it.

Second, the daimyo. Although the han would have lost their fiscal and military independence once an empire was established, the daimyo would most likely have become important imperial officials, with higher incomes and without the personal burdens and worries of managing fiefdoms in perpetual fiscal crisis. Managing an empire would have been simpler because the abolition of samurai stipends would have solved the state's major financial problem.

Third, the merchants. The major oppression of merchants under the Tokugawa system related to their exclusion from landholding, the officialdom, and the han and bakufu monopoly structures that acted as barriers to the free pursuit of economic opportunities throughout the land. In an imperial system, merchants would have been permitted to buy land and to enter government freely, and nationwide economic opportunities would have been opened.

Fourth, the peasants. Although the masses of the peasantry probably would have gained little, rich peasants would have been able to "get ahead," joining the ex-samurai and the merchants in a new gentry-merchant-official upper class.

How would the transformation have come about? Through gradual evolution or revolution? Changes leading to an imperial structure were gradually occurring within the old order. Changes that are usually interpreted as the decline of feudalism and the rise of capitalism are just as easily interpreted as leading to an imperial structure. For instance, the use of "merit" in schools and in recruitment to officialdom, which allegedly was increasing, is compatible with transformation to a Chinese-style political system. Merchants were buying and selling land, rich peasants were beginning to demand that they be permitted to become intendants, and so on; these phenomena are also compatible with a trend toward an imperial system.

However, it seems that these trends would most likely have been hastened by a revolution, perhaps after a prolonged economic crisis. A "Meiji Restoration," led by lower-status samurai from the tozama han and joined by merchants, might easily have occurred and might have culminated in the establishment of an imperial order. The restoration of the emperor to power would have meant the re-creation of an imperial state, not the national state that the actual Meiji rulers created. The real Meiji Restoration occurred, however, in a different international situation:

European capitalism and the competitive state system had moved into Asia.

It might be legitimately askéd: Was Japan headed *anywhere?* Would the contradictions have resolved themselves? As Jansen points out,

At the mid-point of the nineteenth century, the shogunate had two and a half centuries of prestige behind it. It was in every sense the longest, most stable, and most successful system of social and political organization Japan had yet known. Its economic crises and social dislocations may well have been becoming more troubled, but these were variants of problems with which Japan's rulers had been dealing since the seventeenth century. . . . It required . . . some new, extraordinary, and external problem to bring to the surface all the latent dissatisfactions which had awaited articulation. This challenge was supplied by the advent of the West.[38]

We shall never know, of course. However, it may well be that recent "traditional society" scholarship, which has concentrated on the internal development of China and Japan in order to correct the excessively one-sided external emphasis of earlier diplomatic history, has exaggerated, in its turn, the extent to which these societies were changing. The Ch'ing dynasty might have held on for another 200 years. The Tokugawa feudal system might have remained intact for another 200 years.

It is impossible to say exactly what would have happened in the absence of the Western impact. However, it is possible, I believe, to speculate on what would *not* have happened, and it seems to me highly unlikely that the various trends summarized by many scholars as the "decline of feudalism" in Japan would soon have culminated in the "rise of industrial capitalism," as happened in Europe.

Part II

China and Japan in the nineteenth-century world economy

The China trade must be viewed as the keystone of that magnificent arch which connects the Anglo-Eastern and western realms, and affords a medium for the annual transmission of 4 million sterling of tribute to a small island in the Atlantic, from the territorial revenues of one of the most splendid empires that ever were subjected to the dominions of man – as having yielded to the British Exchequer, at a mere nominal expense, and without trouble, the immense sum of *sixty-seven million sterling!* during the last *eighteen* years, – derived from an innutritious leaf collected on the mountains of a distant continent; as procuring for the Indian Government an impost of more than *one million sterling,* which is levied on the Chinese consumer of opium; requiring *another million sterling* worth of cotton, and of British manufactures for the Canton market; employing from thirty to forty thousand tons of the finest shipping in the world; giving profitable occupation to a respectable community of *seventy-thousand* dealers in the United Kingdom.

(R. Montgomery Martin, *The Past and Present State of the Tea Trade of England and of the Continents of Europe and America* [London, 1832.])

As the studies of world economy scholars have revealed, the rise of capitalism in Europe coincided with the creation of a world-wide economic system. Beginning in the sixteenth century, the emerging capitalist nations of Europe drew successive areas of the world into the orbit of their economies, until by the nineteenth century much of the non-European world occupied a satellite status in relation to Europe. The non-European world had become a vast source of foodstuffs and fuel for the European nations, an area for the investment of their capital, and a market for their manufactures. Along with the economic incorporation of the non-European areas went their political incorporation. Structures of domination, ranging from formal colonies to informal "spheres of influence," were created to prevent the non-European countries from slipping out of orbit.

In the earliest stages of its development, the world economy encompassed only a small part of the globe – fringes of Europe, such as the Mediterranean islands and parts of the Americas.[1] By the nineteenth century, although a vast part of the world had been incorporated, some areas remained relatively outside the world economy. It will be argued below that Japan was one of the areas that remained relatively free from economic and political incorporation as a satellite in the world economy during the nineteenth century. China, in contrast, was intensively and continuously incorporated.

This part of the study explores how and why this was the case. In what sense was China more incorporated than Japan? Why was China incorporated to a greater degree than Japan?

The development of the world political economy from about 1800 to about 1918 could be divided into two phases: one in which linkages were based on trade or flows of commodities between the metropoles and their satellites, and one in which the linkages were based on flows of capital investment. In each phase the dynamics of world economy development led to China's incorporation, but were such as to exclude Japan from intensive incorporation. The first phase, which has been termed the *imperialism of free trade*, lasted until the 1880s.[2] In this phase, the major integrating factor was trade, especially trade of Western manufactures for tropical staples such as sugar and for traditional products such as tea and silk. At this time, fewer efforts were made than there were made later in the century to establish formal colonial control over satellite areas. This is in part because Great Britain, the world's major industrial and naval power, was so strong that it was able to maintain hegemony in many areas of the world, even though it lacked formal colonial powers.

During this first phase, Japan was shielded from strong incorporation by other Asian areas of the satellite world that were geographically closer to the Western European nations and had been reached first, especially India, Indonesia, and China. Moreover, it was widely believed that the effort of "opening" Japan to trade would not be worth the cost because Japan was relatively poor in resources and small in population, possessing few articles of trade of interest to the West and evincing only a small demand for Western manufactures. Western merchants explored and exploited the possibilities for trade and profit in the larger and richer areas for quite a long while before they turned to small, resource-poor Japan. Even after Japan was opened in the late 1850s, China, India, and other areas of the East still bore the brunt of Western exploitation in Asia.

Also, fortunately for Japan, the country escaped the "new imperialism" that began in the 1880s and was of a different nature. In this second phase, other Western nations – the United States, Germany, France, Russia – began to industrialize and to give England increasing competition. Simultaneously, Western industry, increasingly concentrated into monopolies, was shifting from a base of coal and iron to one of steel, oil, chemicals, and electricity, and the new base depended far more than the old one on a continuing supply of materials and sources of energy from the non-Western world, such as oil, nickel, nitrates, rubber, and tin. Ideologists increasingly stressed the need for integrated, self-sufficient empires, which would eliminate dependence on enemies for supplies and provide secure colonial markets for surplus capital. The result was a competitive struggle among the Western nations to carve up and control the world. Not only the lucrative areas but many territories quite barren of resources were annexed by one or another Western power. China was hard hit by this phase of imperialism as the various powers divided the country into "leased areas" and "spheres of influence", and seized large portions of the economy as "concessions."

During this second phase, many areas of the world that apparently were just as small and poor as Japan were incorporated into the world economy as colonial satellites and deprived of their autonomy. Had the Western nations reached Japan at *this* time, rather than in the 1850s, Japan, though smaller and poorer than China or India, might today be burdened with a British, French, or German colonial heritage. This, however, was not to be.

By the 1880s, Japan's new army and navy, though probably not formidable enough to withstand a serious European effort at conquest, were strong enough to make such an effort relatively costly and therefore to deter it. At the same time, Japan's military forces had proved themselves formidable enough to defeat China in the 1890s and thus had proved that Japan was a likely candidate as an ally or "junior partner" of some European power in the competitive race to carve up China and the rest of the world. Fortunately for Japan, Great Britain was looking for such a partner in Asia by the mid-1890s, and Japan, rather than being conquered, as it might have been, was bolstered.

Chapters 4 and 5 will examine the processes of Japan's and China's incorporation in some detail. First, however, let us define the concept of incorporation more closely.

It seems that incorporation has two basic dimensions: an economic and a political dimension. The world political economy that has emerged since the sixteenth century constitutes a world division of labor between more advanced industrial nations (the metropoles) and their predominantly agrarian and industrially dependent satellites. A political division accompanies this economic division: between the dominant industrial metropoles and the subordinate satellites, whose sovereign powers have been reduced or eliminated.

The economic dimension

The degree to which a Third World country is incorporated as a satellite might be seen as depending on its importance to the metropolitan countries in terms of the size and nature of the latter's trade with and investments in the former. The larger the trade, the more that it is staple in nature, and the larger and more interrelated the investments, the more pronounced the country's satellite status.

Trade

Not only is the size of the trade important but also its nature – above all, whether the traded items are important *staple* items. Staples may be defined as commodities that are either consumed or produced on a large scale in the Western nations or are otherwise vital to the functioning of their economies. Staples are distinct from *preciosities,* luxury items that are of less significance in the function of the economies of the Western nations.

It is the exchange of staples, rather than preciosities, that has formed the foundation of the world division of labor and the basis for imperialist efforts to subordinate satellite nations politically. The mere existence of trade relations with the West has never meant that a non-Western area was significant in the world political economy. For example, in the sixteenth century the nations of the West traded with many countries around the world, but only a small part of the globe (the Mediterranean islands and parts of the Caribbean) had become a satellite area to the West, producing a large trade in staple products. Trade with the rest of the world was still an exchange of precious and luxury items, not yet of vital importance to the Western economies, and did not lead to efforts at political incorporation.

Investments

Again, not only the size is important but also the character – especially whether the investments form an interrelated complex or large "stake," as opposed to random, isolated ventures. For example, investment in oil fields, in refineries in nearby seaports, in shipping from the seaports to the metropole, and in docking and ship-repair facilities in the ports constitute an interrelated investment complex of considerable significance, as compared, say, with investment in an oil well here and a factory there. Significant and interconnected investments are the hallmark of a strongly incorporated satellite.

The political dimension

World economy theorists have noted that political incorporation has usually accompanied and promoted economic incorporation. Two aspects of political incorporation seem to have been important in the nineteenth century.

Political encroachment

This term refers to the degree to which the industrial capitalist nations assumed rulership or otherwise encroached on the fiscal, administrative, legal, and military powers of native governments. It includes encroachment not only on the home territory of the country but also on colonies and hinterlands that the government of the country has historically claimed to rule. This latter encroachment is sometimes considered irrelevant to a discussion of economic development in the country "proper"; however, since the conception of an obligation to defend or expand national territory has internal political and economic consequences, it cannot be neglected.

Missionary encroachment

This term refers to the degree to which an area was penetrated by Catholic or Protestant missionaries, those "pickets or advance guards for the . . . phalanx of national power."[3] It is an important indicator of the economic and political importance of a satellite. Nineteenth-century European governments provided missionaries with the military protection that was essential to their activities only when the governments had important national political-economic aims that they hoped might be furthered through missionary influence.

The direction of economic incorporation, as here defined, must be emphasized. The degree to which a society has been incorporated as a satellite (compared to others) is measured by the importance of that society (compared to others) for *metropolitan* economic and political interests, not vice versa – that is, not by the internal economic importance that the society's ties to the metropole assume. By the latter definition, it might be argued that China was less incorporated than Japan (or some other area) because the foreign trade or investment *per capita* was less.[4] Although this distinction is of interest, it seems less important from the point of view of the *political* economics of development. This is because the importance of a satellite to the metropole determines how hard the metropole will fight to take and to hold the satellite, which in turn determines the difficulties the people of the satellite nation will face in their efforts to liberate themselves and to develop the nation's economy.

Having defined somewhat more precisely the concept of incorporation, let us consider the evidence for the nature of incorporation in China and Japan. It will be argued in chapters 4 and 5 that China was more strongly incorporated than Japan in terms of these four dimensions, as follows.

The initial Western interest in China was trade. The China trade was large and, for the nations concerned, it was a staple trade. The development of trade was soon accompanied by the development of a large and interrelated structure of investments, at first in shipping, shipbuilding and repairing, and in manufacturing and, finally, in mines, railways, and loans to the Chinese government for railway construction and military purposes. Trade and investment were accompanied by an intensive invasion of missionaries. Also, the Western nations developed trading and investment interests and extended their control over areas outside China proper that had been under Chinese suzerainty, such as Annam, Mongolia, and Burma.

As these interests developed, there were intensive, ruthless, and progressive encroachments on China's political autonomy in order to secure them. China's incorporation followed a consistent pattern throughout the century: economic incorporation preceded political incorporation. As Western economic interests built up, there was more or less active resistance by the Chinese government and population. This resistance was then broken down, usually through war or "gunboat diplomacy," followed by further encroachments on China's autonomy in the form of (1) treaties or agreements that legitimized the economic incorporation and facilitated its progress and (2) indemnities, levied on China as punishment. The indemnities were usually secured on Chinese revenues, especially the foreign customs revenue, which, after

1853, was administered by Westerners. (When an enormous indemnity was levied after the Boxer Rebellion in 1900, the revenue from the domestic customs taxes also came under Western control.)

Encroachments on Japan's political autonomy, in the form of treaties patterned on the early Western treaties with China, preceded rather than followed the development of Western economic interests in that country. After these initial encroachments, significant economic interests in Japan did not develop for twenty to thirty years. This is the period that E. H. Norman called Japan's "breathing space."[5]

Trade with Japan was not a staple trade for the nations concerned, nor was it as large as the China trade. During the "breathing space," Western investments in Japan were few and isolated. Nor did the Western nations develop important economic interests in Japan's outlying territories. And in the absence of a build-up of economic interests, missionaries were not protected by the Western governments, as they were in China.

After the initial period, there were no further political encroachments on Japan's autonomy. In fact, Japan was encouraged to recover the rights it had lost. Also, the Western nations frequently encouraged the Japanese government to gain or regain control over outlying areas.

During this "breathing space," Japan's industrialization got under way. Trade with Japan subsequently became important to Western nations, and Western investments in Japan also became significant. But Japan's integration into the world economy was then as an equal: trade was an exchange of manufactured and primary products in more or less equal proportion and investment by foreigners was in industry as well as primary production and did not dominate the economy.

Chapter 4 will trace China's incorporation into the world economy during the nineteenth century in terms of the four variables mentioned above. Chapter 5 will consider the case of Japan.

4

China's incorporation into the world economy

Trade

Chinese-Western trade during the seventeenth and eighteenth centuries was basically an exchange of preciosities. Western gold, silver, *sing-songs* (fancy timepieces), and the like were exchanged for Chinese goods that were regarded as luxuries in the West, such as silk, porcelain, tea, and *nankeens* (cotton fabrics). The trade was small and grew only slowly prior to the end of the eighteenth century. As discussed in chapter 3, Western merchants were restricted by the Chinese government to the frontiers of the country (the seaports of Canton and Macao and the "landports" of Kiakhta and Nerchinsk on the Russian frontier), and their activities were closely supervised in order to ensure a steady flow of revenue and to prevent the Westerners from doing anything that might endanger the government's provisioning policy.

In the late eighteenth and early nineteenth centuries, China's trade relations with the West were totally transformed. The trade became a staple trade, it expanded by leaps and bounds, and the Chinese government's controls over it were toppled. This transformation took place primarily under the initiative of Great Britain, which was, until the late nineteenth century, the world's major industrial and colonial power.

The first aspect of the transformation was an enlargement of tea consumption in Britain, which changed tea from a luxury to a staple commodity. This was brought about by an enforced shift in the activities of the East India Company related to Britain's growing industrialization. Prior to 1700, the East India Company, which monopolized British trade "between the Cape of Good Hope and the Straits of Magellan" until the nineteenth century, had concentrated on the import of Indian textiles and Asian spices. In 1700, however, the import of Eastern fabrics was prohibited by Parliament in order to protect the English manufacturers of woolen, silk, and linen textiles. The company then turned to the mass marketing of Chinese tea.[1]

In the seventeenth century, tea was a luxury good in Britain, and beer was the staple drink of the poor.[2] By the mid-eighteenth century, however, "the drink was not uncommon in the country-side, even among labourers," and about a pound per capita was consumed each year.[3] In the nineteenth century, tea became the British national drink. The East India Company was required by an act of Parliament to keep a year's supply in stock at all times.[4] Consumption reached almost five pounds per capita in the 1860s, six pounds in the 1880s, and nearly eleven pounds in the 1920s.[5]

As tea became a staple, it also became an important source of revenue for the British Exchequer. In 1855, for instance, about 10 percent of the gross revenue of the British government was derived from duties on imported tea. This amount is comparable to the revenue collected from duties on such important colonial staples as tobacco, sugar, and molasses.[6] Almost all British tea was imported from China in the first half of the nineteenth century.[7]

The establishment of a mass market for Chinese tea in Britain immediately posed two problems for the British government. First, there was a continual drain of silver to China to pay for the tea. This contradicted the mercantilist aims of the British government, which at first attempted to solve the problem by requiring the company, as a condition of its charter, to export a certain amount of British woolens to China each year. However, these goods sold very poorly in China, and specie continued to be the vehicle of exchange.[8]

Second, the citizens of other nations and private British dealers began to cash in on the expanding tea trade, depriving the government of revenues from it. Because British import duties were very high, smuggling was a profitable activity. French, American, and Dutch merchants smuggled almost as much tea into Britain each year as the East India Company imported. And in Britain itself, tea smuggling was a lucrative and large-scale business that came to occupy the efforts of entire coastal communities.[9]

Thus, as tea consumption increased, the British government confronted two questions: How could the smuggling be halted so that the entire proceeds of the trade might be taxed? What would provide a return for tea so that the steady drain of silver to China could be avoided?

The first step toward a solution was to reduce the import duties on tea so that smuggling was no longer profitable. The Commutation Act of 1784 reduced the import duties from over 100 percent ad valorem to only 12.5 percent. This eliminated the foreign competition to the East India Company's monopoly. But because the price of tea was thereby brought down, it expanded British consumption of tea and increased the problem of finding a return.[10]

The solution was finally found by linking the China trade to the interests of the emerging British colony in India. It was discovered that there was a market in China for Indian raw cotton and, above all, opium. When the British gained control of the opium-producing territories of India after the 1750s, they applied themselves vigorously to increasing the output of opium in India and, simultaneously, preventing its consumption by the Indian producers and increasing the market for it in China.

In becoming opium producers and sellers, the British were doing nothing new. Opium had long been produced in the Near East and in India, where it was a monopoly of the Mogul government. When the Portuguese appeared in the East in the sixteenth century, they found Indian and Arab merchants selling opium in Burma, the Malay Peninsula, China, and the East Indies. The Portuguese took the opium trade away from the Arab and Indian merchants in the seventeenth century, lost it in part in the eighteenth to the Dutch, who in turn lost it to the British at the end of the century when the British replaced the Mogul emperors as controllers of the production monopoly.

The novelty is that the British both produced and sold opium for the first time on a large scale. The Chinese were as little traditionally opium smokers as the Indians were traditionally opium producers or the British tea drinkers. All these habits are a product of the mass production and marketing style of nineteenth- and twentieth-century capitalism.

Poppy seeds appear to have been consumed in China in the form of a beverage at least since the eighth century. This practice was probably introduced to China by the Arabs. Genuine opium, made by extracting and dehydrating the juices of the seed sac, had been consumed in China since the fifteenth century. However, the drug was used primarily for medicinal purposes (i.e., as a household remedy to relieve pain), and addiction was not widespread. Moreover, the practice of smoking opium appears to have been confined to Taiwan and Fukien until the British took over the mass marketing of the drug in the late eighteenth century. Although opium was produced in India prior to the eighteenth century, it was neither intensively cultivated nor produced on a large scale. The British efforts succeeded in raising output in India and in making opium so readily available in China that far larger numbers of people used it than ever before and large numbers became addicted.[11]

Opium provided a return for the tea trade through an indirect mechanism that was known as the *country trade*. This term referred to trade between India and other parts of Asia that was carried on by private merchants under license from the East India Company. (Some of these merchants were Asian, especially Indian; and some of them were American and British, especially Scotch.) The country traders bought opium and other produce in India, carried it to China, and exchanged it for specie. They then turned the specie over to the East India Company at Canton in exchange for bills of exchange on London or the government of Bengal. Because the East India Company controlled the export trade from China to the West and India and the private traders were deprived of return cargoes, they were eager to get the bills of exchange. It was the simplest and least risky way to transfer their profits back to places where they could be reinvested. The East India Company then used the specie it had collected to pay for the Chinese tea, etc., that it was exporting.[12]

The tea and opium trade also provided a solution for a third problem: how to transfer Indian revenues to Britain. As the statement by Martin cited in the introduction to Part II indicates, the tea and opium trade played an important role in the India–Great Britain balance of payments. Greenberg explains this as follows:

Almost 4 million pounds had to be transferred annually from Indian to Great Britain . . . in one way or another; 3 million of this sum represented Government remittances, the obligatory "home charges" of the Company, and the other million the accumulation of private British fortunes, official and mercantile, pensions, etc., seeking return to England. The Company was compelled to make the China trade the channel of remittance from India to London. This was partly because a considerable proportion of the Company's surplus territorial revenues was obtained in kind, in such goods as could be sold profitably only in Canton; partly because by remitting through China via the Country Trade the Company was able to gain a large advantage from its control over the rate of exchange of its Bills. The surplus of *Indian* revenues were thus sent home in teas from China, a procedure made possible by the development of the Country Trade from India to China. The private Country merchants were, indeed, mere licensees of the Company; but the latter had to depend on them not only to redress the balance of trade at Canton, but to convey its own funds to England.[13]

Opium came to provide the Indian government with a handsome source of revenue. As opium production expanded, it soon provided one-seventh of the annual revenues of the British government in India.[14]

Because the opium-tea trade solved all these problems, the system expanded rapidly. In 1729, only about 200 chests of opium had been imported into China each year; in 1767, the number had grown to 1,000; from 1800 to 1820, it reached 4,000; it rose to almost 19,000 in the 1820s, to 40,000 in 1838 and 1839, and hit a peak of 87,000 in 1879, after which it declined due to Chinese *import substitution*.[15] As a result of the expansion of opium consumption, the export of specie to China declined, and by the mid-1820s the outflow of silver from China actually exceeded the inflow, probably for the first time in modern history.[16]

Thus the first aspect of China's trading incorporation into the world economy was that China became the source of an important staple consumed in Great Britain and the major market for a staple produced in one of Britain's major colonies. The large complex of interdependent interests that emerged rested ultimately on the British mass consumption of Chinese tea and the Chinese consumption of Indian opium. On the British side, these included the interest of the British government in the revenue from the import of tea, the interest of the Indian colonial government in revenue from the taxation of opium production and in utilizing the China trade as a means of remitting the Indian surplus to Great Britain, the interest of the East India Company in the profits from importing tea, and the interest of the private country traders in the profits from the export of opium to China. On the Chinese side, they included the interests of merchants involved in importing opium and exporting tea, of opium smokers, and of officials taking bribes to ignore the opium trade (which was illicit until the 1860s). (The laws prohibiting the opium trade will be discussed in the section "Trade and political incorporation.")

The second aspect of China's trading incorporation was related more directly to British industrialization in the late eighteenth and early nineteenth centuries. As Britain industrialized, there was a strong drive to find foreign markets for her products, above all, cotton textiles, and eyes fell upon China, with its population of "400 million," as a vast potential market. After the 1870s, as

France, the United States, and Germany also began to industrialize rapidly, they joined Britain in the effort to open the China market.

The cotton textile industry was the key industry in the British industrial revolution.

The British Industrial Revolution was by no means *only* cotton, or Lancashire, or even textiles, and cotton lost its primacy within it after only a couple of generations. Yet cotton was the pacemaker of industrial change, and the basis of the first regions which could not have existed but for industrialization, and which expressed a new form of society, industrial capitalism, based on a new form of production, the "factory." [17]

The development of British cotton manufacturing, perhaps more than that of any other industry, was intimately related to the development of the British world empire. Raw cotton was almost entirely derived from colonial sources, mainly the slave plantations of the West Indies and the United States. And, what is more important for our purposes here, the British cotton textiles industry was essentially an export industry. After the 1790s, the British cotton industry exported most of its output; by the late nineteenth century, almost 90 percent of it. "From time to time it broke into the rewarding markets of Europe and the U.S.A., but wars and the rise of native competition put a brake on such expansion and the industry returned time and time again to some old or new region of the undeveloped world." And the East – above all, India and China – came to consume a large part of the industry's exports.[18]

The creation of an export market for British textiles in the East was the result of a two-step process. First, the early eighteenth-century prohibition on the import of Asian textiles into Britain, which had been designed to benefit the linen, woolen, and silk manufacturers, also protected the nascent cotton industry. Without protection from the competition of cheaper and better-quality Chinese and Indian goods, it probably never would have succeeded. Second, having deprived Indian and Chinese industries of their export market in Britain, the British now deprived them of their home markets and substituted British manufactures.

As India came under British control after the mid-eighteenth century, efforts were made to secure India as a market for British cottons. "British manufactures were forced into India through the agency of the Company's Governor-General and Commercial Residents, while Indian manufactures were shut out from England by protective tariffs."[19] As a result, the value of British cotton goods sent to the East (mainly India) increased tremendously, from £2,501 in 1797 to £108,824 in 1813.[20]

Attention soon turned to China. British manufacturers hoped that the 400 million Chinese would come to be dressed in British cottons. They were soon joined in these hopes by the manufacturers of other nations. France, Germany, and the United States were industrializing rapidly in the late nineteenth century and catching up with Great Britain. As they industrialized, they also turned their attention increasingly to the non-Western world.

Pamphleteers and manufacturers in the United States and on the Continent began to formulate a theory of the relationship between colonial markets and industrial expansion. This theory appeared first in Europe in the 1870s and 1880s. At the core of the theory was the idea of *overproduction*. Industrial output, it was argued, tended to expand beyond the capacities of the home market to absorb it. If colonial markets were not found to absorb the surplus, crises and depressions would recur, and social revolution would be an immanent threat. In the 1890s, the theory was popularized in the United States. "It is nearly impossible," writes McCormick, "to find *any* prominent members of the power structure who did not, by 1898, think and act within such a conceptual framework." [21] Inevitably, China became a target of the search for colonial markets.

This vision of Western manufacturers – of the entire Chinese population dressed in Western textiles – never materialized. The Chinese handicraft industry continued to provide the bulk of China's needs. However, China's consumption of Western goods was not small, and it expanded greatly during the century. Textile exports to China increased slowly prior to the 1860s, but after the opening of the Suez Canal (in 1869) they expanded rapidly.[22] Yarn imports, for instance (most of which were from Britain), increased thirty-two times between 1871 and 1910, from 70,000 to 2,282,000 piculs; and their value increased about thirty-three times, from 1,877,000 Haikwan taels (the Chinese customs unit of valuation) to 62,831,000. Although cloth exports to China exceeded yarn exports in value, they grew more slowly, increasing only about two times in the period 1871–1880 to 1900–1910.[23]

Thus the second aspect of China's trading incorporation into the world economy was that China was regarded as an important present and potential market for the major staple product of British nineteenth-century industry, cotton manufactures, and that, as the century wore on, China came to be regarded as an important export market by the emerging industrial powers: the United States, France, Germany, and (somewhat later) Japan.

Trade and political incorporation

The Chinese resisted the expansion of both the opium and the textiles markets. This resistance was countered by the Opium War (1840–1842) and by a second war, which Westerners term the Arrow War and Chinese term the Second Opium War (1858–1860). After China's defeat in these wars, encroachments on political autonomy were established in treaties that formed the general framework for Chinese-Western trade relations during most of the nineteenth century. The two wars also established a pattern that was to be repeated in China throughout the century: the levying of high indemnities on the Chinese government after a defeat as punishment for resistance. The practice scarcely halted resistance, but it resulted in a large drain of Chinese revenues out of the country.

The sale of opium was opposed by the Chinese government for several reasons. First, there was the threat of addiction among officials and soldiers. These groups seem to have constituted the highest proportion of opium smokers in the early days of the trade, before massive imports and, later, native production brought the price down to a level that peasants and urban workers could better afford.[24] Second, for complex reasons (see the section "China's incorporation and the Taiping Rebellion" in chapter 6) the trade appeared to be increasing the tax burden on the populace and thus giving rise to the threat of peasant rebellion.

From its inception, the opium trade had to be a smuggling trade. The Chinese government had issued edicts against opium smoking as early as 1729. These edicts were repeated, with additional edicts against the sale of opium, as the trade expanded in the late eighteenth century. Many provincial and local officials were bribed to facilitate the import of opium into Canton and from Canton into the interior of the country.

In the 1820s the government began a campaign of suppression at Canton, which was not, however, successful. Western ships moved out of Canton but anchored at one of the islands in the estuary of the Canton River and along the coast, and the opium smuggling continued from the ships. In the 1830s, trade was booming and Chinese merchants hired fast, heavily armed boats, sometimes rowed by as many as 100 men, to carry the cargoes to shore. The opium was carried into the interior (to the west and north) along several main trade routes by groups of men who were heavily armed for protection against pirates.[25]

During the 1830s an intensive debate went on among imperial officials over how the problem of the opium trade might be solved. Some officials argued that the trade ought to be legalized and taxed. However, their arguments were convincingly refuted by those who pointed out that the British would doubtless continue to smuggle the drug anyway and that the trade constituted such a danger, because of the effects it was having on the economy, that legalization could not be a solution.

In 1837 a larger campaign of suppression began; many Chinese dealers were arrested, chests of opium were confiscated and destroyed, opium dens and brokerage houses were closed, smuggling boats were wrecked, and provisions for the foreign ships were blockaded. The government utilized whatever means of control it had over the population to stop the trade, and the suppression was extremely successful. By 1839 the trade had been almost completely halted.[26]

This effort by the Chinese government to assert control over the Chinese economy led to British retaliation in the Opium War of 1840–1842, which China lost. The British had sixteen warships, four armed steamers, twenty-seven transports, and about 4,000 soldiers. China possessed no modern warships and its ports were defended with antiquated weapons. The war was carried on in several phases, culminating in the British occupation of Amoy, Tinghai, Ningpo, Woosung, Shanghai, and Chinkiang – the latter a central city at the juncture of the Grand Canal and the Yangtze River, over which the grain tribute passed to Peking.[27]

The Treaty of Nanking and the Supplementary Treaty of the Bogue were imposed on China after the war. Similar agreements with the United States and France soon followed. These treaties constituted a significant encroachment on China's political autonomy. Their major features were:

1 The abolition of tariff autonomy. Tariffs were reduced and fixed at rates that ranged from 4 to 13 percent ad valorem.
2 The "opening" of five Chinese seaports (in addition to Canton) to Western trade and residence: Amoy, Ningpo, Shanghai, Hongkong, and Foochow. The Chinese government lost authority over the sectors of the ports settled in by Westerners, and Hong Kong became a formal colony of Great Britain.

3 Extraterritoriality was established. The Chinese government lost the right of jurisdiction over Western residents in China.

4 Free trade was established; all Chinese commercial monopolies were abolished.

In addition, Western warships were permitted to anchor at the treaty ports to "protect commerce" and each nation was granted most-favored-nation treatment, whereby any subsequent privileges granted to one nation would automatically accrue to the others.[28]

The treaties did not legalize opium import; nevertheless, opium was freely imported after the war. For a time it was carried into the new treaty ports, but this was later prohibited by the Western consuls as a minor concession to the Chinese government. However, it was openly imported all along the coast.

The British also imposed an indemnity of $21 million after the war, the first of many in China's nineteenth-century history.

The Chinese government offered little resistance per se to the import of British textiles. The major factor hindering more rapid development of the market was the resistance of the Chinese pre-industrial economy. The Chinese population continued to purchase Chinese products in preference to Western goods because Chinese textiles continued to be cheaper and more durable than the Western products. The former were produced by local peasant families or in tiny workshops where labor was much cheaper than in the West. Also, the price of Western merchandise was inevitably raised by the high cost of transporting it from the coast into the interior on China's premodern transport system.[29]

In neither China nor India did Western goods replace native handicrafts. For instance, in China in 1933 the share of handicrafts in total manufacturing in terms of net product was still 72 percent on the average, and the share of textiles was about 63 percent.[30]

Their inability to demolish China's handicraft industry was a continual disappointment to Western manufacturers and merchants. However, they did not believe that the reasons for this were economic (i.e., related to costs of labor and transport). Arguments to the effect that the market for Western manufactures was inevitably limited for economic reasons were put forward by numerous statesmen in both India and China during the nineteenth century, but to little avail.[31] British merchants and manufacturers were convinced that the only obstacle to clothing all of the 400 million Chinese in their textiles was the obstinacy of the Chinese government.

Western capitalists claimed that they could sell more goods in China if only they might live and engage in business anywhere in China, or if more ports were opened for business, or if Chinese internal transit taxes on Western goods were abolished. The latter were of particular concern. It was argued that Western goods were more expensive than Chinese goods primarily because greedy Chinese officials heaped taxes on them as soon as the goods left the treaty ports.

Western merchants had anticipated an enormous expansion of exports to China after the Treaty of Nanking, which followed the First Opium War. When this did not materialize, the pressure mounted for "opening" China further. In addition, there was interest in finally legalizing the opium trade. These pressures converged in the Second Opium War (1858–1860), which China also lost. This time the British were joined by the French in the military operations, and Russia joined the United States as a beneficiary in treaties that were concluded after the war. These were the Treaty of Tientsin and the Conventions of Peking, which

1 Further reduced China's tariffs, to about 5 percent ad valorem.

2 Provided that Western imports might pass into the interior of China outside the treaty ports) duty free, after payment of import duties at the port plus a small extra charge.

3 Opened ten new ports, including some on the Yangtze River as well as the coast, to Western trade and residence (Nanking, Newchwang, Tengchow, Hankow, Kiukiang, Chinkiang, Taiwanfu, Tamsui, Swatow, and Kiungchow). In addition, the Russian Supplementary Treaty of Peking opened the Manchurian towns of Urga and Kashgar. (Another Russian treaty, concluded in 1851, had opened the towns of Ili and Tarbagatai in Turkestan.)[32]

4 Permitted Western merchants, missionaries, politicians, etc., to travel outside the ports and into the interior of China for trading, proselytizing, etc., upon acquisition of passports from their consuls in the ports.

5 Legalized the opium trade and subjected it to import duties similar to those on other articles of trade.

6 Ceded more territory to the British (part of the Kowloon peninsula opposite Hong Kong).

7 Established the right to maintain Western diplomatic corps in Peking.

In addition, an indemnity of 16 million taels was levied, of which half went to Britain and half to France. This was secured on the

Chinese customs revenues, which, in the meantime, had come under the control of the Western nations.[33]

Western control over the customs had originated in 1854, when the Chinese customs superintendent was driven out of Shanghai during an attack by the Taiping rebels. The British and American consuls in Shanghai undertook to supervise customs collection and refused to return control to the Chinese official when he returned to Shanghai. In 1861, after the Second Opium War, the system was expanded to the other ports. The customs administration was nominally under Chinese control (the superintendent was appointed by the head of the new Chinese Foreign Affairs Office), but it operated quite independently and was staffed almost entirely, especially at the higher levels, by Europeans and Americans.[34]

However, these privileges still did not satisfy Western manufacturers and merchants. Throughout the century there was steady pressure to open more ports and to eliminate China's ability to tax Western goods entering the interior, which was believed to persist in spite of the treaties.

The desire to eliminate China's internal fiscal autonomy was never realized, primarily because no government, not even the British, was willing at that point to take on the enormous task of conquering and ruling China, which this would probably have entailed.[35] As the century wore on, however, increasing numbers of ports were opened.

The Chefoo Convention of 1876 between Britain and China, concluded after a British official was murdered while traveling through Yunnan (during an upsurge of rebellion and against official Chinese urgings), opened four other ports to Western trade and residence and six other places on the Yangtze as ports of call for steamers. It also provided that an indemnity of 200,000 taels be paid to the family of the victim.[36]

A treaty with Russia concluded after the Ili affairs in the 1870s (see "Attack on China's dependencies" in this chapter) opened several Mongolian and Tibetan cities to Russian trade and residence.[37]

In 1887, conventions were concluded between China and France after China's defeat in a war over French encroachment on Annam, which had been a Chinese tributary state (see "Attack on China's dependencies"). These conventions opened the cities of Mengtze and Manhao in Yunnan, Lungchow in Kwangsi (provinces on the border with Tonkin), and the town of Szemao (near the border of Laos) as treaty ports.[38]

In 1894 and 1897, following British conquests in Burma, Tang-yueh (on the border), Wuchow, Samshui, and Kongkun were made treaty ports and four ports on the West River were made ports of call.[39]

The Treaty of Shimonosekei with Japan (1895) opened the cities of Soochow, Hangchow, Chungking, and Shasi.[40]

Thus by the end of the century a large number of China's cities had become treaty ports – enclaves in which Western traders, politicians, and their families lived, protected by warships and out of reach of the Chinese government's fiscal and judicial control. Westerners, moreover, could travel into the interior of the country, shielded by their governments from Chinese law and justice. And the Chinese government had lost control over its foreign customs revenues, which were collected by Westerners at rates determined in the interests of the West and garnished for the payment of indemnities.

Investments and political incorporation

As the nineteenth century progressed, certain elements of China's trading incorporation waned. After 1870 the British began growing tea in India on a large scale, and Indian tea eventually eclipsed Chinese tea on the British and other markets of the world. Opium began to be grown in China, and this, plus the end of the British market for Chinese tea (which had given rise to the opium trade), made it possible for Britain to concede to pressures from China and within Britain to halt the opium trade. Indian exports of opium to China were stopped between 1900 and 1918. However, China continued to be a market for Western manufactures, and new articles of export to the West, such as eggs and egg products, hides, and straw and braid products, also appeared.

Moreover, China's trading incorporation was joined by incorporation in terms of investments. A large and interrelated complex of Western (and later also Japanese) investments developed in shipping (not only of exports and imports but articles of China's domestic commerce), in shipbuilding and repairs, in manufacturing in the ports, in banking, and in railways, mines, and loans to the Chinese government. These investments were accompanied by political incorporation in the form of concessions, leased areas, and spheres of influence and by indemnities secured on Chinese revenues.

Shipping

China's foreign commerce was carried largely on Western-owned ships throughout the nineteenth and early twentieth centuries. In addition, Westerners – mainly the British – came to control more than half of China's modern domestic shipping industry, which was "one of the chief foreign stakes in China."[41] Between 1909 and 1913, the Chinese share of capital in total shipping (including steamers, sailboats, and junks) in Chinese ports was only 23 percent, and the share of capital in shipping between Chinese and foreign ports was only 19 percent.[42]

Western participation in Chinese domestic commerce dates from the 1840s. The ports of Amoy, Ningpo, Shanghai, and Foochow, opened by the Treaty of Nanking in 1842, were not selected at random. They were chosen because the British hoped to penetrate China's domestic commerce, and these ports were important points in that commerce (and in China's trade with Southern Asia as well).[43]

Although Western participation in Chinese commerce was not permitted by the 1842 treaties, it expanded steadily throughout the 1840s and 1850s, primarily in trade among the five treaty ports, although Western ships continually tried their luck elsewhere. Little distinction was made between many of the articles for foreign trade and those entering into commerce among the five ports, and Western ships carried Chinese produce from one port for sale in another, as well as abroad.

Chinese merchants soon began to rent space in Western ships for their cargoes. This was promoted by a large increase in piracy during the 1840s, related to the lucrative booty of the opium trade. Chinese merchants desired to ship their goods on the better-armed Western ships. Moreover, fishing and cargo junks began to hire Western armed schooners and lorchas to convoy them to their destinations. For similar reasons, the disturbances of the Taiping Rebellion encouraged foreign shipping.[44]

As Western shipping along the Chinese coast increased in the 1840s and 1850s, British consuls in the treaty ports did much to encourage it. In 1847, for instance, when Chinese officials at Amoy forbade Chinese merchants to transport their wares on foreign ships, the British consul protested to the Chinese foreign commissioner, threatening reprisals if the order was not revoked, and the commissioner complied. British consuls also intervened in disputes between shipowners and Chinese officials over whether Western ships engaged in coastal trade should pay duties in accord with the treaty tariff or with the rates levied upon native Chinese. The treaty rate was not necessarily the lowest for domestic commerce, and Western shippers tried to apply the most advantageous rate rather than abide by the treaty rates.[45]

When the Treaty of Tientsin opened more ports (on the Yangtze River as well as on the coast), Western shipping expanded accordingly, although it was not legal in terms of any treaty. Legalization of Western participation in Chinese trade between treaty ports came in an 1863 treaty with Denmark, whose privileges were extended to the other treaty powers as a result of the most-favored-nation clause.[46]

After legalization, several foreign steamship companies were formed in China, the first by an American company in 1867. For a time it "virtually monopolized steam traffic on the Yangtze River and enjoyed a very dominant position in some routes on the China coast."[47] However, in the 1870s it sold its ships and properties to a new Chinese-government-sponsored steamship company, the China Merchants' Steam Navigation Company. After that, foreign participation was dominated by the British until the twentieth century, especially by the two most powerful British trading firms in China, Jardine Matheson & Company and Butterfield and Swire, which founded shipping lines in 1875 and 1872, respectively.[48]

In the following years, more and more ports were opened and Western shipping expanded accordingly. In addition to the Yangtze, the Pei Ho, Siang, and West rivers were opened to foreign shipping. Finally, in 1898, all remaining limitations on foreign shipping in China were removed. Under pressure from Britain, the Chinese government established the Inland Steam Navigation Regulations, which permitted foreign ships to sail on any waterway in China.[49]

Manufacturing and public utilities

Manufacturing in China by foreign firms was not made legal until the 1895 Treaty of Shimonosekei with Japan, which followed China's defeat in the Sino-Japanese War of that year. However, Western and Japanese firms had engaged in manufacturing in China long before it was legalized. As in the case of shipping, treaties legitimized what the industrial powers had begun to do.

The growth of Western shipping in China led to the establishment of one of the most important Western industries, shipbuilding and ship repairing. Western firms had constructed large shipyards in the treaty ports as early as the 1860s, and by the 1930s over half the tonnage built in China was the work of foreign-controlled firms.[50] This industry, like shipping generally, was controlled by the British.[51]

Another significant activity was the processing of goods for export. By the late 1860s, most of the tea shipped to Russia and Central Asia was processed in factories under Russian supervision.[52]

Western firms were also heavily involved in the processing of bean oil and cake, egg products, and hides.[53] They were less successful in silk processing. Many times during the nineteenth century Western merchants attempted to set up modern silk-reeling factories in China; however, Chinese merchants refused to supply them with the needed cocoons. When the modern silk-reeling industry expanded, after the turn of the century, it was primarily under Chinese control.[54]

Western firms were also involved in manufacturing for the domestic market.

Since the 1850s, foreign firms had engaged in a number of activities to supply the needs of foreign residents of the treaty ports. They established flour mills, breweries, and brick, glass, and furniture factories; they manufactured drugs, baked bread, and made ice and soda.[55]

After markets for Western goods had been opened up through imports, foreign firms manufactured the goods inside China. By the 1880s, Western firms were producing paper, matches, and soap in China for the domestic market. The most important industries were cotton textiles and cigarettes.

American and British merchants attempted to establish textile factories in several treaty ports in the 1860s but gave up in the face of Chinese official opposition. After the Treaty of Shimonosekei, however, they again entered the field, along with German and Japanese manufacturers, and by the 1930s almost 70 percent of the power looms and more than 40 percent of the yarn spindles in China were owned by foreign mills.[56]

Cigarettes were first imported into China in 1890 by the American Tobacco Company. They were readily accepted, and import substitution soon began. The dominant firm was the British-American Tobacco Company. Chinese farmers were induced to grow American tobacco, and by the 1930s cigarette factories in China were largely supplied by domestic leaf. Chinese tobacco consumption increased from 300 million cigarettes in 1900 to 88.5 billion in 1933, which were supplied almost entirely by the factories in China.[57]

The Chinese government prevented foreign participation in public utilities, such as telephone and telegraph service. When these services were constructed, after the turn of the century, they were largely under Chinese government control. It was otherwise with gas, electricity, waterworks, and bus and tram companies, in which Westerners and, after the turn of the century, Japanese were particularly active.[58]

Railways and mines

In no other area of investment were the Western powers so persistent or the Chinese government so adamant in its refusal to permit such efforts. And until China's defeat in the Sino-Japanese war of 1895 unleashed what has been termed the *scramble* for railway and mining concessions, the Chinese government was largely successful in keeping foreign investment out.

Since the 1860s, Western merchants and statesmen continually sought out Chinese officials and urged railroad and mine construction. They offered to construct railways and to open mines or to lend the money to the government to do so. Western merchants were especially interested in coal mining so as to have a cheap and readily accessible source of fuel for their steamships that operated in China's waters. Their urgings appeared to Chinese officialdom as a scarcely veiled threat.[59] They saw foreign-controlled railroads as a means for foreign military penetration (as in India) and for opening the entire continent of China to Western trade and and residence. The dangers of foreign control in borrowing money were well known from the example of Egypt.[60]

Although a faction within Chinese officialdom opposed railways and modern mines under any circumstances, many officials appear to have favored building them if they could have been built by Chinese and without borrowing money from the West. The latter, however, seemed unlikely in view of the enormous costs and China's distressed financial situation.[61]

In 1876 a company formed by British and American merchants attempted, despite opposition from Chinese officials, to build a railway linking Shanghai and Woosung. Many merchants had desired such a railway because silt in the river between the two ports often made passage difficult. The firm finished part of the railroad and began service in June 1876 in the face of continued official opposition. In August, however, when a Chinese soldier was struck and killed, popular opposition forced the investors to give up. The Chinese government purchased the railway but did not operate it, apparently as a gesture of defiance, to show that railroads would be built where the government wanted them built. The line was torn up and shipped to Taiwan, where the government had been planning to build a railroad.[62]

The Sino-Japanese War marked the end of the government's ability to resist foreign investment in railroads and mines, as it had in manufacturing. After 1895 the Chinese government was forced to grant railway and mining concessions to various Western nations and Japan (a concession granted the sole right to construct railroads or open modern mines within a specified territory). France received railway concessions in various places on the borders between Indochina and China, Russia obtained concession in Manchuria and Liaotung (whose railways ultimately came under control of Japan), the Germans in Shantung (which also came under control of Japan after World War I), and the English in the Canton area.

By 1911, 41 percent of the railway mileage in China was owned by foreigners and the remainder had largely been built by the Chinese government with foreign loans. Between 1895 and 1911, loans of about £34 million were floated on foreign money markets by the government to pay for railway construction.[63] When railroads were built with foreign loans, they came under such stringent external control that they were virtually indistinguishable from concession railroads. Loans had strings attached, which usually gave a monopoly over construction to foreign agents (which gave these agents some degree of monopoly power in supplying materials for construction) and control over the administration and part of the profits until the loans were paid off.[64]

Numerous mining concessions were granted from 1896 to 1913 to the British, Germans, Russians, French, Americans, Belgians, and Japanese. The French received concessions in Yunnan, Kwangsi, and Kwangtung; the Russians in Manchuria (later lost to Japan); the Japanese in Manchuria and Liaotung; the Germans in Shantung (also later lost to Japan); and the British in Honan and Shansi. Coal mining was generally the main objective, but the Japanese had significant interests in iron mining.[65]

An interesting aspect of the scramble for mining concessions is that the Chinese government was permitted in several cases to recover by purchase the rights that had been obtained from it by force. Because the concessions brought bitter opposition from local miners in many places, the government, in response, purchased the British concession in Shansi (in 1908) for 2,750,000 taels, the two French concessions in Yunnan for 1,500,000 taels, and the German concessions in Shantung for Chinese $210,000.[66]

The railway and mining concessions were accompanied by large territorial encroachments on China in the form of *leased areas,* which were completely controlled by foreign powers for the term of the leases, which was usually ninety-nine years. China lost all sovereignty in a leased area and all foreign powers had to submit to the authority of the lessee. The major leased areas were Kiaochow, to Germany; part of the Liaotung peninsula, to Japan; an area at Kwangchouwan, to France; and more of Kowloon, to Britain.

At the same time, *spheres of influence* were established, usually through agreements between China and foreign powers rather than among the powers, as happened elsewhere in the world. In these agreements, China promised not to alienate any of the pertinent areas to another power and it granted the claiming power the sole right to receive mining and railway concessions, to supply China with advisers or technical experts, and so on. Between 1895 and 1899, Britain obtained the Yangtze valley as a sphere of influence, France obtained Southern China along the Indochina border, Russia obtained Manchuria, and Germany obtained Shantung.[67]

Loans and banking

The Chinese government borrowed from the West several times prior to 1894, primarily to finance a military campaign against Moslem rebels in the 1870s and the war with France over Annam in the 1880s. However, the government was generally very reluctant to borrow because of fear of foreign control and the sums it borrowed were small. Up to 1894, the Chinese government had borrowed only about £13 million from the West.

Between 1894 and 1911, China borrowed seven times more than it had borrowed in the entire previous century of contact with the West (about £90 million). The cause of the multiple increase was the utter inadequacy of China's internal revenues in the face of (1) the enormous expenditures required by the war with Japan and the indemnity levied after it of some £48 million, (2) the expenditures required by the government's railway construction, and (3) the indemnity demanded by the

Western nations in punishment for the Boxer Rebellion of 1900 (450 million taels).

The government borrowed £61 million between 1894 and 1898, mainly to pay for the war with Japan and the indemnity; another £31 million between 1899 and 1911, mainly for railway construction and the Boxer indemnity; and another £118 million between 1912 and 1926 for railway construction and "administrative" purposes (much of which was for interest on the previous debts).[68]

Prior to 1894, most of the loans were from foreign merchant firms or banks inside China and the interest rates (8 to 9 percent) were high because they corresponded to prevailing interest rates in China. From 1894 to 1915, the loans were floated on foreign money markets, especially British, and the interest rates tended to be lower, around 5 percent. (At that time, however, British domestic borrowers generally paid 3 to 3.5 percent and the average rate paid by foreign borrowers was 4 to 4.5 percent.) The effective rate, however, was higher than 5 percent. For instance, railway loans were usually granted on a discount, so that China received less than the nominal amount. By this method, a thirty-year loan at 5 percent interest was, effectively, a loan at 5.7 percent interest. Also, railway loans were frequently granted on the condition that construction would be carried out by specified foreign companies, which charged 2.5 to 5 percent commission fees on the construction costs.

The earlier mechanism, designed to ensure that China would pay the indemnities (securing them on the European-controlled customs revenues), was now applied to the securing of loans. The foreign customs revenues, the salt revenues (which in 1913 also came under foreign control), and even internal customs taxes were taken as security for loans during this period, as China's fiscal autonomy was progressively reduced.[69]

Foreign banks had been established in the treaty ports since the 1840s. Until the end of the century, British-owned banks were dominant, but after 1890, German, Japanese, Russian, French, American, Dutch, and Belgian banks also were important. The banks furnished most of the capital for the export and import trade and handled foreign-exchange transactions. They also furnished short- and long-term loans for manufacturing by foreigners in the treaty ports (only a few Chinese were able to borrow from the banks). Foreign-government establishments in China and foreign and Chinese business firms held accounts in them, and upper-class Chinese deposited their savings there. The banks also issued banknotes, despite the opposition of the Chinese government, and these notes were widely used in the latter part of the nineteenth century.

Important sources of capital for the foreign banks were the sums deposited by the Chinese government, related to loans and indemnities. After 1911 and 1913, customs and salt receipts were pledged as security on loans; railroad revenues were pledged as payment on railway loans. Other deposits were payments on the indemnity levied after the Boxer Rebellion of 1899–1900 and various payments for interest or principal on foreign loans.[70]

Foreign banks began to decline in importance only in the 1930s, when modern Chinese banks began to appear, encouraged by the Nationalist government. But even then, large amounts of banking capital were still in foreign hands.[71]

Investments, indemnities, and drain of capital

As the number of foreign investments in railways, mines, utilities, manufacturing, shipping, and banking in China increased, profits increasingly ended up in foreign hands. As loans to the Chinese government mounted, increasing amounts of revenue went toward the payment of interest. The multiplying indemnities added to the revenues flowing into foreign hands. It has been estimated by Hou Chi-ming that, as a result, "there was not only no net inflow of capital, but a considerable net *outflow*" during the nineteenth and early twentieth centuries. The case of China, like that of other satellite countries today, demonstrates the dubiousness of "foreign aid" as an addition to domestic resources. (As we shall see, however, in the case of Japan, less incorporation led to a net *inflow* of capital.)

Thus, over the course of the nineteenth century, a large and interrelated complex of investments developed in China: in the shipment of goods in the export-import trade and in China's domestic commerce, in treaty ports' manufactured products that once were imported, in public utilities that served the merchants and manufacturers in the ports, in investments in railways for the transport of foreign trade goods to and from the treaty ports, in mines for the production of coal to supply the shipping lines, and in banks for financing and servicing commerce and manufacturing. Where these investments could not be made because of Chinese opposition, the Western powers, and finally Japan, eventually forced China to submit, and further encroachments on Chinese autonomy were made in the form of treaties, concessions, leased areas, and spheres of influence. Accompanying all this were the indemnities and the attachment of Chinese revenues to pay for them.

Attack on China's dependencies

In the eighteenth century the Chinese government ruled (in addition to China proper) the island of Taiwan off the China coast (as a province) and Manchuria, Mongolia, and Tibet (through a system of residents and garrisons of troops), and claimed a degree of control over such places as Annam, Korea, Siam, Burma, and the Ryukyus through the tributary system.

In the nineteenth century the Western states, followed by Japan, encroached steadily upon all these territories: Britain from the south and west, France from the south and east, Russia from the north and west, and Japan from the north and east. By the twentieth century, China had lost one territory after the other; Korea, Annam, Siam, Burma, the Ryukyus, Taiwan, and much of Manchuria passed entirely out of Chinese control. And China preserved only a weak hegemony in Mongolia and Tibet.

There is a tendency in Western scholarship to regard these losses as unrelated to what was happening inside China at the same time. When China is compared with Japan, the fact that Japan's territories were little infringed upon is not mentioned. Yet defense is a typical response to foreign encroachment on what a state has claimed as part of its territories. And defense against encroachment has important internal consequences: fiscal, military, and so forth. These factors will be considered in part III; here we will simply examine the extent of the encroachment on China.

Russia

The Russian government's encroachment on China constituted an attempt to take control of the territories bordering Russia: Mongolia, Turkestan, and Manchuria. China's frontiers with Russia in the Northeast (in Manchuria) and in the Northwest (in Mongolia and Turkestan) had been delineated in the late seventeenth and early eighteenth centuries by the treaties of Nerchinsk and Kiakhta. These treaties had been "equal" in nature; that is, each nation gave something and got something. And the Treaty of Nerchinsk was concluded after China had won several military victories over Russia.

By the nineteenth century, however, encouraged by Britain's

victory in the First Opium War, the Russians determined to advance their eastern borders. As we have seen, Russia had signed two treaties with China in the 1850s and 1860s, that had opened several towns in Sinkiang and Manchuria to Western trade and residence. It soon began to seek territorial gains in these areas as well.

The first target was Manchuria. In the 1850s the governor general of eastern Siberia had occupied land along the lower reaches of the Amur River, and by 1858 he had got a Manchu general to conclude a treaty that signed away some of the territories that, according to earlier treaties, belonged to China. The Chinese court had refused to ratify the 1858 treaty, but in 1860 a Russian diplomat who had become involved in diplomatic negotiations between the Chinese court and the British and French after the Second Opium War got the court to sign over to Russia the lands north of the Amur and east of the Ussuri rivers to the sea: some 300,000 to 400,000 square miles of territory.[72]

The next Russian move was against the prefecture of Ili, in northern Sinkiang, in the 1870s. Ili was a rice farming and mining area, and was strategically important because of a mountain pass that linked southern and northern Sinkiang. The population was mainly Moslem. A considerable trade with Russia and Central Asia had grown up since the towns of Ili and Tarbagatai had been opened to trade in 1851.

After the conquest of Ili by the Manchus in the seventeenth century there had been continual uprisings by the Moslem population, many in conjunction with invasions by the former rulers of the territory, who had been banished to Khokand. Such a revolt occurred in 1870, apparently backed by the British, who were interested in containing Russia's southern expansion in order to protect India. The Russians thereupon occupied Ili, pacified the rebels, and announced to the world that they planned to hold Ili "in stewardship" for China until such time as China would be able to defend it.

China's effort to regain Ili proceeded in two stages. First, a Manchu noble, who was sent to Russia to negotiate, signed a treaty that returned Ili to China but, at the same time, gave seven-tenths of it to Russia, including the pass. The treaty also granted an indemnity of 5 million rubles to Russia and gave Russia the right to navigate the Sunguri River in Manchuria. Second, this treaty was repudiated by the Chinese court and the noble who signed it was put in prison. When many Chinese officials urged that China declare war, Russia responded by send-ing twenty-three warships to cruise along the China coast. The matter was finally settled by a treaty, concluded in 1881, in which China regained all of Ili except a few towns (in which Moslem refugees might settle) and paid the Russians 9 million rubles in return.[73]

Later, the Russians encroached on Mongolia. The treaty of 1881 had also opened several towns in Mongolia to Russian trade and residence, and trade there was growing. At the same time, the Chinese government was sponsoring a colonization move-ment into the area. In the eighteenth century the Chinese govern-ment's policy had prohibited Chinese immigration into Mongolia and Manchuria, but in the nineteenth century, because Japanese and Russian expansion in those areas threatened Chinese control, this policy had been reversed. By 1909, about 100,000 Chinese immigrants were entering Mongolia each year and bringing large areas into cultivation. Some districts of Inner Mongolia were in-corporated into the Chinese province of Chihli.

In 1911, during the revolution in China, the rulers of Outer Mongolia declared independence, a move in which they were en-couraged by Russia. Step by step, Russian influence was extended in the area. A treaty was signed that declared Russia's respect for Mongolian independence and affirmed that Mongolia had the right to keep Chinese immigrants out of the area. Russia ob-tained a concession to build a telegraph line and an agreement that it would be consulted first if railway construction was con-templated.

The Chinese government attempted to prevent all this, but was forced by treaties of 1913 and 1915 to recognize Mongolia's autonomy and to pledge not to interfere with its internal ad-ministration. The same agreement was made by Russia. "Russia had become co-suzerain with China over Outer Mongolia, as Great Britain had become, to all intents and purposes, in Tibet."[74]

France

As the Russian government approached from the north and west, the French approached from the south, taking control of the Chinese tributary states of Annam and Siam. The French gov-ernment had been trying to extend its control over Annam since the 1840s, when the area had been divided into three parts: Cochin China in the south, Annam in the center, and Tonking in the north. In 1862 France gained control over the eastern part of Cochin China and in 1867 over the western part. In 1874

Annam was made a French protectorate (France took control of Annamese foreign relations).

In the following years the Annamese rulers attempted to thwart the French by strengthening their ties with China. They continued to send tributary missions to China and they asked the Chinese Black Flag army, a band of irregulars along the southern borders of Kwangsi and Yunnan, to help them defend the Annamese territory in various battles against the French.

In 1884 France and China went to war over Annam. Although there was some fighting in Tonking, the main battles were fought in China. The French attacked Foochow, destroying eleven new warships and a modern dockyard that had been built in 1866 by the Chinese government. They also blockaded the Yangtze River and several ports, halting the grain tribute to Peking.

The outcome was a treaty in which China recognized French control over Annam. Although no indemnity was paid, China suffered losses of around 100 million taels as a result of military expenditures and the destruction of the ships and dockyard.[75]

Siam also came under French control. In 1855 the British had saddled Siam with a treaty based on the 1842 Nanking treaty with China, and in 1856 the United States had negotiated a similar arrangement. In the 1890s the French took part of Siamese territory and gained a large measure of control over what remained by the principle of extraterritoriality, which meant that France would protect not only French nationals in Siam but Chinese immigrants and many other groups. By 1896, according to Morse and MacNair, there were 30,000 French consulates in Siam for that purpose.[76]

Britain

The British conquered the tributary state of Burma in 1862 (Lower Burma) and 1886 (Upper Burma). In 1886 they negotiated an agreement with China in which China recognized British sovereignty, but Britain agreed to permit Burmese tributary missions to go to the Chinese court every ten years.

Late in the century, when it began to look as if the Russians might do so, the British began to encroach upon Tibet. In 1904 they sent an expedition into Tibet from India. A treaty was signed in which three towns were opened to trade, an indemnity of £500,000 was to be paid, and a British sphere of influence in Tibet was recognized. This treaty was confirmed by China in a convention it signed with England in 1906; however, the Chinese government then tried to reassert sovereignty over Tibet, paying the indemnity and tightening administrative control. Britain continued to encroach on Tibet through the 1910s and 1920s, China continued to resist, and the matter remained unsettled.[77]

Japan

The rulers of Japan soon joined the other nations in encroaching on China's dependencies. Japanese designs were mainly on Korea, Taiwan, and the Ryukyus. The Japanese government began to try to undermine Chinese hegemony over Korea, Taiwan, and the Ryukyus as early as the 1870s.

In 1873, when Ryukyuan sailors who were shipwrecked on Taiwan were murdered by aborigines, the Japanese government asked China to punish the aborigines, raising the question whether China exercised sovereignty over Taiwan and whether the Japanese exercised hegemony over the Ryukyus and thus were the protectors of Ryukyuan sailors, or whether the Chinese were. The outcome was that the Japanese sent a military expedition to Taiwan to punish the aborigines and to China to threaten the Chinese government. China ended by paying Japan 500,000 taels, ostensibly in compensation for buildings and roads that Japanese troops had built in Taiwan during their expedition. The Japanese gained effective control over the Ryukyus; the king was made a Japanese noble and given a residence in Tokyo. However, formal control over the islands was established only by the 1895 treaty, after the Sino-Japanese War.

In the 1870s, the Japanese imposed a treaty on Korea by which several treaty ports were opened and Japan gained territorial rights. The treaty also stated that Korea was an independent state, but Korea continued to claim to be a vassal state of China. Much as the Annamese had done when the French began to encroach on their territory, the Koreans appealed to China for help against Japan.

In the 1880s the Western nations moved in and imposed similar treaties on Korea. From then on, a series of rebellions in Korea aimed at ousting the dynasty. In 1894 both China and Japan sent troops to Korea to aid the dynasty against rebels, but the Japanese and Chinese soon turned against one another. The Sino-Japanese War was fought on land and on sea, and China lost.[78]

The Treaty of Shimonosekei concluded the war. By this treaty China gave Taiwan to Japan, abandoned claim to the Ryukyus, ceded the Liaotung peninsula (Japan was later forced to return it by the joint pressure of Russia, France, and Germany), and granted Japan commercial privileges in Korea equal to what the

Europeans and Americans had obtained in their treaties. As we have seen, the treaty also opened additional Chinese ports to trade and residence, granted Japan the right to manufacture in the treaty ports, and gave Japan an enormous indemnity of 200 million taels.

After the war, Korea gradually came under Japanese control. Russian designs on Korea were checked by Russia's defeat in the war with Japan in 1905, and in 1910 Korea was formally annexed by Japan as a colony.[79]

Missionaries

During the Ming dynasty a Jesuit mission had been established in Peking. The imperial government employed Jesuit priests as astronomers and, toward the end of the dynasty, as technical advisers in cannon manufacturing. Missionary activities were carried on throughout the empire, a native priesthood developed, and many Chinese were converted to Christianity. It is not known exactly how many converts there were but there may have been as many as 200,000 to 300,000 by the early eighteenth century. Converts included high officials and members of the imperial family, but most were peasants.[80]

The early Ch'ing rulers continued the practices of the Ming. However, in the eighteenth century, as Western rule expanded elsewhere in Asia and the connections between Christianity and imperialism became known, the Ch'ing government changed its orientation toward Christianity. In 1724 the Yung-cheng emperor issued an edict proscribing Christianity; missionaries were to be deported to Macao, church property was to be confiscated, and Chinese Christians were to renounce their faith. Periodic persecutions of Christians and expulsion of missionaries continued throughout the century at various places in China, and by the early nineteenth century Christian activities were very much diminished.[81]

In the early nineteenth century there were still perhaps 200,000 Christians in China who practiced the faith. They were scattered throughout the country (in most of the eighteen provinces and in Taiwan, Mongolia, Sinkiang, and perhaps Manchuria) and most of them were peasants. The preservation of Christianity was helped by its communal character: whole villages had been converted and there were proscriptions against intermarriage with non-Catholics. Little else was in its favor. Becoming a Christian brought no wealth or advantage, and the threat of persecution was always at hand.[82]

Christian missionaries, Protestants as well as Catholics, accompanied the expansion of Western trade and investment in China during the nineteenth century. Quite literally, as the opium ships were driven out of Canton to anchor along the coast, a certain Reverend Gutzlaff dispensed Bibles from one side of a ship while his companions dispensed opium from the other.[83]

No special rights were granted to missionaries in the Treaty of Nanking, but around that time the French got the Chinese government to issue an edict lifting the ban on Catholicism. Subsequent edicts confirmed toleration of Protestantism.[84] Toleration later became a treaty obligation. It was written into the Treaty of Tientsin that the Chinese government must tolerate Christianity and protect missionaries and converts in the exercise of their faith. The Convention of Peking further opened China to missionary activity, granting French missionaries the right to buy or rent land and to erect buildings in the interior of China, outside the treaty ports. Missionaries of other powers soon claimed this right under the most-favored-nation principle.

It is questionable whether this privilege was really legal; it appeared only in the Chinese version of the treaty, not the French, and the original French treaty stipulated that the French version was to apply in case of disagreement. However, the French government acted as if it were legal and the other governments, with a show of reluctance, followed suit.[85]

Missionaries proceeded to penetrate China, reviving old Christian communities and establishing new ones. In 1853 there were only a few hundred Protestant converts; by 1876 there were over 13,000, by 1898 over 80,000, by 1906 almost 180,000, and by 1914 about 235,000. In 1875 there were only about 400 Protestant missionaries in China; in 1889 there were about 1,300.[86]

Catholics, because of their earlier start, outnumbered Protestants throughout the century. By 1870 the number of Catholic converts had increased to 300,000 or more, by 1890 there were over 500,000, and by 1910 the number had doubled. In 1870 there were about 250 European priests in China; by 1896 there were about 760 European and 400 Chinese priests.[87]

Missions were established in most major cities in China, but Christianity remained primarily a rural phenomenon, with converts coming mostly from the peasantry.[88]

Through the mechanism of extraterritoriality, conversion to

Christianity was transformed from a risky into a profitable business. A major motive for conversion in China appears to have been the protection that missionaries offered their converts. The missionaries used their extraterritorial status whenever they exerted power locally. Above all, they intervened in lawsuits to aid their parishioners.

This threat to the status quo of landlord and gentry activist rule over local society prompted the former to organize the peasants to engage in antimissionary riots and attacks on church property. Officials, dependent on cooperation with the local upper classes for their political survival, closed their eyes to the situation. Even the imperial government was incapable of stopping the outbreaks, however much foreign consuls might urge it to do so.[89]

Antimissionary incidents were almost continuous after 1860, and much of the correspondence of Western legations in Peking was concerned with protecting missionary affairs.[90] Cohen's work on Christian missionaries in China during the 1860s lists thirty-four major incidents during that decade that involved personal injury and/or property damage in twelve different provinces, where twenty-four foreigners and 130 Chinese Christians were killed.[91]

Outbreaks related to missionary activity culminated in the Boxer Rebellion of 1899–1900. It was a peasant rebellion, and the first rebellion since the onset of China's incorporation that was consciously and predominantly an antiforeign rebellion. It occurred on the heels of the scramble for railway and mining concessions, in the Northern Chinese provinces of Chihli (where the capital was located) and Shantung (site of the German concessions).

At the outset the Boxers were not only antiforeigner and antimissionary but anti-Manchu. As they burned churches and killed converts and missionaries, they fought skirmishes with government troops who were sent out to stop them. At some point, however, the Boxers became pro-Manchu, perhaps after they suffered a major defeat by government troops.[92] About the same time, elements in the central government determined that they might use the Boxers in their own effort to resist the imperialist powers. War was declared, the Boxers entered Peking, and foreign legations and churches were besieged.

However, the rebellion was short lived and remained a sectional effort; the viceroys of the Southern and Eastern provinces and the governor of Shantung withheld support for the movement. After the Western powers moved in, the siege of the legations was ended after fifty-nine days and the Boxers were defeated.

The immediate outcome of the Boxer Rebellion was the imposition of a large indemnity (450 million taels) and a further incursion on China's sovereignty in order to secure it. The indemnity was secured on foreign customs and Western control was extended over domestic customs as well. This was an extension, on a grand scale, of what had been done over the century whenever there were missionary incidents.[93] Antimissionary activity almost invariably ended in the imposition of indemnities. For instance, during the 1860s, as Cohen notes, over 877,000 taels were imposed as indemnities for the thirty-four incidents of the decade.[94] I have not been able to calculate the total amount of indemnities levied over the remainder of the century for antimissionary incidents, but it seems likely that they were at least equivalent to those in the 1860s.

5

Japan's incorporation into the world economy

Commercial treaties between Japan and the Western nations were established prior to the development of trade relations, and these treaties were not signed until the late 1850s, when China's incorporation had been under way for over a generation. What accounts for the delayed "opening" of Japan?

As we have seen, the Tokugawa rulers placed more restrictions on foreign trade than did the Ch'ing. The only foreign traders who were permitted to come to Japan were the Dutch and the Chinese. Merchant ships from other countries, seeking trade, became numerous after the turn of the century due to the increased trade with China, but were forced away. Its *seclusion policy* made the opening of the country possible only if one or more Western governments could be persuaded to send sufficient warships to open it by force. And this no government was willing to do before the 1850s. Why not?

First, as Baran emphasized, the Western powers were preoccupied with other areas of Asia, such as Indonesia, India, and China, where significant trade and investments were already established. These areas had become a "buffer" (E. H. Norman) shielding Japan from the West. Second, it was widely believed that the effort of opening Japan would not be worth the cost because Japan had few articles of interest to trade in the West and no demand for Western manufactures.

In the early nineteenth century, for instance, the British and the Dutch were preoccupied elsewhere in Asia: the British were expanding their control in India and developing the tea and opium trade with China, as we have seen; the Dutch were preoccupied with Indonesia. The Dutch had turned this country into a vast plantation during the eighteenth century, producing coffee and other staples, and had ruled it indirectly through dependent native rulers; during the early nineteenth century they established direct rule over Indonesia. The other Western countries, such as France, the United States, and Russia, were still developing their trade with China at this time.

It must also be remembered that the military resources of the capitalist metropoles were not unlimited. Then, as now, it was not possible to hold the entire non-Western world at once. For instance, in order to fight the Second Opium War the British had to wait until ships that were used to fight the Indian Mutiny of 1857 were available. Japan could not be opened if other areas of the world were centers of attention.

Moreover, Japan did not appear to be a tempting prospect. The belief that Japan had no articles of trade of interest to the West stems from the nature of the trade the Dutch had built since the early seventeenth century. As noted above, Japan's major trading partners were China and the countries of Southern Asia, and the Dutch traders in Japan, like the Chinese, were only the vehicle of Japan's trade with these places. There was no trade to speak of between Japan and Holland. The Dutch and the Chinese imported Chinese silk, cotton, iron, and gold into Japan, as well as Indonesian and Indian cloth, spices, and sugar, and exported Japanese copper and sea products.[1] The Dutch did not try to develop a trade in Japanese tea and silk, which became the major export items of the nineteenth century.

The character of the trade the Dutch had developed seems to have been a function of Japan's backwardness, compared with China, during the seventeenth and eighteenth centuries. Japan did not produce sufficient quantities of the various raw materials that were essential to the standard of living to which the bakufu and han rulers aspired; thus Chinese raw silk, pig iron, and cotton were major import items. There was little surplus of Japanese produce for export, and the government's provisioning policy led it to prohibit the export of goods that Japan required from the outside. In time, imports of such items had declined as domestic production increased, but the domestic output was insufficient to supply both the home market and foreign commerce, as was the Chinese. When Japan began exporting raw silk and tea after the treaties were signed in the 1850s, it was at the expense, at least initially, of domestic consumption and was bitterly resisted by the government and certain sectors of the population, especially the samurai.[2]

The British East India Company's brief period of trade with Japan, prior to the seclusion policy, seemed to confirm the Dutch experience and did nothing to promote British interest in Japan. The East India Company had established a "factory" or trading post in Japan in 1613, which was closed in 1623 primarily because it had failed to make profits. At that time the British had not had much success in Asian trade, which was still largely the province of the Dutch, Portuguese, and Spanish. The factory was closed because the British were unable to supply the Japanese with the products they wanted, especially Chinese goods. The East India Company's factory in Canton had not yet been opened, and what the British had to offer, British woolens, the Japanese did not want, any more than the Chinese wanted them later.

The company subsequently made a few efforts to reopen its factory in Japan but was rebuffed by the Japanese, apparently without too much disappointment. In its important 1792 report on the nature of the Japan trade, the company stated that the trade would never become "an Object of Attention for the Manufactures and Produce of Great Britain." There was no demand in Japan for British goods, the report argued, and even if a demand could be developed, the Japanese would have to pay for the goods in copper, which would compete with the output of British mines. Thus the profits of the company would be made at the expense of British national interests.[3]

The idea that Japan was of little interest persisted in Britain into the nineteenth century. After the company gave up its effort to trade with Japan, it permitted private merchants to trade there. Many British merchants crossed from China to Japan and attempted to engage in trade but were turned away by Japanese officials. British journals discussed whether the trade was valuable enough to warrant reprisals and concluded that it was not. For instance, the *Quarterly Review* commented in 1819 that it regretted Britain's inability to establish commercial relations with Japan "not so much because we lost the opportunity for extending our commerce (for we believe the wants of this people are few and their superfluous produce neither great nor valuable), as that we let slip the occasion of convincing this proud and jealous government that the few Dutchmen, on whom they were long accustomed to trample, are not the best specimen of Christian Europe."[4]

The United States and Russia made the first serious attempts to break the Japanese seclusion policy. They were as little interested in trading with Japan as the British had been; like the British, their eyes were turned toward China. For America and Russia, however, Japan lay on the route to China.

Japan, moreover, was an obstacle to Russia's steady eastward expansion of its borders, which was engulfing China. Russian in-

terest also was related to Japan's claim over the largely unin-
habited Kurile and Sakhalin islands. As early as the late 1700s
the Russians had been exploring these island groups, setting up
boundary posts, and there had been clashes between Russians
and Japanese. Sakhalin, northernmost island in the chain of islands to which Japan belongs, lies off the coast of China, adjacent to the territories north of the Amur River that were taken
by Russia in the treaty of 1860. After these territories were taken,
Russian interest in Sakhalin became intense.[5]

American interest in Japan was related primarily to the development of commercial interests in China, which became more
intensive in the 1850s. There was little interest in trading with
Japan per se. As Commodore Perry's instructions for his expedition to Japan put it, Japan lay *"in the route of* a great commerce
which will be of importance to the United States" (my emphasis). That is, Japan, first and foremost, was not an object of commerce but a way station for merchant, naval, and other vessels
going elsewhere: to China.

In 1844 the United States acquired California; construction of
the transcontinental railroad was planned and interest in the
Pacific mounted. If the United States was to participate in the
China trade to the greatest advantage, Pacific steamship lines
would have to be established. Japan, which lay across the U.S.
route to China, appeared to be an ideal port of call for refueling
steamers. It was also believed (falsely) that there were large supplies of coal in Japan.

A second aspect was military. As American trade with China
increased, the American naval presence in the Pacific had also increased, which increased the need for secure fueling and provisioning stations. Moreover, American naval vessels had been
using the British colony of Hong Kong as their major port,
though it was hardly secure from the point of view of American
naval interests.

A third interest was related to the development of American
whaling in the northern Pacific. Sailors were frequently shipwrecked in the waters around Japan. Because of the seclusion
policy, the Japanese often imprisoned and mistreated them, and
there was an interest in making an agreement with the Japanese
government about the care and return of shipwrecked sailors.[6]

The first treaty with Japan was concluded by the United States
after Commodore Perry led a naval demonstration. He arrived
with a fleet of two steamships and two sailing ships and demanded that ports be opened in which American ships might be

provisioned, that arrangements be made for humanitarian treatment and the return of shipwrecked sailors, and that commerce between Japan and the United States be permitted.

Perry had been instructed to achieve the first two demands and that he might back down on the third, if the Japanese did not give in.[7] He announced that he would return in a year to receive the answers, with a much larger force. By only a few weeks, Perry's expedition beat an expedition led by Count Putiatin of Russia, who demanded that seaports in Japan be opened and that boundaries in Sakhalin be settled. The entrance of the Russians on the scene prompted Perry's early return, only a half-year later. His enlarged fleet consisted of three steamships, four sailing ships, three supply ships, 129 guns, and a force of 1,800 men.

The outcome was that the Japanese signed a treaty – not a treaty of commerce, for the Japanese refused to do so – but a treaty that was "not much more than a shipwreck convention."[8] It provided for shipwrecked sailors and opened Shimoda and Hakodate (the latter on the northern island of Hokkaido, near the whaling grounds) as ports where American ships might stop for provisioning or repairs. The treaty also established the most-favored-nation principle for the United States and provided for the residence of an American consul in Shimoda.[9]

As was usually the case in those days, other powers soon concluded similar treaties with Japan, and the British were first. Their treaty was similar to the U.S. treaty except that it opened Nagasaki rather than Shimoda. The Russians were next. Their treaty included Nagasaki and Shimoda and settled Russian-Japanese boundaries, giving the island of Urup to Russia, part of the Kuriles and Iturup to Japan, and providing for joint occupation of Sakhalin. The Russians also added extraterritoriality, a privilege the Dutch also secured when they concluded a new treaty.[10]

The first commercial treaty with Japan was negotiated by the new American consul at Shimoda, Townsend Harris, who arrived in 1856. Harris had not been provided military backing for his negotiations; however, he argued that signing a treaty with the United States would protect Japan from conquest by the British. He pointed out that the British were preparing for a second war against China and that they would force a treaty upon Japan as soon as they had finished in China.[11] The argument was persuasive, and the Japanese-American treaty was signed in 1857. Similar treaties with other Western nations followed the American treaty in 1858. The British later imposed an additional settlement on Japan, the Tariff Convention of 1866, which completed the formal framework that determined Western-Japanese relations for most of the rest of the century.

The 1858 treaties and the 1866 convention were patterned on the Chinese treaties of Nanking and Tientsin and were designed to re-create the features of the Chinese treaty port system in Japan. Treaty ports were opened to Western trade and residence and the principles of the most favored nation, extraterritoriality, and free trade were established. Japan's tariff autonomy was abolished and tariffs were fixed at low rates, about 5 percent ad valorem. The taxing of imported Western goods in the interior and Japanese goods that were bound for export was also restricted, as it had been in China.[12]

These similarities between the Japanese and Chinese treaties were tips of very different icebergs, however. Evidence will be presented below to show that Japan was not incorporated into the world economy to the same degree that China was, even after the treaties were concluded. Although some items of trade between Japan and the Western countries were similar (after 1858) to those of the China trade (tea, silk, Western textiles), the character of the former trade was different. It was not as large as the China trade, nor was it a staple trade for the Western nations. Western investments in Japan turned out to be few and far between. Missionaries were not protected by Western governments in the same way as in China, and their activities did not expand as they did in China. Nor was there such an intensive attack on the outlying territories of Japan as there was on China's. Because Japan was not incorporated economically to any significant degree, there were no further encroachments on Japan's political autonomy after the initial treaties were concluded and no cycles of encroachment and indemnities, as in China. Moreover, the Western powers cooperated with Japanese efforts to remove the restrictions established in the early agreements and they encouraged Japanese attempts to expand control over outlying territories.

Japan's smaller degree of incorporation was manifested in the treaties, which despite great similarities to the China treaties, are not the same. The major differences are that

1 The import of opium was prohibited. This clause was introduced in the American treaty because the United States "thought it advantageous to exclude trade in opium, chief item of British

Oriental trade, from the market of the Far East."[13] The British acquiesced in this, for reasons examined below.

2 European and American traders and missionaries were not permitted freely to travel or live or to purchase property in the interior of Japan (i.e., outside the treaty ports). They could travel in the interior, but only for "educational or scientific" purposes and upon application for a passport from the Japanese government. They could live in the interior, but only if they were employed by a Japanese citizen.

3 No territory was ceded; there was no Japanese equivalent of Hong Kong and Kowloon.

4 There was no treaty obligation to tolerate Christianity.[14]

Trade

As soon as Japan was opened, her trade with the Western countries grew rapidly. Why did this occur, given the widespread belief of Western merchants that trade with Japan would not be worthwhile? According to Allen and Donnithorne, this was due to several fortuitous events.

First, the Japanese government had evaluated gold (relative to silver) at an artificially low rate, unleashing a feverish burst of speculative activity that brought Western merchants to Japan when they might otherwise have stayed away. The gold–silver ratio was about 1:5, compared with 1:16 in the outside world. Western merchants flocked to Japan with silver, which they exchanged for gold, carried the gold to Shanghai, where they exchanged it for silver, and returned to Japan and repeated the process. Thus a considerable amount of gold left the country, although the drain was probably not as great as the outflow of silver from China in connection with the opium trade (see "The Meiji Restoration" in Chapter 6).[15]

Second, the artificially high value of silver made the prices of Japanese tea and silk relatively low, compared with the Chinese. As a result, an export trade developed more rapidly in the early years than it might otherwise have. At the time, one writer even remarked that "foreign commerce could not have begun in this country without the aid of the blunder by which foreign silver was admitted at the overvaluation . . . it enjoyed in 1859."[16]

Third, at the time that trade with Japan was opening up there was an outbreak of silkworm disease in France and Italy. The demand for silkworm eggs and raw silk exceeded what China could provide, and merchants turned to Japan. During the late

1860s, silkworm eggs and raw silk amounted to about two-thirds of the value of Japan's export trade.[17]

However, although Western trade with Japan grew rapidly, it was smaller than the China trade during most of the century. Let us take two of Japan's major trading partners, Great Britain and the United States, as examples. The value of British exports to Japan as a percentage of total British exports lagged behind the value of exports to China throughout the nineteenth century (see table 1). Exports to Japan grew, but became as large as those to China only at the end of the century, when Japan was rapidly becoming an industrial power. This phenomenon repeats itself throughout the history of Japan's trade relations with the Western countries: a sizable trade grew up only as a consequence of Japan's growing industrialization, and then the trade was of a sort that is typical of industrial nations. Japan was exporting raw materials and manufactured goods in more or less equal amounts, in contrast to China, which exported mainly primary products and imported mainly manufactured products.

The figures in table 1 underestimate the value of British exports to China by a large and unknown amount. First, they do not include British exports to China after 1861 that entered

Table 1. *Value of British exports to India, China, and Japan as a percent of value of total British exports, 1855–9 to 1905–8*

	India	China	Japan	Japan as a % of China
1855–9	12.1	1.7	—	—
1860–4	13.0	2.0	—	—
1865–9	10.9	3.0	0.8	26
1870–4	8.5	2.6	0.9	34
1875–9	11.3	2.3	1.2	52
1880–4	12.9	2.1	1.0	47
1885–9	13.7	2.5	1.4	56
1890–4	12.9	2.4	1.5	60
1895–9	12.0	2.4	2.2	91
1900–4	12.2	2.5	1.8	72
1905–8	12.8	3.2	2.8	87

Source: Compiled from Great Britain, Board of Trade, *British and Foreign Trade and Industry, 1854–1908* (London, 1909), pp. 40–43. Figures not available for Japan prior to 1865–69.

Table 2. *Value of British imports from India, China, and Japan as a percent of value of total British imports, 1855–9 to 1905–9*

	India	China	Japan	Japan as a % of China
1855–9	9.3	5.3	0.07[a]	1
1860–4	14.5	4.8	0.47	1
1865–9	11.3	3.6	0.14	3
1870–4	8.7	3.3	0.10	3
1875–9	7.6	3.6	0.10	4
1880–4	8.7	2.6	0.20	8
1885–9	8.5	1.9	—	—
1890–4	7.1	1.0	—	—
1895–9	5.8	0.6	—	—
1900–4	5.7	0.5	—	—
1905–9	6.1	0.5	—	—

Source: Figures for India and China are compiled from Great Britain, Board of Trade, *British and Foreign Trade and Industry, 1854–1908* (London, 1909), pp. 30–33. Figures for Japan are taken from Fox, *Great Britain and Japan*, p. 368. Figures for Japan after 1885 are not supplied because Fox did not include them and I have not been able to acquire her source, *Annual Statement of the Trade of the United Kingdom*.
[a] This figure is for 1859 alone.

through Hong Kong or Macao, and such goods were an important part of China's total trade.[18] Second, they do not include the value of exports to China from India, and since the opium trade must be included in any calculation of the size of British exports to China, this is an enormous omission. Opium accounted for 43 percent of China's imports in 1870, 39.3 percent in 1880, and almost 20 percent in 1890.[19]

British imports from Japan also lagged behind imports from China (see table 2). Again, the figures are an underestimate for China due to the omission of Hong Kong.

U.S. trade with Japan, as compared with China followed the same pattern. Trade with Japan was smaller than with China, but it caught up at the end of the century as Japan industrialized (see tables 3 and 4). Again, it is likely that the value of the China trade is underestimated. The source for tables 3 and 4 does

Table 3. *Value of U.S. exports to China and Japan as a percent of value of total U.S. exports, 1855–9 to 1905–9*

	China	Japan	Japan as a % of China
1855–9	1.6	less than 0.1	6
1860–4	2.8	less than 0.1	7
1865–9	0.9	0.2	22
1870–4	0.3	0.1	33
1875–9	0.3	0.2	66
1880–4	0.5	0.3	60
1885–9	0.9	0.5	55
1890–4	0.6	0.4	66
1895–9	0.9	1.0	111
1900–4	1.0	1.6	160
1905–9	1.8	2.0	111

Source: Compiled from figures in Bureau of the Census, *Historical Statistics of the United States, Colonial Times to 1957* (Washington, D.C., 1960), pp. 550–551.

Table 4. *Value of U.S. imports from China and Japan as a percent of value of total U.S. imports, 1855–9 to 1905–9*

	China	Japan	Japan as a % of China
1855–9	3.0	less than 0.1	3
1860–4	3.0	less than 0.1	3
1865–9	2.7	0.6	22
1870–4	3.7	0.1	2
1875–9	2.9	2.3	79
1880–4	2.9	2.0	68
1885–9	2.6	2.3	88
1890–4	2.3	2.7	117
1895–9	2.8	3.5	125
1900–4	2.6	4.1	157
1905–9	2.3	4.9	213

Source: Compiled from figures in Bureau of the Census, *Historical Statistics of the United States, Colonial Times to 1957* (Washington, D.C., 1960), pp. 552–553.

not indicate whether the figures for China include Hong Kong. Indeed, it is highly likely that they do not. Dennett, for instance, has remarked that American trade with China always surpassed the trade with Japan, atlhough official statistics do not reflect it because of the omission of Hong Kong.[20]

To get the full picture, it is necessary to examine the significance of the traded commodities in terms of the Western economies as well as the size of the trade. Were they staples?

Interestingly, the British did not attempt to import Japanese tea into their country. Tea, which, with silk, was Japan's major export commodity, went mostly to the United States. Tea was a staple commodity in Great Britain but not in the United States.

In 1821, for example, per capita tea consumption in the United States was only about one-half pound, approximately what it had been in Britain in 1750. By 1882, consumption had risen to only one and one-half pounds per year. At the same time, per capita coffee consumption in the United States rose from 1.29 pounds in 1821 to 8.25 pounds in 1882.[21] The United States has been a nation of coffee drinkers since the nineteenth century and coffee has been closely connected with U.S. imperialism, whereas tea has not. (British coffee consumption in 1926 was about what American consumption had been in 1821, something over a pound per capita.)[22]

Why were the British not interested in exporting Japanese tea to their country? The reason seems to lie in what was happening in India during the 1860s and 1870s. Ever since the British began to import tea from China, they had been smuggling tea plants out of China and trying to grow them in India. In the 1850s, large grants of land for tea estates were made in Assam, and after a speculative boom and bust in the 1860s the Indian tea industry got under way and progressed steadily. As noted above, Indian tea began to supplant Chinese tea on the British market. In 1866, only 4 percent of the tea imported into the United Kingdom was from India; the rest was from China. By 1903, 60 percent was from India, 30 percent from Ceylon, and only 10 percent from China. Given this trend toward importing tea from British colonial territories, it is not surprising that there was not an effort to import Japanese tea.[23]

Nor did the British try to develop a market for opium in Japan. I believe that the lack of interest in exporting tea probably accounts for this failure; however, it is usually ascribed to other causes: a lesser demand for opium by the Japanese vis-à-vis the Chinese (e.g., due to the "fierce martial Japanese feudal character" and the "soft bureaucratic" Chinese character), or the prohibitions on opium consumption that were issued by the "stern" Japanese government, or the "felicitous" American embargo on opium. None of these reasons is very convincing.

After all, as we have seen, the Chinese were not traditionally opium smokers, yet they became addicted once the British imported the drug on a large scale. The Chinese government, like the Japanese, issued stringent prohibitions on opium importing and smoking and successfully enforced them for a time, but this did not stop the British once they had decided to push the drug. And it seems unlikely that the United States could have prevented the British during the nineteenth century from pushing opium in Japan (or found it in its interests to marshal the forces to attempt to do so) had the British really desired to do so.

Another reason might be thought to have been the development of a British moral crusade against opium trading. However, this did not get under way until the 1870s, after Japan had been opened for over a decade, and significant support in Parliament for the movement did not occur before the 1890s.[24] Thus it could not have had much impact on policy relating to Japan.

The silk industry was not an unimportant industry in either the United States or Europe, and the United States, in particular, imported large quantities of Japanese silk during the latter part of the nineteenth and the early twentieth century (before the industry declined from the competition of synthetics). However, most of the silk required by the Western silk industry was supplied by China, rather than Japan, right down to the twentieth century. From 1885 to 1900, China each year exported two times more raw silk than Japan and provided 42 percent of the total Western supply. Japan overtook China only in the twentieth century. By the 1930s, Japan supplied 75 percent and China only 10 percent of the total amount.[25]

The same is true of Japan's major import items, cotton textiles. Although this industry of course was of enormous importance in the economies of Great Britain and the other Western nations, the China market was larger than the Japan market during the nineteenth century, and the potential of China was always seen as much larger.

Investments

Japan's foreign trade, like China's, was carried largely in foreign ships until the twentieth century. Japan broke out of this pattern only as she developed a trade, on her own initiative, with China, Korea, and other non-Western underdeveloped satellite areas.

There was little expansion of Japanese shipping in foreign trade in terms of inroads on the established trade with Europe and the United States.[26]

Foreign participation in Japanese domestic shipping, however, seems to have been more limited than in China. Several steamship companies that established lines between China and Japan or Japan and Europe stopped at various points along the way in Japan. For instance, the Jardine Matheson Company established a line linking Yokohama, Kobe, and China and the Pacific Mail Steamship Company, an American firm, established a line that stopped at Yokohama, Kobe, and Nagasaki on the way to Shanghai. But if companies of any importance engaged exclusively in the Japanese coastal trade (as they did in China), the standard economic histories of Japan have failed to record them.[27]

Western manufacturing in Japan also was limited during the nineteenth century, compared with China. Just as trade with the West became important only as Japan industrialized in the late nineteenth and early twentieth centuries, foreign investment in Japanese industry became important only later. "Direct participation by Western firms in Japan's industrial expansion, though always limited to a small number of industries, was considerably more important in the twentieth century, especially after the First World War, than at any time during the nineteenth century."[28] And by this time it amounted to participation rather than domination, in the typical pattern of relations between equally advanced industrial powers.[29]

In 1861 J. Mitchell built a schooner in Nagasaki,[30] but shipbuilding and ship repairing generally remained in Japanese hands throughout the nineteenth century. Western investment in the processing of tea, silk, and other export goods occurred in Japan, as well as in China, but was much more limited.[31]

There was no railway construction by Westerners in Japan nor foreign opening of mines, and thus, of course, there were no railway or mining concessions. An exception is a coal mine that was opened in 1868 (prior to the Restoration, in the Saga domain) with funds from Glover and Company, a subsidiary of the Jardine Matheson Company. (This mine was turned over to the Mitsubishi Steamship Company in 1881.) As we shall see below, the Glover firm was unable to protect itself – as it could have done in China – sustained heavy losses, and therefore desired to sell out.[32]

Compared to China, Western loans to Japan were smaller during most of the nineteenth century. Before 1894, the Japanese government had probably borrowed less than half the amount the Chinese had borrowed to that time. After that, however, Japan's borrowings soared: by 1914 Japan had borrowed about 200 billion yen, perhaps twice as much as China had borrowed by that time.[33]

The Japanese government willingly went into heavy indebtedness because by this time it was able to get loans on better terms. Japan's loans, like China's, were mostly floated on the money markets of London and Paris; but the interest rates were 4 to 4.5 percent, rather than the 5 percent charged China, and there do not appear to have been "strings" attached that made the effective rates much higher. Nor do the loans appear to have been secured on Japanese revenues in the same way they were in China. Nor were the loans generally tied to imports of materials from foreign areas.[34]

There were foreign banks in Japan, as in China, from the outset of Japan's opening, but their operations were much more circumscribed. They financed foreign trade and handled exchange dealings, as they did in China, but they never issued banknotes, as they did in China.[35] They could not make profits on handling revenues placed in security for indemnities because there were no indemnities, nor on handling revenues placed in security for loans, because security was not demanded. And because there was little foreign manufacturing or other business enterprise in Japan, they were also deprived of profits from holding the accounts of such firms, making loans, and the like.

The smaller amount of foreign investment in Japan, the absence of multiplying indemnities, and the smaller charges on foreign loans, coupled with a growing inflow of indemnities, profits, and interest from satellite areas (including China), meant that for Japan – in contrast to China – there was a considerable net inflow of foreign capital. Hou points out:

The net inflow of foreign capital was quite substantial relative to the Japanese economy at the time. . . . The net contribution of foreign capital in this period (1896–1913) constituted 12 percent of the entire net real-capital formation in Japan or 20 percent of the net real-capital formation of the "productive" type. Similarly the net real foreign contribution was about 2.3 percent of the average national income.[36]

Missionaries

Catholic missionaries had been active in Japan as well as in China during the sixteenth and seventeenth centuries. Before the Tokugawa rulers expelled the Spanish and Portuguese and banned Christianity, there had been many Japanese converts. In the early seventeenth century there may have been as many as 300,000 Japanese Christians – as many as in China.[37] By the nineteenth century there were only some 20,000 Japanese Catholics, compared with 200,000 in China. Persecution had been highly effective.

The Japanese Catholics resided primarily in the countryside and had their own priests, many of whom would later resist returning to the fold of the church. These so-called crypto Christians were "rediscovered" by Catholic missionaries in 1865.[38] However, there were many obstacles to renewed missionary activity in Japan, compared with China.

As we have seen, it was written into the China treaties that missionaries might travel, live, and buy property in the interior and that the Chinese government must tolerate Christianity among its subjects. In Japan, however, the treaties did not demand toleration, nor were missionaries permitted to travel and live inside the country. Because of this, the Chinese pattern of aggressive missionary enclaves, which were hostile to local authorities, precipitating violent outbursts against them that led to indemnities and further foreign control, did not emerge in Japan.

Missionaries attempted to proselytize inside Japan by obtaining passports to travel on educational pretexts, but once they left the ports they appear to have behaved with a caution toward the authorities that was quite different from their counterparts in China. As van Hecken explained: "Arriving in a city, they introduced themselves first to the police, who examined their passports, received them as hosts of the government, and most frequently indicated the hotel where they had to stay. Then, if requested, the police permitted them to convoke a more or less numerous audience and to give . . . lectures to those willing to hear them."[39]

Discussions of Protestant and Catholic activities in Japan inevitably mention persecutions of missionaries and converts during the nineteenth century. It is significant, however, that only a few incidents are cited and that different texts repeat the same incidents (see Cohen's book on China [cited above], which devotes a long section to detailing incident after incident). According to Treat, it was rare for legation correspondence to be concerned with missionary incidents in Japan.[40] Western governments refused to come to the aid of missionaries. For instance, in one of the often mentioned instances of persecution (in 1867 and 1868), the Japanese government deported several thousand Japanese Catholic crypto Christians from Uragami (near Nagasaki) to remote regions because they had contacted Catholic missionaries. The Western governments merely protested this action and did nothing to stop it. In fact, they promised that "if the expelled Christians were returned to their villages, they would do their best to prevent the missionaries from doing their work outside the treaty settlements."[41]

As a result of restrictions on the movement of missionaries into the interior, Protestantism was almost exclusively a coastal, urban, and upper-class phenomenon in Japan and Catholicism only somewhat less so.[42] Whereas missionaries in China seem to have converted peasants by offering them legal immunity and economic opportunities, the urban missionaries in Japan concentrated upon founding schools for the children of the upper classes. Since Christianity did not threaten the power structure in Japan, as it did in China, many upper-class Japanese could favor it, in a utilitarian way, and urge its adoption (like Western commercial law) as an aid in attempting to obtain a treaty revision that would end extraterritoriality and restore tariff autonomy.

In 1873 a Japanese government edict ordered toleration of Christianity. Indeed, Christianity had a brief period of popularity among the urban upper and middle classes in the 1880s, before the government-subsidized compulsory school system was established and before the failure to achieve a treaty revision (in 1889) inspired popular hostility against the West and created a wave of revulsion against the adoption of Western culture. Thereafter it ceased to expand.[43]

When treaty revision failed there were a number of anti-Christian incidents, such as smashing the windows of a Tokyo church and inflicting injuries on members of the congregation. Also, the government became more exacting about missionary passports. Western missionaries and teachers who had taken up residence ouside the treaty ports were required to return to the ports. Despite this, there was no intervention by the Western powers to protect missionary activity.[44]

Japan's dependencies

In addition to the three main islands of Japan proper, eighteenth-century Japan claimed the northern island of Hokkaido and the Kurile and Sakhalin islands; the Ryukyus, as we have seen, were a dependency of Satsuma. In the nineteenth century, Japan's claim to the Kuriles and Sakhalin was disputed by Russia, and

Hokkaido appeared to be on the agenda of Russian expansion. The Bonin Islands, which are near Japan but had not been claimed by it, were claimed by both Britain and the United States. And the ownership of the Ryukyus was disputed by China.

In contrast to what happened in China, these periphery claims of Japan were not vigorously attacked by the Western powers. Disputes were settled through negotiations on a relatively equal basis and Japan was encouraged by Western nations, especially the United States, in its efforts to maintain or regain territories. The United States also encouraged Japanese efforts to control Taiwan.[45]

The 1855 treaty between Russia and Japan had divided the Kurile Islands and left Russia and Japan in hazily defined joint possession of Sakhalin. After 1870 they negotiated the issue, and in 1875 a treaty was concluded in which the northern Kuriles were turned over to Japan and Sakhalin became Russian. (After Russia's defeat by Japan in the War of 1905, Japan gained control of southern Sakhalin.)

Both the United States and Britain claimed to have discovered the Bonin Islands, and in 1853 Commodore Perry landed on the Coffin group and claimed it. In 1861 the Tokugawa bakufu sent an expedition to the islands, established a unit of government, and left about thirty settlers, who remained there until 1863. In the meantime a group of Americans and other Westerners (of about the same number) had settled on the islands and in 1873 asked the U.S. government for protection. The United States decided, however, not to claim the islands, and when the British decided the same, the Japanese government took them over.

Japan's efforts to gain control of the Ryukyus and Taiwan were greatly encouraged by the United States. The American consul in Japan was sympathetic to what Japan was doing and recommended General Charles LeGendre, American Civil War hero and former U.S. consul in Amoy, as an adviser. LeGendre, who had taken part in an episode of American gunboat diplomacy off Taiwan in 1867, was made adviser to the Japanese Foreign Affairs Ministry. A number of other Americans also became involved as advisers, and a steamship of the Pacific Mail line, together with a British steamer, was hired to transport troops to Taiwan.

American encouragement began to flag, however, when it looked as if Japanese expansion could hurt American interests in Asia. Toward the end of the century, when the Japanese seizure of Korea appeared imminent, the United States dropped its earlier term for Japanese expansion, *consolidation,* and began to speak of "aggression."[46]

In the 1870s the Japanese government undertook a colonization project in Hokkaido, much as the Chinese had done in Manchuria and Mongolia in response to Russian encroachment. However, the Russians did not make an effort to take Hokkaido and the colonization project was permitted to succeed, in contrast to what happened in China.

Thus, although both China and Japan were subjected to the treaty port system, China was tightly integrated as a satellite of the Western world economy throughout the nineteenth century and Japan was not. In China, an important trade in staple products developed, as well as a large and interrelated body of investments. In Japan, trade remained peripheral to the Western economies and their investments in Japan were few and isolated. The industrial powers steadily encroached on China's dependencies but did not encroach on Japan's. China was subjected to a large influx of Western missionaries, who were protected by their governments, but Japan was not. And China increasingly lost political autonomy whereas Japan did not.

Part III

Incorporation, development, and underdevelopment

Japan was incorporated into the world economy during the nine-teenth century to a lesser degree than China. As the twentieth century began, Japan was fast becoming an industrial nation while China remained agrarian. Part III analyzes the influence of Japan's greater autonomy within the world system and China's incorporation as a satellite on their internal situations. Did Japan's "breathing space" promote industrialization and did China's more intensive incorporation hamper it?

Numerous social changes are involved in the transition to an industrial economy. I will examine two changes that seem to be among the most significant: first, the emergence of a centralized national state; second, state efforts to encourage national indus-trialization. As was argued in part I, these are two important de-velopments that did not occur in China and Japan prior to the Western capitalist intrusion but had been an important aspect of the modernization of Western Europe.

Before going on it should be noted that two arguments are made by world economy theorists about the relationship between incorporation and underdevelopment that do not seem to explain the divergent cases of China and Japan. The first set of argu-ments pertains to the negative effects on industrialization of certain consequences of trade with the industrial nations: the de-struction of native handicrafts, export price instability, and de-clining terms of trade. The arguments go as follows:

The decline of native handicrafts, which is caused by an influx of foreign manufactured goods, hampers industrialization be-cause it destroys native centers of industrial initiative. It also impoverishes the peasantry, which is dependent upon supple-mentary income from handicraft activity for its livelihood, and thus reduces the surplus available for industrial investment. In-dustrialization is also hampered by another consequence of trade: the skewing of the rural economy toward production of a few primary products for export to the industrial countries. Because the prices of primary goods on the world market tend to fluctuate wildly, the underdeveloped countries are deprived of a steady, predictable flow of funds that would facilitate industrial investment.

Moreover, as the economy is skewed toward production of a few primary products for export, it becomes more vulnerable to the effects of the declining terms of trade (i.e., the decline in prices of primary products relative to the prices of manufactured goods). This hinders industrialization because it becomes increasingly difficult to purchase essential producers' goods that cannot yet be manufactured at home.

The second group of arguments is concerned with changes in class structure and the character of the state, which some theorists seem to see simply as an automatic result of the onset of trade relations with the industrial nations. Trade with the industrial nations inevitably gives rise to a group of export-import merchants, landlords, and others who have a vital stake in the country's relations with the industrial nations. As this class grows in wealth and power, it may block government policies that aim at encouraging industrialization because these aims are contrary to its interests. For instance, the government may attempt to raise taxes on imports, exports, or land so as to increase the funds available for industrial subsidies, but fail to do so because of the opposition of landlords and merchants. The state becomes more and more the instrument of an upper class that is dependent for its survival upon the country's subordinate status within the world system.

Moreover, since the state is an instrument of these landowning and commercial groups, if the government establishes any national industries, these industries tend to aim at providing a privileged source of profits for certain merchants or state officials, or both. They are made into monopolies, and thus they tend, like all monopolies, to stagnate rather than to expand and furnish a starting point for industrial development.

In Japan, all these consequences of the opening of the country to trade with the industrial nations appeared, just as they did in China. Yet Japan industrialized anyway.

The decline of handicrafts may have been more rapid, more general, and more severe in Japan than in China after Japan was opened to trade.[1] The prices of China's export goods fluctuated during the nineteenth century, but so did Japan's, because the two countries were exporting, in the main, the same kinds of goods: tea and silk.[2]

Moreover, the Japanese economy was, if anything, skewed more toward the export of crops than was the Chinese. A higher percentage of silk and tea crops was exported from Japan than from China. About half of Japan's tea production was exported and about two-thirds of its raw silk production.[3] China exported only 30 to 40 percent of its tea and silk production.[4]

The pattern of the terms of trade was similar in both countries. If anything, Japan's situation seems to have been worse than China's. In China, the terms of trade were unfavorable and remained more or less stable up to 1900; then they declined markedly.[5] In Japan, the terms of trade were also unfavorable, declining between 1876 and 1880, remaining stable to 1900, and declining markedly thereafter, just as in China.[6]

In both countries the development of trade with the West led to the emergence of groups with a vested interest in the trade: landlords, export-import merchants, industrialists who produced luxuries with imported raw materials, upper-class consumers of luxury imports and import substitutes, and so forth.

In Japan from the 1860s to the 1880s, entrepreneurs profited from the booming tea and silk industries and the import of textiles, just as in China.[7] And if a larger proportion of the Japanese tea and silk crop was exported, a larger percentage of Japanese merchants may have been dependent on maintaining this relationship with the outside world for their survival. Moreover, they began importing goods from the West to manufacture Western-style articles, from shoe polish and hats to cigarette cases and liquor: luxury articles that the population eagerly consumed but that did little to further national industrialization.[8]

Such groups opposed government tax policies that were designed to channel funds out of their hands and into subsidizing heavy industry, and they participated in a popular movement that threatened Meiji rule.[9]

Finally, it is not true that modern industries were monopolies in China but not in Japan. In *both* countries industries that were subsidized or sponsored by the government became monopolistic. For example, the Mitsubishi Steamship Company, which was heavily subsidized by the government, had a virtual monopoly of Japanese shipping during the nineteenth century, and it was continuously criticized throughout this period of its hegemony for the high rates and poor service that allegedly grew out of its monopolistic character.[10]

One author has contrasted the rapid expansion of this Japanese firm with the stagnation of the major Chinese shipping firm, blaming the Chinese firm's stagnation on its monopolistic character but not noting that the Japanese firm was equally monopolistic.[11]

The problem with this line of argument is that it focuses too narrowly on the economic aspects of incorporation and, within them, on the aspect of trade. These aspects are only parts of a total relationship between Japan or China and the Western nations that developed over time, and to understand Japan's development or China's underdevelopment it is necessary to focus on that total relationship.

Japan's industrialization occurred *despite* a focus on production for export, despite the displacement of native products by imports, despite declining terms of trade, despite fluctuating export prices, despite the emergence of strata with a vested interest in the export-import trade, and despite the opposition of these strata to government tax policies.

This, I believe, was possible in large part because of Japan's greater autonomy vis-à-vis the world system. The absence of strong Western trading and investment interests, of strong missionary pressures and other political encroachments, promoted state centralization in Japan and gave Japan's rulers an opportunity to further national industrialization, an opportunity they seized. The government undertook policies that increasingly wrenched the economy along industrial lines, counteracting the seemingly inevitable consequences of the onset of trade relations. In China, this opportunity was lacking. China's incorporation led to an increasing dismantling of the state and prevented or undercut effective policies that would have encouraged national industrialization.

6

Transformation of the state

By the early nineteenth century, both the Manchu and the Tokugawa regimes no longer had the firm grip on society that they had had during the seventeenth. In China, provincial civil and military officials and the landlord class were appropriating an increasing share of the surplus. Peasant revolts were increasing in size and frequency, and the Ch'ing armies that were sent out to battle them were increasingly ineffective. In Japan, the han had benefited disproportionately from the economic growth of the seventeenth and early eighteenth centuries. And as the economy's rate of expansion slowed during the eighteenth century, the bakufu faced increasing discontent in all sectors of Japanese society, from samurai, merchants, and rich and poor peasants alike.

Until the arrival of the Europeans in the nineteenth century, however, both regimes had proved themselves capable of dealing with whatever opposition appeared. It was the onset of relations with the West that turned the tide. The fortunes of various groups and classes changed rapidly, mostly for the worse. Hitherto suppressed conflicts broke out into the open and discontent grew into revolutions directed against Tokugawa and Manchu rule.

These revolutions were very different in character. The Chinese revolution was a great peasant revolt: the Taiping Rebellion (1851–1864). Peasant armies, numbering in the hundreds of thousands, marched through the country, conquering numerous cities and provinces, and very nearly overturned the dynasty. In Japan, peasant unrest remained localized, and although peasants became involved, the revolution was primarily an upper-class event: several of the tozama han and the imperial court united to return the emperor to power in the Meiji Restoration (1868–1869).

The revolutions had one thing in common, however: the revolutionaries had centralizing or rationalizing aims. That is, they aimed not merely at replacing the existing rulers but also at strengthening state control over society. The Meiji rebels intended to overcome the loose Tokugawa hegemony and establish a unified empire. The Taipings aimed at expropriating the landlord class and destroying the entire structure of official privilege.

Despite this, the outcomes were very different. The Japanese revolutionaries not only came to power and established a unified empire but succeeded, during the two decades from 1870 to 1890, in the enormously difficult task of transforming that empire into a modern, centralized, national state. The Taiping revolution was defeated, and China emerged from the war more decentralized than before.

The following pages will discuss the two revolutions, their divergent characters (a peasant war in China versus an upperclass struggle in Japan) and their divergent outcomes (the defeat of the Taipings versus the victory of the Meiji rebels and the strengthening of the state in Japan versus its weakening in China). These events have frequently been analyzed primarily as a function of the inherent tendencies of Chinese and Japanese traditional society. I will focus on the relationships of the two countries to the world economy.

China's incorporation and the Taiping Rebellion

Despite the upsurge of peasant revolts in the late eighteenth and early nineteenth centuries in China and the weakness of the Manchu military forces, most of the rebellions were small in scale and the Ch'ing regime was able to hold on. After the White Lotus Rebellion (1796–1804) had been defeated, there was no large-scale revolt for over a generation.[1]

The Ch'ing government might have held on indefinitely without serious opposition had not the onset of relations with the West changed the situation in two ways that greatly increased the likelihood of large-scale revolt. First, the expansion of trade led to a dramatic increase in the hardships suffered by peasants throughout China and in South China in particular. Second, it increased the frequency and intensity of contacts among dissident groups – merchants, lower gentry, peasants, and artisans – thus facilitating the spread of revolt.

The expansion of trade, in turn, had two consequences for the peasantry: a decline in the price of copper relative to silver that, for complicated reasons, raised the peasants' tax burden and a price deflation that reduced the peasants' income and thus also contributed to raising their tax burden.

After the turn into the nineteenth century, there was a decline in China in the price of copper, relative to silver, that the government and many contemporary analysts attributed to the outflow of silver that accompanied the expansion of the opium trade.[2] The Ch'ing economy was bimetallic: major commercial transactions and tax payments were negotiated in terms of silver while smaller transactions, such as wages, were paid in copper. Prior to the expansion of the opium trade, the exchange rate between copper coins and silver had fluctuated around an official exchange rate of 1,000 copper coins to one tael of silver. After the expansion of the trade, the value rose from 1,500 to 2,000 copper coins per tael, and in some places to 2,600.[3]

This placed a greater burden on lower-class taxpayers. Their income was often received in copper, which was worth less and less in terms of the silver in which they had to pay taxes, and thus a peasant's land-tax burden was often effectively doubled.[4] In some places the government halted the commutation process and again collected the land and grain taxes in kind, but, for the most part, adjustments were not made rapidly enough and the burden was borne by the populace.[5]

During the expansion of the opium and tea trades there was also a drastic and general deflation in the prices of major commodities, including rice. In the latter part of the eighteenth century, prices had been slowly rising; "then in the 3½ decades before 1850 prices fell by a half." [6] This threatened the peasants' economy. In general, slow and steady inflation benefits peasants because it increases their incomes, especially insofar as they are self-sufficient and independent of the market for the purchase of many consumer necessities. Deflation, however, reduces peasant income. As Ramon Myers points out in his analysis of the twentieth-century North Chinese peasant economy, "If the price decline continued for long, households reduced their purchase of new capital and replacement of existing capital. The effects could be serious." [7]

Because of its beneficial effects on the agrarian economy, promoting inflation had been a major principle of Chinese government economic policy.[8] The deflation, however, increased the peasants' tax burden, forcing them to sell more of their crops to pay the same amount of taxes.[9]

The causes of the deflation are unclear. One Chinese official attributed it to the falling demand for all other commodities, brought on by the increased demand for opium:

Reporting to the emperor in late 1838, Governor-General Lin Tse-hsu revealed that from his own investigation in Soochow . . . and later in Hankow, he had found that there was a depression in almost every area of trade. The merchants informed Lin that they could sell only half of the volume of the commodities . . . that they had sold twenty or thirty years ago; opium had taken the place of the other half.[10]

The idea that the demand for opium versus the demand for other goods were mutually exclusive finds support in the views of a nineteenth-century British parliamentary committee that argued that the major hindrance to the expansion of the market for British textiles in China was the opium trade. Since the Chinese were buying so much opium, it was not surprising that they could not afford to buy much cloth and yarn.[11]

Others attributed the price deflation to the outflow of silver, which as we have noted, they believed was caused by the opium trade. Classical Chinese monetary theory linked commodity price levels to the quality of the money supply. It was believed that commodity prices rose or fell in response to a decline or rise in the value of money, which in turn might be determined by an increase or decrease in its supply.[12]

Hardship became especially acute in South China after 1840. The South China economy had at first benefited from the expansion of trade with the West; prior to the 1840s, most of the opium entered China through the Canton area, and most of the legitimate trade goods as well. All of these commodities were shipped from Canton over several main trade routes to the north and west. As the trade expanded, there was increased employment and business all along the routes, for carriers, shippers, innkeepers, and the like.

The opium trade had important employment-generating features that legitimate trade lacked. Since it was a smuggling trade and the Western ships could not unload their cargoes as usual, large numbers of people were employed in transferring the opium from the ships onto shore. In addition, the lucrative cargoes incited piracy and banditry and therefore had to be guarded aboard the ships and convoyed over the trade routes by large groups of armed men.[13]

All this changed after 1842, when the Treaty of Nanking opened additional ports to trade. Shanghai, because of its proximity to the areas of silk and tea production and its site on the

Yangtze, rapidly became the new trade center, replacing Canton in importance. The amount of opium imported through the Canton area rapidly declined and from 1842 to 1850 it declined not only relatively but absolutely, to about one-eighth its former volume.[14] The amount of other goods that moved by way of Canton also declined.[15] People in South China who had carried these goods and protected them were thrown out of work, and all along the old trade routes a depression set in as the inns, post stations, wharves, and other facilities that had become dependent upon the development of the routes lost customers.[16]

Many of the unemployed turned to banditry, preying on village communities, and the village communities, arming themselves in response, began to feud with one another.[17] Rural banditry was increased by the activities of the British navy in suppressing pirates because, after the Opium War, when opium no longer had to be smuggled ashore, former smugglers frequently turned to piracy along the coast, where the British attacked them and drove them into the interior, along the West River. By 1851 there was a "proliferation of bandits" in the Southern Chinese provinces of Kwangsi and Kwangtung.[18] And it was in Kwangsi that the Taiping Rebellion (actually a revolution) began, in a village at an important river crossing on one of the major trade routes leading north into Hunan province.

The leader of the rebellion, Hung Hsiu-ch'üan, was the son of a rich peasant and of Hakka origin. The Hakka are ethnic Chinese who migrated to South China in the Southern Sung dynasty (1127–1278) but were never completely assimilated into the population (*Hakka* means "guest people"). They frequently engaged in mining and charcoal production, as well as farming. Conflicts were constant between the Hakku and the Punti ("natives"), and were intense during the nineteenth century. Originally, the Hakka farmers had occupied the poorer and hillier land, but eventually they gained an ascendancy, so that in many places Hakka settlements had displaced the Punti. Hakka and Punti villages were often armed camps, prepared to battle one another at any moment.[19]

Hung was educated, but he had repeatedly failed the government examinations for the lowest degree and remained a village schoolteacher. He may also have been employed for a time as a protector of opium convoys moving out of Canton.[20] In trips to Canton to take the examinations between the years 1828 and 1847 he became acquainted with Christianity and studied for two months at an American mission.

Hung became convinced that he was the younger son of Jesus Christ. He prepared religious tracts based on Protestant pamphlets and Confucian-utopian writings. He converted his relatives and many Hakka peasant villages to his beliefs and enrolled them in an organization called the Society of God Worshipers. Like many other Hakka groups in the area, the God Worshipers armed themselves for protection against bandits and the depredations of Punti villagers.

Unlike the other groups, however, the society proclaimed itself in revolt against the dynasty. In 1852, over 10,000 strong, the rebels marched north toward the Yangtze provinces, gathering tens of thousands of adherents along the way. The Taipings defeated all the imperial armies that were sent against them and in 1853, with an army of over 500,000, established their capital in Nanking, where Hung ruled as Heavenly King for over a decade.

The earlier expansion and contraction of trade in South China probably contributed greatly to the rapid growth of the Taiping Rebellion. The Taipings were made up primarily of the unemployed, miners, the landless, and secret society members. It is said, moreover, that the rebels were guided in their journey northward, through the difficult mountain terrain of Hunan, by "bandits and organized hoodlums" who, as Miyazaki suggests, were very likely former opium smugglers who were out of work.[21]

The Taiping program envisioned radical changes in Chinese society, and many of these changes or proposals presage the changes that were introduced by the Chinese Communist party after 1949. Landlordism was to be abolished and the land divided equally among the peasants. Surplus beyond individual needs was to be gathered in public storehouses and allocated in accord with community goals. The peasants were to be divided into uniform organizational units of various size and these units were to be ruled by a hierarchy of officials who were, simultaneously, soldiers and administrators. Western forms of administration might be adopted.[22] Equality between the sexes was to be established. Opium smoking, as well as drinking and gambling, was forbidden.

The Taiping revolutionaries, strongly anti-Western, adopted the imperial government's form of addressing Westerners. When a British envoy wrote a letter to Hung, requesting that he be allowed to visit Nanking, the reply was "curiously condescending, stating that the Heavenly King, pleased with the coming of distant people from the 'dependencies', graciously granted them permission to trade or to serve in Nanking. Accompanying the communication were several Taiping tracts which the British were asked to read to learn the Truth."[23]

The Ch'ing, as it turned out, defeated the Taiping revolution only at the cost of further weakening the Chinese state. As word spread of the Taipings' program and their military successes against the imperial troops, landlords and gentry all over China organized the peasants into local militias. The imperial government, fearing for its survival, soon overcame its reluctance to delegate further power to the provinces and upper classes and sanctioned the organization of these militias into provincial armies. The first of several such armies was organized by a prominent Chinese official, Tseng Kuo-fan, in his home province of Hunan.

The organization of these armies was strongly personal. Tseng, for example, chose his officers among his friends, neighbors, relatives, and former classmates. These officers, in turn, selected the men who would serve under them. Local militias were often taken into the armies intact in order to make use of their local loyalties.

At first the leaders of these armies were purely military commanders. They controlled no tax funds and were compelled to turn to the regular provincial officialdom for the revenue to support their armies. However, they were soon appointed to the leading civil positions in the provinces, such as governorships and governor generalships. They thereby gained control over provincial taxes and, in the turmoil of war, over civil appointments as well. The personal character of their military organizations was then extended to the civil administration, and the entire personalized civil-military complex attained a fiscal base that was independent of the central government.[24]

Fiscal independence was furthered by the introduction of a completely new tax, the *likin*, on goods in transit (*likin* means "a thousandth," but the rate was generally higher). The likin was almost completely under provincial control during the war years; neither the quota system nor central audits were applied to it. Moreover, unlike the land and other taxes, the likin, because it was new, was highly flexible: it could be utilized for any purpose the provincial rulers decided upon and the rate could easily be adjusted upward.

After years of fighting, the provincial armies turned the tide against the Taipings. The reasons why the Taipings lost and the Ch'ing won are not very clear. Among the mistakes that authors have retrospectively attributed to the Taipings are strategic errors, such as their tendency to move on rather than administer areas they had conquered and their failure to take Shanghai or to march on Peking; internal conflicts within the Taiping organization, such as rivalry among the leaders and within the ranks among groups from various provinces; their failure, when retreat was necessary, to protect their peasant-converts who were left behind from the depredations of the Ch'ing troops; the growing separation of the Taiping rulers and officials from the masses of their followers; the tendency of Taiping troops to follow the Manchu practice of looting peasant communities instead of trying to convert them; and the failure to seek support among the Western nations.[25]

The latter deserves special consideration. It is sometimes held that the Ch'ing defeated the Taipings because the Ch'ing had Western aid, and it is true that the Western powers extended aid to the Ch'ing government; but did this affect the outcome of the war?

At the beginning of the rebellion, many Westerners in China had been sympathetic to the Taiping cause because of the Taipings' connection with Christianity and because they hoped that the Taipings, because of this connection, might be more susceptible than the Manchus to Western influence. The Western governments therefore declared neutrality. Later, however, their views changed, when the rebels showed themselves to be hostile to the West. Their prohibition of opium smoking became known; trade was increasingly disrupted as the conflict dragged on; and the Taiping armies attacked Shanghai.

In 1860, after defeating China in the Second Opium War, the Western nations had helped in a coup d'etat in Peking that brought a new group of rulers to power who promised to uphold the treaties and to communicate more openly with the Western diplomats.[26] At this point the West began to give military support to the imperial government and its regional armies. British and American officers trained and led Chinese and foreign mercenary soldiers, defending Shanghai and aiding Chinese forces in several campaigns. As H. B. Morse put it:

In defense of their own interests, the Western powers were impelled more and more to intervene in the measures taken to suppress the rebellion and were driven from step to step in supporting the imperial government, which, with all its faults, was yet the power to which they were bound by treaties . . . trade was the principal, almost the only Western interest, and for this the restoration of peace and order was essential. To secure this, it was seen that an attitude of benevolent neutrality was not sufficient and in the end measures were adopted to allay that state of disorder which prevailed generally throughout the empire.[27]

In retrospect, however, it appears that Western support for the government may have come at a time when it was no longer necessary. The Taipings were probably losing when the Western nations stepped in.[28] Indeed, it may be precisely *because* the scales were tipping that the Western powers determined to step in. As we shall see below, Western policy toward the Japanese revolution was very similar; the Western powers remained neutral until it became clear that one side was winning, and then they supported the winning side.

The major consideration of the Western nations vis-à-vis China and Japan appears to have been that there should be *some* central government in power that they could put pressure upon to enforce their treaty rights. They did not care very much about who that government was and how it got to power.

Dismantling the imperial state

After the war was over, the Ch'ing state did not return to its prewar level of centralization. The provinces retained enhanced financial and military autonomy and the central government's efforts to restrict it were feeble and unsuccessful. The provinces became so independent that the imperial court almost became one among many centers of power in China.

In chapter 2 it was pointed out that the Ch'ing government's fiscal control over the provinces was manifested in four ways: (1) the provinces reported to the center on the taxes they collected; (2) they remitted a fixed quota of funds to the center; (3) the expenditure of the remainder of the reported funds was audited at the center; and (4) the central government frequently ordered provinces to transfer surplus funds (beyond expenditures) to provinces where they were needed. Provincial independence, on the other hand, was manifested primarily in adding surcharges (which were not reported) to the basic tax rate and to juggling figures or procrastinating in transferring funds. After the rebellion, there appears to have been an increase in the number of taxes that were not strictly subjected to reporting or central auditing, an increase in unreported surcharges on the other taxes, and greater resistance not only to relinquishing funds to other provinces but also to remitting the fixed quotas.

In the latter part of the nineteenth century, commercial taxes provided the largest part of China's revenues. The land tax, which in 1750 had provided the bulk of the revenues, shrank to about 35 percent by 1908.[29] The land tax had always been more rigorously audited than commercial taxes, and, as commercial taxes expanded, revenues that were not subject to central control also expanded.

Miscellaneous taxes, mostly commercial in nature, grew in the nineteenth century from about 7 percent of government revenues to about 22 percent. They, too, were almost entirely unreported and not subject to central control.

The likin, which was almost entirely under provincial control during the Taiping revolution, continued to be collected, and although the central government tried to bring it under scrutiny, the effort was not very successful. Wang estimates that in 1908 about 40 percent of the likin was not reported (the likin accounted for about 14 percent of government revenues in 1908). Almost as large a share of the salt tax, which accounted for 15 percent of revenues in 1908, was also unreported.[30]

Foreign customs was about 11 percent of government revenues in 1908.[31] Collected in provincial ports, it was supposed to be divided 40 percent to the central government and 60 percent to the provinces. In theory, the central government had the right to allocate foreign customs revenue collected in one province to another province if it so desired, just as in the case of domestic taxes. In practice, however, provincial governments resisted such transfers and also successfully resisted sending the central government its full share.[32]

Provincial and local officials continued to add surcharges to the land tax. By 1908, according to Wang's estimates, only about one-half of the land revenues were reported to the central government. However, although scholars seem to be in general agreement that land-tax surcharges increased during the dynasty, it does not seem to be known whether the increase was continuous or whether it accelerated after the rebellion. I imagine the latter was the case, since there must have been less fear after the rebellion was defeated, at least for a time, of peasant opposition to tax increases.[33] However, this must remain a speculation for the time being.

Military forces remained largely regionally controlled after the rebellion was over. In the North, Li Hung-chang controlled a large army and navy that protected the capital, and he became so independent and powerful that he practically held the status of a shogun in relation to the court at Peking.[34]

Regional military commanders frequently refused to cooperate with one another at critical points or to respond to central commands, with disastrous results from the national point of view. For instance, during the war with France in 1884 the Northern Fleet and the Southern Fleet failed to come to the aid of the Fukien provincial navy when it was under fire. During the war with Japan in 1894 and 1895, the Southern Fleet refused to aid the Northern Fleet. And during the Boxer Rebellion, the Southern forces refused to participate when the court declared war on the Western nations.[35]

The imperial government's efforts to assert its authority over the provinces were weak, and when they had any effect, the unanticipated consequence was usually that the Chinese state became less rational and more decentralized. The major method used by the central government in trying to break provincial power structures was the old one of transferring or rotating officials from one province to another. This was usually ineffective, however, because when an official was transferred he would often move part of his staff or troops with him. But even when his staff or troops did *not* move with him, their loyalties proved impossible to break, and frequently they sent revenues from the old province to the official at his new post.

When Li Hung-chang moved from Southern China to the Northern province of Chihli, for example, he took his army with him, but its financial support came not only from Chihli but also from comrades Li had left behind in Kiangsu, Chekiang, Hupeh, Hunan, and other places where he had formerly served. Li's struggle to maintain his army and navy and to support the industrial and modernization projects he undertook after 1870 involved a continual effort to acquire funds from sources up and down the China coast, in competition with other regional commanders.[36] Given this weakening of imperial control, it is surprising that one or another (or a coalition) of China's regional commanders did not move to increase his strength and attempt to reunite China in an effort similar to the Meiji Restoration.

Li Hung-chang would have been the likely candidate for such an endeavor. He was Chihli governor general and commissioner of trade for the Northern ports in Tientsin during the latter part of the nineteenth century. As commissioner of trade, he practically monopolized the conduct of China's foreign affairs, thrusting into relative obscurity the imperial government's Bureau of Foreign Affairs, which had been instituted under Western pressure. Li controlled the revenues of Chihli province and, with the help of friends, part of the revenues of distant provinces. He commanded the Northern Fleet, as well as a provincial army and his personal Huai army, which he had organized during the Taiping revolution. He controlled a number of arsenals, mines, factories, a shipping company, and other enterprises. He was reputed to be the most powerful and the most wealthy man in China.[37]

A major reason why such a coup did not happen during the nineteenth century, I suggest, is that the imperial government, though enormously undermined by the rise of the regional commanders, was by no means moribund. It received a large, though declining, share of China's revenues and had regained the final say on many official appointments, although provincial officials might increasingly suggest the candidates. As long as the court was able to distribute patronage and revenues among the commanders, the latter found that it was to their advantage to maintain the imperial structure – unlike the situation in Japan, where the bakufu, even at its height, provided few benefits for the powerful tozama domains. When the imperial government was toppled by the 1911 Revolution and China collapsed into fragmented warlordism, the way was paved for Chiang Kai-shek's drive to reunite the country.

A drive toward centralization, coming from the center or from one or several regions, was hampered during the nineteenth and early twentieth centuries primarily by the combination of foreign encroachment and rebellion. Centralization occurs only when great effort and energy are devoted to it, since it inevitably meets resistance from those who are losing power. Yet the incorporation of China had the effect of sending the energies of China's ruling class into many other directions. (As we shall see, the case of Japan was quite different.)

China's rulers were engaged in almost continuous battle from the 1830s on, against both the Western powers and the Chinese peasantry. Much of the energy of China's regional commanders was devoted to fighting foreign encroachments and coping with their aftermath. (The very onset of China's incorporation was signaled by two major military conflicts with Western nations.) After 1860, encroachments continued, with the missionary incidents, the Margary affair (which led to the 1876 Chefoo Convention), the Russian move in Ili, the war with France over Annam, the Japanese moves on Taiwan and the Ryukyus, negotiations over the 1869 treaty revision, the Shanghai–Woosung railroad, and many smaller incidents.

The Chinese ruling class fought not only against the Taiping revolution but against other revolutionary movements it had inspired: the Nien in the Huai region, which was not suppressed until 1868; the Moslem revolt in Yunnan, which lasted from 1855 to 1873; and the Tungan revolt in the Northwest, from 1862 to 1878. All of these movements required the attention of the imperial government, many of China's regional commanders, and a large expenditure of funds and energy.

In addition, in an effort to prevent revolution from recurring, officials all over China turned to the problems of reconstructing the agrarian economy. The rebellions had laid waste vast territories; millions had been killed; canals and dikes were in disrepair and the land was returning to wilderness.[38] Officials moved settlers into abandoned areas, helping them bring land under cultivation by distributing seeds and tools, organizing the repair of waterworks, and so forth.

In Japan, in contrast (it will be argued below), there were no great peasant rebellions comparable to the Taiping for the rulers to fight or recover from. Nor did the battles of the Meiji Restoration lead to widespread destruction. Moreover, Japan faced a lesser effort at political incorporation by the Western powers than did China. Thus a situation more conducive to centralization existed in Japan. I will return to this after considering the character and outcome of the Japanese revolution.

The Meiji Restoration

In chapter 3 I argued that there were two major currents of opposition within the Tokugawa social order. The first, the opposition from above, was the resistance of the han to the Tokugawa hegemony, together with the discontent of merchants, rich peasants, and lower-ranking samurai arising from the limited opportunity structure within the Tokugawa system. The second current, the opposition from below, was the resistance of the peasantry to exploitation through high rents, high taxes, commercial monopolies, and the like. The opposition from above was the predominant form of resistance during the seventeenth and eighteenth centuries. In the absence of an imperial structure, which in China facilitated the transformation of peasant revolt into dynastic wars, peasant opposition was primarily small scale.

By the nineteenth century, as the discontent of the other classes with the restrictive feudal system mounted, peasant opposition threatened to become an important factor in national politics. The effect of the onset of relations with the West, however, was to swell the first current of opposition, rather than the second.

The beginning of relations with the Western nations had two major consequences in Japan. First, it led to an inflation that created hardship among the samurai because their incomes were fixed. Second, it quickly increased the power of the han relative to the bakufu. Compared to China, many of the peasants in Japan were insulated from the negative effects of the onset of trade. The major negative effects in Japan were felt by the samurai, whose discontent with the Tokugawa order mounted as their incomes declined. There was no large outflow of specie from Japan as a result of the onset of trade, and no deflation, no depression, and no absolute loss of employment for peasants and workers over a large area of the country.

It was noted in chapter 4 that there was an outflow of gold from Japan in the early days of the trade. Indeed, the "gold rush" of 1859–1860 is often mentioned in texts on Japanese history and its negative effects on the Japanese economy are stressed. However, the quantity of gold that left the country has been exaggerated. McMaster's evidence shows that the amount could not have been as vast as was claimed by the British consul, Sir Rutherford Alcock, whose word has been taken at face value by later historians.[39]

McMaster argues that Alcock, supervising a community frightened by increasingly frequent Japanese attacks on Europeans but unable to get additional military protection because British forces were fighting the Second Opium War in China, was attempting to blame Western merchants for precipitating the Japanese attacks by their speculative activities.[40] Moreover, the gold rush had lasted less than a year before the Japanese government halted it by changing the exchange ratio to the one that prevailed outside Japan. Compare this to the decades-long outflow of silver in China and the inability of the Chinese government to do anything about it against British determination to push the opium trade.

Since there was no large outflow of specie in Japan, there was no deflation and no depression. The major consequences of the expansion of trade were a boom and inflation. The sudden increase in demand for such commodities as tea and silk for export increased their prices dramatically. The inflation spread to most goods and to most areas of Japan. From 1858 to 1867, prices of rice and oil, as well as for tea, silk, silkworm eggs, etc., rose 200 to 400 percent.[41]

The major negative effects of the inflation, again, were felt by the samurai because of their fixed incomes. The rising prices were a source of profits to merchants, to the peasant producers, and to the rulers of producing territories, who taxed the various commodities. Only the most highly specialized peasants suffered, along with the samurai, from the inflation. Peasants who were not highly dependent on the marketplaces always had the option of cutting their market purchases and supplying their needs themselves. In China, in contrast, the price changes and the depression that resulted from the onset of trade seem to have hit all classes, including the masses of the peasantry.

After other ports were opened in Japan (in addition to Nagasaki and Shimoda), Yokohama began to displace Nagasaki as the major foreign trade center. However, this shift was not as dramatic as the rise of Shanghai and the decline of Canton in China. Miyazaki, who has attempted to compare the Satsuma revolt and other minor revolts against the new Meiji state in the 1870s to the Taiping revolution, argues that these samurai-led rebellions against Meiji authority occurred in an area of Japan that was suffering economic depression due to the shift of trade from Nagasaki to Yokohama.[42] This, however, seems exaggerated.

Although the Nagasaki trade declined *relatively* after Yokohama was opened, it did not decline *absolutely,* as the Canton trade did. According to Fox, exports and imports from Nagasaki *increased.* Some commodities, which had traditionally been exported to China from Nagasaki, continued to be shipped to China, and Nagasaki became a center for the export of coal that was used by steamships in East Asia. It also became a center for the import of Western ships and arms.[43]

The revolts in western Japan, I believe, were primarily in opposition to Meiji policies, such as the incorporation of the han into the nation and the abolition of samurai stipends (see "Creation of a national state," below), rather than to an absolute loss of employment and profits caused by a shift in trade centers.

The power of the han, relative to the Tokugawa bakufu, had been growing since the seventeenth century, but the han and the bankufu had not yet come into open conflict. The appearance of the Western powers and the opening of Japan to trade enhanced this shift in power and caused the han opposition to the bakufu to emerge into the open.

The process of Tokugawa disintegration began almost as soon as Perry's ships had sailed away.[44] There was widespread opposition to the treaties of 1854 and 1858, especially by the han who had been excluded from the Tokugawa branch families (especially the Mito han) and then by the large tozama domains (especially Choshu and Satsuma).

The bakufu was continually and increasingly criticized for its failure to throw out the Westerners and uphold the seclusion policy. Both the bakufu and its opponents turned to the imperial court for legitimation of their views. In general, since the court was disposed to use the situation to its advantage, Kyoto rapidly became a center of anti-Tokugawa activities.

The bakufu's earliest response to opposition was to attempt to silence it by force. For instance, in 1858 some members of the Council of State who had objected to the treaties were purged, several prominent daimyo were put under house arrest, and various Kyoto court notables were punished. This did not work, however; but it might have worked had Western pressures stopped at this point. However, the pressures were not to stop until after the 1866 convention had been concluded. Thus the bakufu's effort forcibly to silence the opposition only increased it, and soon there was a rash of assassination attempts on the lives of bakufu councillors.

The next response was to make concessions to the opposition. The bakufu permitted some of its opponents to enter the bakufu government. It promised to cancel the treaties and to push the Westerners into the sea in a few years. The major concession was the elimination of the sankin kotai system. In 1862 the system was practically abolished, ostensibly so that the daimyo might return to their domains and devote themselves to preparing for the bakufu's attempt to drive the Westerners into the sea.

The end of the sankin kotai system marked a tremendous change in the constellation of power in Japan. The daimyo could no longer be supervised by the bakufu; they were now completely free to make increasing expenditures on building han power, and they were free to move about. Many of the daimyo who were released from Edo did not go home but to Kyoto, where they participated in intrigues against the bakufu.

The establishment of trade with the West also enhanced the wealth and military might of the bakufu's opponents. Indeed, the nightmares of the Tokugawa founders about the effects of foreign trade were realized. Inasmuch as the Western nations were indifferent or hostile to the Tokugawa monopolies and made every effort to trade directly with merchants or the daimyo, the proceeds of trade increasingly escaped the Tokugawa coffers. In addition, the military capacity of the han expanded because now they could easily purchase Western arms, ships, and military advisers. The Tokugawa house did so too, of course, but it had no advantage in the race.

After the relaxation of the sankin kotai system, bakufu fortunes slid rapidly downhill. For a few years, struggles among the major han for control of the imperial court prevented them from attacking the bakufu, but in 1866 Choshu and Satsuma agreed to join to fight the bakufu, and in 1868 the revolution began. In early 1868, forces from Choshu, Satsuma, Tosa, Echizen, Nagoya, and Hiroshima seized the emperor's palace and announced restoration of imperial rule. A provisional central government was created. When bakufu forces moved on Kyoto, they were badly beaten by troops from Satsuma and Choshu, and by spring the bakufu had surrendered to the new imperial forces. Fighting continued between supporters of the bakufu and the new imperial forces at Aizu (in northern Honshu) and Hokkaido; but by May 1869, it was all over.

During the Restoration, peasants played a part in national events for the first time during the Tokugawa period. During the 1850s and 1860s, several han had organized militias, enrolling men from the peasant and merchant classes as well as samurai (this was not done by the bakufu.) In fact, the Choshu militia has been termed a "peasant revolt controlled from above" by E. H. Norman. It was armies of this sort, composed of peasants as well as samurai, that defeated the bakufu forces. In some cases it appears that independent peasant armies were coopted and utilized by the revolutionaries. For instance, a Tokugawa army was defeated in battle by 60,000 armed peasants and the commander of the peasant army went over to the Meiji forces.[45] After the Restoration, however, peasant revolts were controlled. As we shall see, peasant rebellions in Japan were pacified throughout the nineteenth century.

As in China, Western support does not seem to have played a decisive part in the success or failure of the Japanese revolution. On one hand, the Western merchants sold arms and ships to the various han, and more and more proceeds of commerce tended to evade bakufu territory. But on the other hand, the bakufu also was able to purchase arms and ships from the West.

Moreover, until 1865 or 1866 the Western nations had dealt with the bakufu as if it were the only legitimate power in the land. There was less flirting with the Japanese han than with the Taipings in China because the Westerners believed the powerful tozama han were the major source of opposition to foreign trade and the treaties, and they hoped to quell this opposition by strengthening the bakufu. It is not surprising that they thought this, because the bakufu officials told them so and because the western han created the major anti-Western incidents of the day and constantly urged the bakufu to expel the foreigners.

For example, when anti-Western incidents were created by the han the Western nations first sought redress through the bakufu rather than by gunboat diplomacy. From 1862 to 1864, major anti-Western incidents were created by Satsuma and Choshu. Samurai from Satsuma murdered several Western travelers who failed to dismount when a daimyo procession rode by and Choshu troops fired on Western ships that were passing through the Shimonosekei Straits. In both cases the Western powers first tried to get the bakufu to punish the han and offered the bakufu forces aid in an expedition against the han. Later, the Western powers retaliated directly against Choshu and Satsuma, but only when it became clear that the bakufu was unwilling to proceed against its enemies in the name of the Western-imposed treaties.[46]

Another example is the postponement of the opening of some of the treaty ports. In 1862 the bakufu requested that the opening of the four cities designated in the 1858 treaties be postponed, saying that it feared the openings would precipitate civil war. This request was granted by the British:

> By granting its request to postpone the opening of the 2 ports and the 2 cities, he [Alcock, the British consul] hoped to strengthen it, to destroy its anti-foreign adversaries, and thus to remove the hindrance to trade. He also believed it was better to give the bakufu the "benefit of any doubt" regarding its ability and desire to overcome its opposition, before risking the high cost and uncertain outcome of hostilities to enforce the rights of the treaty.[47]

But after 1865, when it became more and more apparent that a revolution was in the offing, that the bakufu was probably the weaker power, and that the antiforeignism of the bakufu's opponents was perhaps more a "club to beat the bakufu" than an indication that they were more opposed to the West than was the bakufu, the British (and others) began to withdraw their relatively unqualified support for the bakufu. For instance, Ernst Satow, the British consul's interpreter, published several articles in 1866 that advocated replacing treaties with the bakufu by treaties with the "Confederate Daimios" because the bakufu was not powerful enough to enforce its treaties.[48]

Even after the British had, so to speak, withdrawn legitimation of the bakufu's rule, they did not actively support its rivals. The Western powers generally declared neutrality in the struggle. This meant that certain kinds of aid were given to both sides (e.g., Western merchants were permitted to sell arms and to ferry the troops of both sides) and that other kinds of aid were withdrawn from both sides (e.g., delivery of a warship the bakufu had bought from the United States was held up, but the opponents were not permitted to purchase it).[49] It was only in 1869, when the bakufu had been decisively defeated, that the Western powers withdrew their declaration of neutrality and began to support the Meiji government (e.g., by selling it the American warship, which was used in the final campaigns against the bakufu).

Many writers have argued, in contrast, that the British supported Choshu and Satsuma and contributed to the Meiji success, whereas the bakufu was supported by France, a weaker power. They emphasize the sale of arms to Satsuma by British merchants such as Thomas Glover. Norman has further suggested that British and French support of rival factions was fortunate for Japanese autonomy: since the two "cancelled out" one another, Japan escaped the kind of domination that would have occurred had one of them held sway.

Gordon Daniels argues that this view of French and British support of the opposing factions is somewhat exaggerated.[50] It is based primarily on the memoirs of interpreter Ernst Satow, which stress Britain's shrewdness in supporting the "right" side but do not reflect the actual government policy during the whole period. (Daniels is probably correct, I believe.) Although the British trade strengthened the various han, the government did not stop its support of the bakufu in the ways mentioned above until 1865 and 1866, and even then it was still dealing with the bakufu. It wanted to be sure that it did not alienate itself from the victors, and until it was clear who the victors would be, it did not lean decisively on the anti-Tokugawa side.

Creation of a national state

The Meiji revolutionaries did not rest with establishing a unified empire. During the 1870s and 1880s they undertook major political reforms that resulted in the establishment of a modern national state. The reform had two aspects: (1) abolition of the bakufu-han system and its replacement by a centralized administrative and military structure and (2) a concerted attack on the economic privileges of various strata of society (daimyo, samurai, rich and poor peasants) in order to provide the new state structure with ample and predictable revenues.

Soon after the Restoration, a central Executive Council or Cabinet was established and six central executive departments were created (Civil or Home Affairs, Finance, War [divided into Army and Navy in 1872], Justice, Foreign Affairs, and Imperial Household). The Cabinet and the executive departments were generally dominated by men from the revolutionary domains.[51]

These departments then extended their control over the nation. The independent han armies and governments were abolished and replaced with structures controlled by the central departments of Home Affairs, Army, and Navy. In 1871, forces from the major revolutionary han had been consolidated into a central army, the Imperial Guard. The domains were then ordered to disband their military forces. The central army was greatly enlarged after the introduction of conscription in 1872. Once they had the backing of a central army, the Meiji rulers called for the abolition of the han. The old han boundaries were abolished and replaced by seventy-five prefectures that were governed by centrally appointed salaried governors and administrative staffs.

Central and provincial administrations and the military forces were reorganized and rationalized throughout the 1870s and 1880s. The powers of the prefectural governors vis-à-vis the center were circumscribed and the prefectural administrations became increasingly bureaucratic.

By 1876 the prefectural authorities not only looked to Tokyo for appointment, but had also been made subject to a system of rewards and punishments. They thus became part of a national bureaucracy which depended for its power on central, not local connections and drew its personnel from a variety of sources: former samurai officials of the domains . . . Japanese who despite relatively low birth had acquired special knowledge by travel or study abroad; and some, though they were few as yet, who qualified by possession of commercial and industrial expertise.[52]

In the 1880s, bureaucratic reforms were undertaken in the central departments. Civil service regulations were established that

created a system of examinations to decide appointments and promotions; prescribed the limits of departmental budgets; laid down with precision the number of posts to be filled; and dealt with a host of details concerning the keeping of archives and accounts, such as the issue of warrants to authorize payment, the use of entry books, the numbering of letters, the circulation and approval of drafts.[53]

During the 1870s and 1880s the army also was continuously enlarged, a reserve system was established, and the years of service were steadily increased. In 1878 the army underwent a major reorganization, modeled on the German army.

Financial support for the new civil and military structures and for the industrial undertakings of the new government (see Chapter 7) came in an attack on the various classes of Tokugawa society, increasing the state's capacity to mobilize large and continuous revenues.[54] As we have seen, the capacity of the Tokugawa government to mobilize the wealth of the population and utilize it for central purposes had been very limited. The Tokugawa rulers did not have complete control over han revenues, and both han and bakufu were burdened with the support of the large and unproductive samurai class. Their efforts to increase revenue from the countryside or the city met resistance from merchants and peasants. And revenues were unpredictable, rising and falling with the state of the harvest. The Meiji reforms reduced the funds paid to the samurai, increased the squeeze on the peasantry, commuted taxes to make revenues predictable and unrelated to the condition of the harvest, and brought the revenues under centralized control.

First, the regime encroached upon the incomes of daimyo and samurai. In 1871, in compensation for the abolition of the han, the daimyo were given stipends equivalent to one-tenth the revenues of their former domains; they were thus reduced to the status of very rich samurai. Then the regime reduced the amount it was paying to both the daimyo and the samurai. In 1873 a voluntary commutation of daimyo and samurai stipends to government bonds was announced, and in 1876 the voluntary commutation was made compulsory. The effect of the commutation was to reduce by one-half the yearly amount paid to the daimyo and samurai and thus to increase the revenues available for new purposes. As time passed and inflation continued, this amount, in effect, was further reduced.

The commutation of stipends and the incorporation of the han into the nation, together with other attacks on samurai privilege (such as abolition of the ban on interclass marriage and prohibition on wearing swords) soon led to opposition. In 1876 and 1877 there were samurai-led revolts in Satsuma, Saga, Hagi,

Kunamoto, and other places. The most important was the Satsuma rebellion, led by a disgruntled Meiji official who had returned to his home in Satsuma in 1873. The rebellion, however, was easily suppressed in about six months by the new Meiji armies, primarily because they had superior weaponry and controlled communications and the seas.[55]

Second, the regime encroached upon the peasantry, beginning with a reform of the land tax. The land was resurveyed and the peasants were ordered to pay taxes equivalent to 3 percent of the assessed value of the land (reduced in 1876–1877 to 2.5 percent after outbreaks of rioting). The taxes were to be paid in cash, rather than in kind, and they were not adjusted in accord with the condition of the harvest.

The result was to increase the revenues from the land tax and to make them predictable for the first time. Prior to the reform, the revenues yielded about 36 million yen; in 1877 they climbed to 39 million; and during 1881 to 1885 to an average of 43 million. Moreover, the entire tax yield was now controlled by the central government. The land tax provided the central government with 70 to 80 percent of its revenues during the nineteenth century.[56] In China, land tax as a percentage of revenues available to the central government shrank to about 40 percent and the commercial taxes that made up the difference were under increasing control by foreign powers.

The land-tax reform had negative consequences for the poorer peasants. In particular, it appears to have been a major cause of the large increase in tenancy after the Meiji Restoration. Because the tax was fixed and was not reduced if the harvest was poor, many peasants had to borrow money to pay their taxes and thus started on the cycle familiar to students of peasant societies: of indebtedness leading to more indebtedness and culminating in loss of the land to creditors. In many cases the government simply seized land for nonpayment of taxes. From 1883 to 1890, about 10 percent of the peasants were dispossessed for nonpayment.[57]

As the poorer peasants increasingly became tenants, the rich peasant-landlord-merchant class in the countryside, already on the rise in Tokugawa days, became increasingly prosperous. Their prosperity was enhanced by inflation, which had continued in the late 1870s (after a brief period of stability from 1868 to 1876).[58] However, they too were soon struck by the regime. The more prices rose, the more the government's income was reduced, and in 1881 a new finance minister came to power, who undertook a deflationary policy. He reduced the amount of money in circulation, and this reversed the situation. Rapid deflation replaced inflation, cutting into the prosperity of the rich peasants (and the poorer ones too, of course) and enhancing government income.[59]

The deflationary policy, the land-tax reform, and other encroachments on the peasantry (such as the conscription act) led to an increase in peasant riots. The number of riots, which had been on the increase in the late Tokugawa period, peaked only after the Restoration.[60] The deflationary policy in particular caused widespread peasant rioting and contributed to the formation of a national rural opposition party, the Liberal party, which counted among its members both rich and poor peasants, landlords, rural entrepreneurs, and so forth. The Liberal party's program centered on opposition to deflation, to heavy taxes on the land, and to the government's policy of channeling wealth out of the countryside and into heavy industry.

Despite the fact that the peasant opposition was now on a national scale, and was linked with upper-class opposition and thus potentially more threatening, the Meiji government was able to control it. The activities of the Liberal party were curtailed by censorship of books, periodicals, and newspapers; surveillance of meetings; prohibition of attendance at political meetings by soldiers, policemen, teachers, and students; prohibition of advertising meetings by political groups; regulations permitting the exile of "conspirators" from the capital city; and so forth. The peasant riots were put down without much difficulty by the new army. Moreover, many rich peasants felt their interests might be threatened by the rioting of poor peasants and they increasingly abandoned the alliance with the poor. The Liberal party declined.[61]

Thus by the 1890s the independent han had been replaced by a centralized, bureaucratic state, and that state had been put on a sound financial footing by a series of raids on the income of various classes of society, including the former ruling class of the Tokugawa period.

The most interesting aspects of the centralization of the Japanese state are that it was done (1) on such a grand scale and so rapidly and (2) without a great deal of effective opposition from the expropriated daimyo, samurai, and rich and poor peasants. In many other non-Western countries and in China (as we have seen) the rulers did not make a great effort to carry out centralizing policies.

A major reason for the rapid and relatively unopposed centralization of the Meiji state was the international situation at the time. Due in large part to the nature of the Western impact, the Japanese peasantry did not organize great rebellions comparable to the Taiping. The Meiji Restoration did not lead to combat and destruction on such a large geographic or time scale as did the Taiping. Moreover, as we have seen, Western encroachments on Japan's political autonomy and its dependencies more or less ceased after the mid-1860s. Thus Japan's new rulers did not have to devote great energies to such problems and could concern themselves with the task of strengthening the state.

Hall has raised several hypotheses with special reference to the daimyo and samurai.[62] He has proposed that the old order was replaced only "in easy stages" by the new one, rather than all at once. For example, before the han were abolished and re-replaced by prefectures, they had been nominally placed under central control and the daimyo had been given the title "governor." Before the samurai stipends were compulsorily commuted, there was the voluntary commutation (and so forth).

This argument does not seem very plausible. To the daimyo and samurai of 1869, it is doubtful that the shift of title represented a loss of power; after all, the daimyo still controlled their armies, the han revenues, and the like. In fact, *nothing* had changed. In contrast, the abolition of the han and the han armies in 1872 must have been a startling change. The other changes of this period were equally dramatic. The voluntary commutation of stipends in 1873 in no way prepared anyone for the compulsory commutation in 1876.

Hall's second point is more compelling; it also conforms with what was argued in chapter 3 about the tendencies of Japanese development. Hall points out that the new national system "gave promise of new opportunities for the ambitious."[63] First, the regional construction of the Tokugawa order disappeared, offering myriad new opportunities. Although the highest offices within the central government seem to have been occupied by men from Choshu and from the other major revolutionary han, the state structure was otherwise thrown open to men from all regions. Men who once were restricted to their domains could now serve anywhere; men from regions all over Japan could now achieve power in the central government.

Second, social mobility was no longer constrained by the old Tokugawa divisions of rank: lower samurai were catapulted into high positions; rural and han merchants rose to national power.

"Those who had the competitive instinct," Hall writes, "were not denied a future."[64]

The national system, that is, met little resistance because it accommodated so many of the social pressures that could not be relieved within the closed-opportunity structure of Tokugawa society. An imperial structure might have had the same consequences; however, given the new international context, a national rather than an imperial state was created.

7

The state and national industrialization

It was pointed out in chapter 2 that government economic policies have contributed to capitalist industrialization in a number of areas, including (1) the development of national industries and an industrial infrastructure through policies promoting capital accumulation, colonial expansion, and the protection of national industries; (2) the development of a national market; and (3) the emergence of a disciplined industrial proletariat.

Of the three areas of activity, the first was of primary importance in the creation of national industrial economies. That is, without national industries the creation of a national market would have resulted in the country's becoming a unified market for the consumption of foreign manufactures; without national industries, the industrial proletariat would have been an under- or unemployed urban lumpenproletariat; and so on. This chapter will therefore concentrate on the first type of activity.

After the Meiji Restoration, the Japanese government made vigorous efforts to encourage the development of national industries and an industrial infrastructure, and these efforts were an important contribution to Japan's industrialization. After the defeat of the Taiping revolution, the Chinese government, particularly under the impetus of the regional rulers, also made such efforts. However, the Chinese government's efforts ultimately failed.

It will be argued below that a comparison with Japan shows that the Chinese movement failed for two reasons: it was hampered by greater Western encroachment and by the dismantling of the state.

The state and national industrialization in Japan

Capital accumulation

At the beginning of the Meiji period, private entrepreneurs were very reluctant to invest in modern industry. Both samurai and merchants – large and small, urban and rural – either retained their funds or invested them in forms of commerce that were booming due to the expansion of foreign trade. Industrial investment appeared risky because of ignorance of modern industrial technology and because such investment required large accumulations of capital, which were not readily available. The reluctance was greater in proportion to the investment that was required. Thus investment was made most readily in various forms of light industry, such as silk reeling, but heavy industry was neglected.[1]

The Meiji government took it upon itself to make industrial investment sufficiently profitable and safe that private capital would be forthcoming. This effort took three forms.

First, the government established pilot projects with its own funds and ran them. This demonstrated that industrial investment was possible and could pay off. Second, the government subsidized industries (above all heavy industry, railway construction, and shipping) in various ways, thus guaranteeing profits equivalent to those from investment in land or commerce and making industrial investment a conceivable alternative. Third, the government encouraged the formation of a system of national banks, including industrial banks, that would provide long-term low-interest loans to investors in modern industry.

Projects and subsidies

In the first decade or so of Meiji rule the first method, establishing pilot factories, predominated. The second method, subsidizing private industry, became important in the 1880s and 1890s.

The Meiji government began to promote railway construction in the 1870s. At first the government tried to encourage private capital to enter the field, but was unsuccessful. The Mitsui firm was asked to raise capital for a railway company to build a line from Osaka to Kyoto and the government guaranteed a dividend rate of 7 percent on the capital invested. "In spite of considerable effort on the part of Mitsui, however, the company did not materialize for lack of subscribers."[2]

Thus the government came to engage directly in railway construction. From 1870 to 1874 railways were a major government activity, accounting for about one-third of government investment in modern enterprises. The government railways soon proved profitable, and subsidies turned out to be a sufficient stimulus to private investment after 1874. The government's expenditures on railways then declined to around 4 percent between 1875 and 1882 and around 8 percent in the 1890s. By 1892, Japan had 1,870 miles of railways, of which 550 miles were government owned; the rest had been built by private capital.[3]

By the 1880s six mines were being worked by the Japanese government (iron, lead, gold, silver, copper, and coal). These government-owned mines were only a small percentage of the mines in Japan at that time but they were almost the only ones that were worked on a large scale and with modern machinery. They produced almost all the gold and silver in Japan, about 40 percent of the lead, and 25 percent of the iron.[4] Government participation in the iron and steel industry expanded rapidly, so that by 1913 most of Japan's output of iron and steel was produced by one government work.[5]

The government also became heavily involved in manufacturing during the 1870s, especially textiles. Its degree of direct involvement was related to the technological complexity of the industry and the scale of investment required. Government efforts were not very important in the encouragement of mechanized silk reeling because the mechanization was simple, involving the mere application of steam or water power to the earlier handicraft reel, and the amounts of capital required were not large. In cotton spinning, however, the government played a more important role because the entire process had to be mechanized and large amounts of capital were necessary.[6]

In 1877 there were only three modern cotton spinning mills, and two of them were owned by the Meiji government. (One was built by the Satsuma daimyo before the Restoration; the other was also in Satsuma but was built after the Restoration, in 1870. Both were confiscated by the imperial government.)[7]

In 1878 the government began to subsidize private investment in cotton spinning. It purchased spinning machinery in England, sold it on easy terms (fifteen years for payment, with no interest) to entrepreneurs, and offered long-term loans to other entrepreneurs who wished to import spinning machinery. Two new government mills also were built. Private entrepreneurs quickly responded to the government subsidies, and many cotton mills were built. In 1877 there had been only three mills, with a total of 6,224 spindles; by 1886 there were twenty-three mills, with 89,520 spindles; and by 1890 there were 277,895 spindles, primarily under control of the mills that had been established with government aid.[8]

The Meiji government also established pilot plants during the 1870s that manufactured machinery (steam engines, boilers, and machinery for mines, sawmills, hemp and cotton spinning, silk reeling, and sugar and glass manufacturing) and plants that produced cement, glass, bricks, and armaments (ordnance, rifles, ammunition, gunpowder). Private investment in these industries did not occur until later in the century.[9]

Shipyards were also established by the government, and shipbuilding was subsidized. Before 1880 the three largest shipyards were owned and operated by the Meiji regime (two of them had been built before the Restoration). One of the shipyards built and repaired naval vessels and the other two serviced merchant ships.

When government expenditures on railroad construction declined after 1875, its expenditures on ship construction rose.[10] From 1896 to 1899 the government began heavy subsidies of private industry, which was to carry the Japanese shipbuilding industry to world prominence. Builders of iron and steel vessels of over 700 gross tons were granted large subsidies. The industry was furthered by laws that gave the owners of Japanese-built ships subsidies amounting to twice the amount that was granted to owners of foreign-built ships.[11] In contrast to other arrangements, the Meiji government never *operated* a commercial shipping fleet. But although the largest modern fleet was owned by the Mitsubishi firm, it was dependent on government subsidies for its existence.

Subsidies ranged from monetary grants to outright handouts of ships, usually during or after wartime. For example, during the Satsuma rebellion ten steamships were bought for military operations and given to the Mitsubishi company, together with grants for operating them. The same thing occurred after the war with Russia in 1905.

Mitsubishi maintained a virtual monopoly of Japanese shipping throughout the nineteenth century. It continuously expanded the size and scope of its operations with the help of government subsidies. There was a short period (1882–1885) when a rival firm, also subsidized by the government, engaged in cutthroat competition with Mitsubishi, but under pressure from the government the two combined to form what is still the major Japanese shipping line, Nippon Yusen Kaisha. After it was formed, the government continued to subsidize it by guaranteeing dividends on its capital for fifteen years. After 1896, subsidies were increased about sixfold.

Moreover, the government encouraged the expansion of Japanese shipping in Japan's foreign trade. As mentioned above, Japan's foreign trade was carried almost exclusively by Western shippers until the late nineteenth century; then, in 1896, the government began making special subsidies to Japanese owners of ships of 1,000 tons and over that were employed in foreign trade. In 1893 about 14 percent of the ships entering Japanese ports were owned by Japanese; by World War I the proportion was about 50 percent, and Japan ranked sixth in the world in shipping capacity. As noted above, this development was related to Japan's establishment of trade relations with satellite areas under her control.[12]

After 1880 most of the government pilot projects – with the exception of railways, telegraph lines, the naval shipyard, and arsenals – were sold to private firms at extremely low prices. For example, the government investment in the Shinagawa Glass Factory was about 350,000 yen but the factory was sold for about 80,000 yen, payable over a fifty-five-year period that began ten years *after* the sale.[13] After 1880, the government's efforts to encourage capital accumulation were concentrated in the forms of subsidies and banking.

The reasons for the sale of pilot factories are somewhat obscure but there are three major lines of argument. One is that the government desired to forge an alliance with a clique of powerful capitalists, who were the recipients of the windfalls. A second is that the government wished to placate liberal opponents. A third is that these sales were part of the government's program of retrenchment of expenditures, related to the fiscal problems caused by the severe inflation of the 1870s and early 1880s.[14]

Smith points out that there is little evidence to support the first argument. The sale of the enterprises at low prices enriched a small number of capitalists, but there is no evidence that the government's main intent was to enrich them through the sales. The second argument is not plausible, according to Smith, because the ideological atmosphere in Japan was hardly laissez-faire. In the 1860s and 1870s liberal ideas had had some popularity, but this spirit had soon waned and government ownership of key industries and subsidy of others were widely favored. The liberal opposition focused primarily on issues such as high taxation, civil rights and constitutional government, not on the issue of laissez-faire.

The third argument is Smith's own. As we have seen, the government was trying strenuously to reduce expenditures during the inflationary period, as well as undertaking policies aimed at bringing deflation. It seems very plausible that the sale of government enterprises was part of this retrenchment. The pilot projects appear to have been largely unprofitable to the government; had they been making money, it would have been absurd to sell them so as to cut back on expenses. In fact, many of the pilot firms operated at a loss or at very low profit, and the textile factories were especially unprofitable.

If, therefore, the pilot factories helped the development of Japanese industry, it was not because they had fully demonstrated their profitability. The sale of these enterprises at low prices must be regarded as a subsidy to private entrepreneurs. For a very low price these entrepreneurs acquired, without any effort, a large number of well-run factories and mines: "With so much done by the government in technical experiments and machinery investments, the purchasers of the enterprises, with some additional investments, could overcome the critical stage rather quickly and make these factories and mines the foundations of their own industrial enterprises."[15]

Banking

The third method of encouraging industrial investment was the establishment of a modern banking system. The Meiji government experimented with establishing banks as early as the 1870s, when a system of national banks was created after the American model. The first four national banks were established primarily with merchant capital and only as a result of pressure from the Meiji government:

When the wealthy merchants were invited to establish joint-stock national banks, they were reluctant. The House of Shimada, one of the three official money agents of the Meiji government, flatly refused to cooperate, and it was only as a result of considerable pressure that Ono finally joined with Mitsui and other Tokyo merchants to set up the first national bank. . . . Three other national banks were established in a similar fashion; one was a direct continuation of the Yokohama exchange company; one was established in Niigata with a rich landowner as its principal shareholder; and one was founded by a group of nobles and samurai from Satsuma.[16]

Their reluctance was understandable for these banks were quite unprofitable because of the arrangements dictated by the government. The banks had to deposit government paper money in the Treasury equal to three-fifths of their capital and to hold gold equal to the other two-fifths as a reserve. In return for the paper money the government gave the banks paper-money exchange bonds, bearing 6 percent interest, and the banks were permitted to issue their own notes up to the amount of the bonds they possessed. Six percent was a low rate of interest, compared with the rate on other investments. Moreover, unlike the government's paper money, the banks' money was convertible into specie. Since merchants involved in foreign trade preferred to pay for imports with specie, they continually exchanged their notes for specie and the banks' reserves were quickly drained. No more banks were established under these regulations.

After 1876 a new set of regulations led to the foundation of numerous national banks. They were founded primarily with samurai capital, derived from the commutation of stipends. Eighty percent of the banks' capital had to be deposited at the Treasury, about three-quarters of it in commutation bonds and the rest in government paper money. In return the banks received government bonds at 4 percent interest, and could issue their own notes. The banknotes were inconvertible because the banks had no specie reserves. Despite the low 4 percent interest rate, as many as 153 banks were established within two years under this system.[17]

The rush of samurai capital to the national banks appears to have been partly a result of government compulsion. For example, in Sendai it is said that "all samurai were compelled to offer their bonds as foundation capital, and 308 samurai gathered a total of 83,865 yen in bonds and cash."[18] It was also partly a result of the peculiar economic situation of the samurai (their lack of experience in business): "man samurai eagerly grasped the unique opportunity to invest their bonds in enterprises that received close governmental attention and thus were considered quite safe."[19]

At the same time, numerous private banks were founded and 204 were in operation by 1883. However, the private banks were less successful than the national banks, and many of them closed. Hirschmeier suggests that this may have been due to a lack of "public confidence" in them, because of less stringent government supervision.[20]

The national banking system, however, did not prove to be highly effective for mobilizing capital and channeling it into industrial investment, and in the 1880s the government's banking policy was again changed. The national banks were dissolved and replaced by a central bank, modeled on the central banks of the European countries, and by several banks with specialized functions: long-term credit to industry and agriculture, foreign exchange, and domestic commercial transactions.

The Industrial Bank of Japan was founded in 1900 to make long-term loans to industry on security of mobile property, such as bonds and shares. Capital was attracted by government guarantees of dividends. The bank made loans to large-scale industries, such as shipbuilding, iron and steel works, chemical plants, machine manufacturing, and public utilities. The Hypotec Bank, founded in 1898 with capital attracted by government-guaranteed dividends, made long-term loans on the security of immovable property: land, forests, fishing waters, etc. Forty-six agricultural and industrial banks, one in each prefecture, were established at the same time. They performed the same functions as the Hypotec Bank and were aided by the government in the same way.[21] This system proved successful.

The subsidizing of industries and the banks involved a heavy commitment of government funds. Where did the funds come from? The major source of tax revenues, prior to 1890, was the land tax. During the 1860s and 1870s any difference between revenues and expenditures was made up primarily by borrowing, mainly through domestic loans and the issuance of inconvertible notes but also through small foreign loans (as noted above). However, during the 1880s, as part of the government's retrenchment policy, most of these debts were paid back and the budget began to be balanced. Thus the burden of financing government expenditures prior to the 1890s fell mainly on the land tax.[22]

After the turn of the century, other sources of tax revenue – especially excise taxes on sake, sugar, textiles, soya, and tobacco – became increasingly important (taxes on sake amounted to about 20 percent of tax revenues) and the land tax declined as a proportion of total tax revenues. By 1900 the land tax had declined to 25 percent of tax revenues and by 1920 to 6 percent. Excise taxes had risen to 29 percent by 1900 and to 32 percent by 1920. Income taxes, taxes on businesses, and customs remained low in the early twentieth century: in 1910, income taxes produced about 7 percent, business taxes about 7 percent, and customs taxes about 8 percent of government revenues.[23]

However, despite the increase in commercial revenues the tax burden on agriculture remained heavy, compared to the burden on commerce and industry. From 1898 to 1902, for instance, taxes on agriculture were about 12 percent of net income while taxes on the nonagricultural sector were only about 3 percent of net income.[24]

After 1895, capital from outside Japan became a critical source of funds. As noted above, it came from foreign borrowing by the Japanese government and from the Chinese indemnity. From 1904 to 1913, foreign borrowing amounted to about one-sixth of the government's revenue.[25] As we have seen, this was a large amount, compared to what was borrowed by China, and most scholars have emphasized the importance of this inflow of funds for Japan's industrialization. Again, as noted above, it has been estimated that there was a net inflow of capital into Japan during this period, while in China, as a result of the indemnities, interest payments on loans, repatriation of profits by Western business firms, etc., there was a net outflow of capital.

Japan's indemnity from China was enormous: about one-third of Japan's gross national product.[26] The total capital invested in all modern manufacturing and mining enterprises in China, both Chinese and foreign owned, was not much greater than the value of the indemnity.[27] The Japanese collected it in gold, and this was of great importance in Japan's ability to change to the gold standard. It also "made possible the expansion of the army and navy, the extension of the railroad, telegraph, and telephone services, [and] the establishment of the Yawata Iron Mill."[28]

Protectionism

Prior to 1911, Japan was deprived of the ability to protect her industries from Western competition and control through the manipulation of tariff rates. The inability to use this mechanism of protection was a substantial handicap in its effort to industrialize. However, the Japanese government followed two other courses of action that had the effect of protecting native industries.

First, government purchase policies favored national over Western industries whenever possible. Second, government-enacted laws and regulations encouraged Japanese citizens to purchase the products and services of native industries and discouraged Western citizens from developing industries in Japan. Neither action would have been possible had Western encroachment on Japan been as great as its encroachment on China.

"The government subsidized private industry by becoming its chief customer."[29] In the early years of Japan's industrialization, there was a large home market for the products of modern industry perhaps only in cotton textiles. The electrical, paper, glass, leather, cement, brick, and other industries had such small markets that large-scale production was not conceivable. Had there been no government purchase policy, most of these industries would not have been formed.

It was purchases by the army and navy, for instance, that permitted the establishment of modern leather and woolen manufacturing in Japan. Modern paper manufacturing also began under the stimulus of purchases by government offices. The cement industry was saved from bankruptcy by purchases related to the construction of railways and government buildings. The manufacture of iron and steel, weaponry, ships, and so forth was of course enormously furthered by the government's build-up of the army and navy.[30] When the government nationalized the railways in 1906, government purchases of iron, steel, and other requirements favored domestic producers.[31]

At the beginning of the Meiji era the government had relied on foreign imports for most of the modern equipment it purchased but as time passed, purchases were increasingly made at home. By the 1930s, imports of foreign machinery and producers' goods amounted to only 20 percent of gross domestic output.[32] This was not an inevitable development, however, and would not have occurred had the Japanese government enjoyed relative autonomy. For instance, had the government's loans from the West after the 1890s been contracted on terms similar to China's, purchase of specified materials and equipment from the Western nations would have been required for rail construction, the army and navy, and so forth. Had much of Japan's railways, shipping, and manufacturing been under Western control, as in China, their supplies and equipment would have been purchased and made in the West indefinitely, not in Japan.

The second method of protecting domestic industries was the enactment of laws encouraging Japanese citizens to purchase Japanese products and discouraging foreigners from investing in Japan. During the nineteenth century Westerners frequently commented disparagingly on the inhospitality of the Japanese to foreign investment; they regarded the Japanese government as mercantilist or protectionist and complained that Japan's economic development was hindered by the government's efforts to prevent foreign capital from entering the country. The effect, in fact, was just the opposite.

The shipping industry is a good example of how a Japanese-owned industry was protected by the encouragement of Japanese nationals to purchase Japanese products. As noted in chapter 5, Japan's domestic coastal shippers had competition during the early Meiji years from American and British steamship lines that plied among Chinese and Japanese ports. The government protected the Japanese industry not only by subsidies but also by putting pressure on Japanese citizens not to use foreign ships. In 1876 the government established regulations that restricted Japanese citizens' use of foreign ships. With the help of these regulations and the subsidies, the Mitsubishi firm was soon able to buy out a major British shipping firm in Japan.[33]

The Meiji government also attempted to prevent Westerners from gaining control over Japanese industries:

Outside of the twenty-five-mile limit of the Treaty Ports of Yokohama, Kobe, Hakodate, Niigata, and Nagasaki, foreigners were forbidden to form partnerships with Japanese, to buy property in Japan, to own stock in a Japanese concern, rent property for business purposes, or even to travel except for "benefit of health or scientific investigation". While foreign mining engineers were tolerated for their knowledge and skills, they were prohibited from acquiring financial interest in mines or from attaching any part of a mine for unpaid salary.[34]

Westerners occasionally slipped through these regulations with the collusion of Japanese businessmen and officials, but when they did they were confronted by another web of obstacles woven by the government.

The Takashima coal mine is an example of the fate of Western investment in Japan. The mine was founded during the very early Meiji years by the daimyo of Saga han together with the British firm of Thomas Glover, a subsidiary of the Jardine Matheson Company. Glover was to lend the han the money to open the mine and would run it for seven years, after which it would revert to the han. In the meantime the two partners were to split the profits equally. Glover would also pay a royalty on the coal produced and the han would give the firm a commission on sales.

In 1874 the mine was taken over by the Meiji government and sold to a Japanese entrepreneur, Goto Shojiro. The capital for its purchase was put up by Jardine Matheson itself. The new contract was for fifteen years, after which the mine was to revert to Goto. Goto and Jardine were to share the profits in the meantime and Jardine was to be the monopoly sales agent for the coal in East Asia. This arrangement was made "apparently with the knowledge and acquiescence of the Japanese authorities in the violation of their own mining law."[35]

The mine had enormous difficulties and was a continual source of trouble to the Jardine Matheson Company. When Goto proved to be insolvent, the mine was plagued by numerous creditors, who won redress in the Japanese courts. The creditors got a Japanese court order, for example, that gave them a concession of

50 cents per ton of coal produced. Every time there was a conflict between Goto and Jardine Matheson, Goto went to the Japanese courts and each time won the case. Finally, the company turned to an extraterritorial court in Tokyo, suing Goto for some of the money the firm had advanced him, and won the case. However, they were not able to collect much of it. The company finally tired of this and attempted to sell out. After years of trying to find a buyer, in 1877 the company sold its share of the mine to the Mitsubishi shipping company, one of the mine's best customers.

The interesting thing about all this is the extraordinary reticence of the Jardine Matheson Company in the face of Japanese opposition: its reliance (at first) on Japanese courts rather than on the aid of the British government and the extent to which it put up with the dealings of Goto Shojiro. Jardine, it must be remembered, was involved at the same time in China, constructing the Shanghai–Woosung railroad in the face of official Chinese opposition. Other Western firms, moreover, were busily engaged in manufacturing in the Chinese ports, also despite opposition. The Western nations would soon begin to strike down the Chinese government's regulations – very similar to those of the Japanese – prohibiting foreign investment in mining, railways, manufacturing, and the like. We will return to this point in "The state and industrialization in China."

Recovery of tariff autonomy

Since the 1870s the Japanese had attempted to recover tariff autonomy. These efforts had often been encouraged by the United States and other powers, especially the smaller European nations, such as Italy. The British had adamantly refused to permit such recovery throughout most of the nineteenth century. In the 1890s, however, Britain's situation in Asia began to change.

Russia had become an increasing threat to British hegemony in East Asia and the British were searching for allies against Russia. Germany was also becoming a strong rival in Asia. Thus when renewed negotiations over treaty revisions began in 1892, the British reversed their policy. As a result, extraterritoriality was ended in 1899 and tariff autonomy was regained in 1911. The new treaties also gave concessions to foreigners that the Japanese government felt it was now possible to make: foreign travel and residence in the interior were permitted since the abolition of extraterritoriality precluded their threat to Japanese jurisdiction. After 1894, coastal shipping by foreigners was prohibited, except between the treaty ports, and was forbidden altogether after 1911 unless on a continuous voyage from a foreign country.[36]

The new tariffs became of great importance in the expansion of certain Japanese industries. Above all, the textile, iron and steel, copper, sugar, and dye industries were aided by tariff protection.[37]

Expansion

As we have seen, the Meiji government had vigorously pursued a policy of expansion almost since its inception, and this policy had been successful. By 1910 Japan had gained formal control over Taiwan, Korea, southern Sakhalin, the Ryukyus, and the various islands around central Japan and was rapidly extending its sway over Manchuria and other parts of Northern China.

Japan's expansion contributed to its industrialization in several ways. First, it provided markets for the growing industries. For example, Japanese textiles in the early years of the industry's development were exported not to Europe and the United States but mainly to China, Korea, and other nearby countries.[38]

Second, it provided raw materials that were in insufficient supply in Japan for Japanese industries. (Japan's meager supply of minerals is well known.) Conversely, the development of modern iron mining in China ended by supplying Japan's rather than China's domestic steel industry (see "The state and industrialization in China").

Third, the growth of satellite areas gave tremendous impetus to the development of the Japanese shipping industry. As noted, Japan's trade with the Western nations was carried largely in Western ships, and Japanese shippers were unable to participate in it; but as Japan's trade with its satellite areas grew as a proportion of foreign trade, the proportion of Japan's foreign trade carried on Japanese ships also grew.

Fourth, Japan's expansion brought many windfall gains from indemnities, colonial taxes, and the like. Again as we have seen, the large indemnity received from China after the 1895 war was very important in furthering Japan's industrial development.

Finally, Japan's defeat of China in the 1895 war proved her capacity to enter the race for control of East Asia, and this was a key element in the British decision to treat Japan as an ally or junior partner, the consequences of which were the end of extraterritoriality, the restoration of tariff autonomy, and the ability to borrow money in the West at lower interest rates and without strings attached.

All of these developments contributed vastly to Japan's industrialization after the 1890s.

The state and industrialization in China

Capital accumulation

Chinese officials, especially regional rulers, such as Li Hung-chang, attempted to foster the establishment of modern industry after the Taiping revolution. In China, as in Japan, there was insufficient capital in private hands during the nineteenth century for the establishment of large-scale industry, and entrepreneurs were reluctant to risk their funds in untried forms of enterprise. As in Japan, the Chinese authorities began by establishing projects under direct government control and ownership and later encouraged private capital investment through forms of subsidy.

In the 1860s and early 1870s, several projects, mainly of a military nature, were established by the Chinese government. Li Hung-chang controlled several gun factories, two major arsenals, and a machine factory. Ts'o Tsung-t'ang, another regional ruler, controlled the large Foochow dockyard and a school for navigation and shipbuilding.

After the early 1870s, the government moved into nonmilitary areas and attempted to encourage the participation of private capital. The institution of the *kuan-tu shang-pan* enterprise was created. This term has typically been translated "government supervision, merchant management," but might be better translated, according to Hsü, as "government-supervised merchant undertakings." Capital was contributed to these enterprises by merchants and by official patrons, but management was usually under control of the official patrons or their appointees, who ranged from government officials to former compradores (i.e., Chinese employees) of Western merchant firms.[39] A wide range of such enterprises was founded from the 1870s to the 1890s, including a shipping company, a machine factory, seven or eight textile factories, two coal mines, a gold mine, several ironworks, iron mines, another dockyard, a paper mill, and a match factory.[40]

The failure of these undertakings has often been told. They often got under way only after protracted delays, production stagnated, profits were small, and so forth. Hsü expresses the majority view of traditional society theorists on why this was so: "These government-supervised merchant enterprises were a hybrid operation which smacked of strong official overtones and the usual bureaucratic inefficiency, corruption, and nepotism. Being profit-oriented, they discouraged private competition and tended to monopolize business through government favor or intervention."[41] Or, as Feuerwerker notes: "The *kuan-tu shang-pan* enterprises remained marginal undertakings within their own environment. Their establishment and operation did not represent a fundamental break with the traditional agrarian economy and the conservative economic outlook which reflected it . . . after longer or shorter periods of initial success, these firms in the end were overwhelmed by the weight of traditional practices, bureaucratic motivation, and official exactions."[42]

The troubles, that is, stemmed from the bureaucratic character of Chinese society. However, a comparison with Japan demonstrates that factors related to China's international situation were of more critical significance. Accounts of the operation of these Chinese enterprises reveal that many of their troubles were rooted in a continuous state of financial crisis, which appears to have been due in large part to the weakness of the government's financial contribution to the enterprises. In contrast to Japan, where the government subsidized industries with outright grants, Chinese authorities tended to rely upon loans and demanded repayment (often with interest) after very short periods.

Why was the Chinese government so ungenerous, compared to the Japanese government? To understand this, we must compare the financial situations of the two governments. Subsidies were limited in China, vis-à-vis Japan, because of the greater costs occasioned by China's political incorporation, because of the greater unpredictability and inaccessibility of its revenues due to their dispersal among a wide variety of authorities, and because of the control of China's revenues by Western powers.

If we are speaking of the comparative availability of funds for subsidizing industrial projects in preindustrial societies, such as China and Japan, we must speak of the surplus available to government agencies after certain "necessary expenditures" were taken care of. The latter included expenditures required by (1) foreign encroachment, as for war, indemnities, and related problems such as rebellion, and (2) ordinary charges on government, such as upkeep of the armed forces, civil administration, tax dependents, and repair of essential roads and canals.

I have not been able to find data on these matters for comparable periods for Japan and China; however, it seems plausible that the Japanese government was required to spend less in the first area than was the Chinese. From 1868 to 1876, Japan was required to spend about 10 percent of its ordinary revenues on foreign encroachment, according to Smith.[43] This included repayment of the foreign debts of bakufu and han, the Restoration war, and pacification of rebellions. Later in the century, from 1876 to 1890, there would have been added expenditures for the Satsuma and the peasant rebellions, but debt repayment would have ceased (we have seen that the debts were paid by the 1880s). In the 1890s, foreign debts and wars would have increased expenditures, but increments were coming in as a result of Japan's success in war with China and as revenues from its new colonies, such as Taiwan and Korea. Thus it seems plausible that the charges against Japanese revenues for the first area of expenditure might have remained at about 10 percent for the rest of the century.

In China, in contrast, expenditures of this sort probably started on a higher level then in Japan and then increased. In the 1850s, 1860s, and 1870s there were the costs of the Taiping and other rebellions, which must have been greater than the costs of the Restoration war and the pacification of rebellion in Japan because the Chinese rebellions were on a much larger geographic scale and lasted from 1853 into the 1870s (instead of only about one year for the Meiji Restoration). China also had to pay the costs of the opium wars, the 1884 war with France, the war with Japan, and the indemnities levied after these wars; there was, moreover, a continual drain of indemnities because of antimissionary incidents and the Boxer Rebellion, as well as the payment of interest on foreign loans. Japan had none of these costs – or they were much lower or were compensated by indemnities and other revenues.

In 1899, when China had borrowed only some £61 million (by 1911 China had borrowed another £90 million), the central government paid about 30 percent of its ordinary tax revenues for the servicing of foreign debts *alone*.[44] A much greater percentage of revenues was spent if the other charges are calculated.

The charges in the second area would have been about the same in both countries, at least in the early years. Smith's figures for Japan for 1868 to 1876 show about 65 percent of its ordinary tax revenues going for these routine expenditures. In most premodern states, West or East, from half to three-quarters of expenditures are usually for the upkeep of the state apparatus, maintenance of communication facilities, and so on. Later in the century, Japan's routine expenditures may have decreased as a proportion of revenues, compared with China. For instance, in the early years of the Meiji regime, salaries of government officials were higher (to secure their loyalty) than they were later (as bureaucratization was introduced).[45] Although I have not been able to estimate such differences, I suspect that they were less than in the first category.

Subsidies were limited in China, compared with Japan, not only by a greater shortage of funds but by their greater unpredictability and inaccessibility. This had two sources: foreign control over China's revenues and the dismantling of the state.

It was of greatest importance for Japan's industrialization that control over revenues was centralized in the Meiji government. As mentioned above, the Meiji rulers had control over most of the revenues derived from internal sources, such as the land tax, and thus the government could dispose of them as it chose. It exercised similar control over the revenue from foreign customs.

Not so in China. Since the 1860s in China, foreign control over the maritime customs not only made it possible for Westerners to secure the indemnities they chose to levy on China, and thus drain the country of funds that might have been used for industrial purposes, but it contributed to the decentralization or dispersal of funds in China. Foreign customs was an added agency to bargain with to get control of money, and the fact that these revenues were under foreign (and thus insecure) control meant that they could not be relied upon in planning for industrial subsidies. The funding of industrial enterprise was also greatly handicapped by China's internal decentralization. The lack of a centralized fiscal structure meant that such financing was always in doubt.

For example, the initial funds for the Hanyang ironworks, established by Chang Chih-tung, one of China's regional rulers (governor general of Hunan and Hupei), came from various provincial sources. The bulk came from provincial funds under Chang's control, from the central government, and from the capital of an arsenal and a textile mill that Chang controlled; substantial amounts were also procured from salt merchants of the Liang-huai district and from the Kiangsu-Chekiang "defense funds." The firm, nevertheless, always lacked sufficient capital; it turned to Chinese banks for credit and eventually began to borrow from the Japanese. After the turn of the century, the firm became a merchant-operated undertaking, and came to be controlled by Japanese creditors. Almost the entire output of the ironworks and an iron mine associated with it went to Japan, where it was fabricated by the Yawata iron and steel mill.[46]

Another example is the China Merchants' Steamship Navigation Company. The initial capital for this kuan-tu shang-pan enterprise came in part from shares purchased by private persons, but the most important part was government loans. These loans were procured from the treasuries of at least four provincial governments, as well as from customs revenues.[47]

In sum, government efforts to encourage capital accumulation in industry in China were limited compared with Japan, not because China was bureaucratic and centralized but because it was not, and not merely because of internal circumstances but because of the very different international situations of the two countries.

Protectionism

Like Japan, China was unable to protect its native industries by manipulating tariffs. However, China did not regain tariff autonomy until almost a generation after Japan, and it is sometimes noted that the Chinese government did not make an equally vigorous effort to achieve this goal. Whereas the Japanese engaged in almost continual negotiations directed toward this goal, beginning in the 1870s, the Chinese hardly raised the question. Although this is true, it would be very misleading to trace it to Chinese bureaucratic backwardness versus Japanese enlightenment.

First, Japan was steadily encouraged to pursue the question by various Western governments. For example, the United States was a great champion of Japan's regaining its tariff autonomy, and the Italians went so far as to negotiate a treaty with Japan in which they made concessions about tariffs and agreed to forgo extraterritoriality in exchange for the right to travel in the interior of Japan. But other powers, led by Britain, would not permit ratification of this treaty. Had it not been for British stubbornness, Japan's tariff autonomy would probably have been restored prior to 1911.

Second, treaty revision in China always called for ruthless pressure on the Chinese negotiators to give up *more* national rights: the Western powers in China were always poised to seize further advantages. Because Chinese officials always struggled to avoid giving away more, it is not surprising that an effort to recover something that had been lost was far from their minds.

Hsü asks: "Why did the Chinese government not press for the abrogation of the treaties when it had become fully aware of the evils of these concessions?" He answers:

Any attempt to recover China's lost rights would necessarily entail a treaty revision which the government was afraid would upset the peace and open to the foreigners new opportunities to make demands. The safest policy was to keep the status quo. . . . The mandarins' fear of new foreign demands was so great that they did not even consider turning to their advantage the official occasions for treaty revision. The Old China Hands' constant clamor for more concessions had created a tense psychological atmosphere that put the mandarins on the defensive. They were terrified by such fire-eating pro-consuls as Harry Parkes, and so busy ferreting out the foreigners' next moves in order to devise means of blocking them, that they hardly had the time or the will to demand restitution of lost rights. Treaty revision was a one-way affair for the officials of the T'ung-Chih period; it was an occasion for the foreigners to make new demands, but not for the Chinese to reduce the foreigners' rights. All China could do was to bargain with the foreigners about the new concessions.[48]

The Chinese government also attempted to compensate for the loss of tariff autonomy by undertaking the same types of protection the Japanese did: government purchases favoring national industries, encouraging the population to purchase the output of national rather than foreign industries, and discouraging foreigners from investing in China. However, these methods were not as successful as they were in Japan, primarily because the Western powers refused to cooperate.

The shipping industry provides a good example of why government efforts at protection failed in China, again in contrast with Japan. Chinese shipping appears to have had a greater amount of Western competition, as we have seen. This competition was not about to give up and go away at the slightest provocation. In the early days of expansion of Western shipping in China, the Chinese authorities attempted to forbid Chinese citizens to ship on Western vessels, but this was objected to by Western consuls and, under pressure, the authorities desisted. Liu points out, in his discussion of the rise of the China Merchants' Steamship Navigation Company in the 1870s and 1880s, that its government sponsors could not think of pressuring Chinese merchants to ship with the company because the Western powers would have objected to it as a violation of the treaties.[49]

The government tried to support the shipping line by certain tax exemptions. Tea shipped north into Tientsin on the way to Russia was exempted from inland duties, for instance, and by purchase of its services: grain tribute to the capital was shipped on the line at double the rate charged by the Western shipping lines. However, the major business of all the shipping companies was domestic commerce, and here the Chinese government was forced to compete with the Western shipping firms without special advantage.

It may have been competing at a disadvantage. The Chinese and the foreign shipping firms attempted to attract business by offering efficient service and regular schedules and by a brokerage system in which commissions, rebates, and the chance to recommend clients for positions on the ship were offered to merchants who brought in the business of others. The Chinese firm appears to have been equal to the Western firms in the first two respects.[50] However, in the third respect the Western firms might have had an advantage. The larger Western shipping enterprises were connected with several major British and American export and import houses that dominated China's foreign trade, such as Jardine, Butterfield and Swire, and Russell and Company,[51] and the network of people who were subject to their influence must have been enormous. Moreover, the Western firms attracted Chinese shareholders and directors, thus multiplying their influence. The Chinese company was under the patronage of Li Hungchang, and thus under the most powerful of China's regional rulers, and its managers included several men who had been compradores of Western firms. However, Li was only one of several sources of power, and the several Western firms probably controlled the largest part of China's foreign trade.

Although the Chinese government forbade Western firms from manufacturing, mining, or building railways in treaty ports or in the interior of China, these prohibitions, as we have seen, like the prohibition on importing opium, amounted to very little. As soon as the Western powers determined to engage in such activities, they ruthlessly proceeded to do so. Prior to the 1890s, manufacturing in the ports was conducted despite opposition, a railway was constructed, and in the 1890s, when the Western nations became seriously interested in investment in China, China's opposition was swept aside in the scramble for concessions. Once the scramble began and the prohibition against manufacturing was lifted in 1895, after the defeat by Japan, the Chinese government still tried to protect Chinese industry from foreign control. New regulations required that a certain percentage of the capital in foreign enterprises must be provided by Chinese citizens, that taxes must be paid to the Chinese government, and that the enterprises must establish schools to train Chinese students. However, like the earlier prohibitions on the entrance of foreign capital, these regulations were violated by the industrial capitalist nations whenever they felt like doing so.[52]

In short, the Chinese government was just as protectionist or mercantilist as the Meiji government in its motives, but since the Western powers had nothing to lose by this in Japan and were preoccupied with pushing their interests in China and elsewhere, they "submitted" to Japanese rules and regulations. Had they desired to invest in Japan, they certainly had the power to do so. Fortunately for Japan's development, they did not choose to exert it.

The Chinese government's ability to protect domestic industries through its purchasing policies was also limited. First, China's fiscal and military weakness meant that the effect of government purchases on the economy was small; that is, the Chinese government simply was unable to buy as much as the Japanese government. Second, when the Chinese government began to borrow from the West, its ability to use its purchasing power to further domestic industrialization was severely restricted. On the other hand, loans to Japan were more freely granted and less encumbered.

For instance, when the Hanyang ironworks was established, the imperial government guaranteed that all government railway projects would purchase iron and steel only from Hanyang. However, when the railroads began to be built with foreign loans, the contracts qualified this privilege granted Hanyang almost out of existence. The supplies had to be imported from abroad. Only the Peking–Hankow line was built with Hanyang iron and steel.[53]

The dismantling of the state, in interaction with the encroachment by industrial nations, further hampered the government's ability to protect native industries. For example, railway construction in China was partly under Western control and partly under the auspices of China's various regional authorities. Since there was no central coordination of even that part of construction that was under Chinese auspices, there was no way of guaranteeing any Chinese industry that its output might be used for railway construction. Again, though the central government had promised to purchase railway supplies from the Hanyang ironworkers, some of the provincial authorities, when the railways were built in the provinces, were persuaded to purchase Western supplies.[54]

Expansion

As the Western nations and Japan expanded, China contracted. China was unable to protect its territories from encroachment during the nineteenth and early twentieth centuries, let alone establish satellite areas under its control.

Although it is obviously true that a nation can industrialize without establishing control over colonial territories – the examples of contemporary socialist nations indicate this – expansion is certainly one of the forces that have stimulated growth in capitalist countries from the sixteenth century to the present. Who knows how much China's textile industries might have expanded had they had unrestrained access to the markets of Korea and Japan? How much might China's machine production have expanded had her ironworks not been given over to the supply of Japanese industry? How much might China's industrialization have been furthered had China been the recipient rather than the provider of indemnities? Had China been a colonizer rather than the colonized during the nineteenth and early twentieth centuries, its history would undoubtedly have been quite different.

In sum, the Japanese government's effort to promote industrialization were critical in the rise of national industrial capitalism. Although the Chinese government made similar efforts, it was hampered or blocked at every turn by China's more intensive incorporation into the world economy. The failure of the Chinese government's efforts has often been attributed to the negative effects of bureaucracy, but such a view is short sighted. Comparing China and Japan, we see that the problem was not that China was *too bureaucratic* but that China was *not bureaucratic enough*. Japan became a modern bureaucratic, national state; China became increasingly decentralized as it was incorporated into the world economy. Despite this, efforts were made to achieve national industrialization. That they failed is not surprising, given China's subordinated international position during the time they were undertaken.

Summary and conclusions

Considerable controversy and confusion surround the question of why Japan was the first – and remains the only – non-Western country to have become a major industrial capitalist power. This study has tried to clarify Japan's unique development by comparing it with Imperial China. The focus has been on the nature and consequences of their ties to the nineteenth-century world economy, a contrast that has been neglected in most other comparative studies of Japan and China.

This study has asked three sets of major questions.

1 Were Japan and China radically different societies prior to the expansion of the Western capitalist world economy to East Asia, as traditional society theorists have claimed? Was Japan's development during the Tokugawa period analogous to European development during the transition from feudalism to capitalism?

2 Was Japan more autonomous within the nineteenth-century world economy than China, as world economy theorists have claimed?

3 Did Japan's autonomy during the nineteenth century contribute significantly to its development, and China's dependence to its underdevelopment, as world economy theorists have argued? Or were differences in their traditional societies more important?

I have argued that traditional society theorists have exaggerated the differences between Tokugawa Japan and Ch'ing China. Although there were political divergences between the two systems – Japan was a more decentralized or "feudal" state than "imperial" China – the overall character of the two economies and societies was more similar than divergent on the eve of the Western capitalist intrusion into East Asia. During the nineteenth century these similar societies were drawn into the world economy. I have argued that the central proposition of world economy theorists is generally correct: Japan remained relatively autonomous within the world system whereas China was incorporated as a dependent satellite.

I have compared the incorporation of China and Japan into the world system in terms of four variables: trade, investment, political incorporation, and missionary penetration. The Western capitalist nations developed a large staple trade with China, exchanging Chinese primary products for Indian opium and Western manufactures, and founded a large and interrelated body of investments in shipping, manufacturing, mining, railways, and lending and banking in China. Japan's economic incorporation was less: trade was smaller and was not of a staple nature, and there were fewer foreign investments.

Accompanying China's ever stronger economic incorporation, and furthering it, was the political incorporation of China proper: the assumption of its powers of government by the Western nations and the penetration of the society by Western missionaries. The Western capitalist nations also developed strong trading and large investments in China's dependencies, which one by one were withdrawn from Chinese control.

In Japan, for complex reasons, political encroachment preceded economic incorporation. Since trade and investment interests did not become important, there was little missionary penetration and political incorporation. Moreover, there was no strong effort by the Western nations to incorporate Japan's dependencies.

What were the consequences of Japan's relative autonomy versus China's incorporation for the two countries' economic development during the nineteenth and twentieth centuries? Did their different relationships to the world economy have significant impact on Japan's development and China's underdevelopment? I have argued that they did.

The major way in which incorporation contributed to underdevelopment in China was the impact on the state. China's incorporation led to the dismantling of the already weak imperial state. Japan's greater autonomy, however, permitted transformation of the weak feudal state into a bureaucratic or national state. In the absence of strong external pressures, the Meiji rulers were able steadily to extend central powers over society. Thus the Japanese government was able to promote national industrialization through policies that promoted private investment in industry (such as subsidies, pilot projects, loans, and the development of banking systems), through protectionist measures, and through colonial expansion. The Chinese government attempted to encourage national industrialization in many of the same ways but failed. It has been argued here that Japan's success was due in part to the greater fiscal strength of the Meiji state but also, and importantly, to the absence of strong Western interests that in China blocked or undermined the success of such policies.

This study has several implications for understanding the development of other Third World nations. What is the lesson of Japan for the Third World today? Does Japan provide a model that other societies may imitate? Since the development of the capitalist world system, most nations of the Third World have had their fate imposed on them from outside, a situation that Japan escaped to an important extent.

Located on the edges of the expanding imperialism of free trade in the early nineteenth century, Japan retained a "breathing space" within which it could strengthen its government and military apparatuses, develop an industrial capitalist economy, and embark on an imperialist path of its own – thus also avoiding incorporation as a satellite during the new thrust of late nineteenth-century imperialism.

It has recently been suggested that Third World countries such as Brazil or Iran may be taking a path that sets them off from the rest of the Third World, a path labeled *subimperialism*. Comparison with Japan's development (to which the concept of subimperialism bears some parallels) may shed light on the possibilities and limitations of subimperialism as a path to national economic development.

According to the theory of subimperialism, slackening ties to the metropoles before World War II led to the growth of independent industries in many Third World nations, providing increased profits to a national bourgeoisie. After the war, new forms of dependency were established, and there were increased profits to foreign capitalists, but economic growth continued, providing increasing-though-lessened profits to the native bourgeoisie. As the local bourgeoisie developed an autonomous capital accumulation, there have been imperialist efforts to expand control over weaker areas of the Third World as sources of raw materials and as markets, and efforts to build a national military apparatus toward these ends. Brazil has been seen as a prime example of subimperialism, with its efforts to control Paraguay, Bolivia, and Uruguay and thus monopolize the rich Rio de la Plata region.

Obviously, there are intriguing parallels to the road taken by Japan in the nineteenth and early twentieth centuries: capital accumulation in the hands of a national bourgeoisie which was closely linked to the state, accompanied by imperialist expansion into weaker areas of Asia. Of course, only a few countries can take such a path; most must stay on the bottom in order for a few to rise. The question is: Can we expect even a few countries to succeed today at what Japan did during the nineteenth century? Or have changed world economic conditions rendered this unlikely?

One basic difference between nineteenth- and early twentieth-century Japan and the subimperialist nations of today is that the latter are far more dependent on foreign capital. In Brazil, for example,

> foreign interests control 100 per cent of the production of tires and other rubber products, 95 per cent of the automobile industry, 59 per cent of the production of heavy machinery and 90 per cent of pharmaceuticals. In 1970, for example, Brazil produced more than 400,000 automobiles, trucks and buses and about 10,000 tractors. Four large companies: Volkswagen, General Motors, Ford and Chrysler, controlled almost all of this production. . . . Three-fourths of the dynamic sector of Brazilian industry belong to U.S. investors.[1]

Such a situation is a great obstacle to autonomous industrial development and would suggest that Brazil (unlike Japan) will probably remain subordinate to the United States, Japanese, and European capital. Subimperialism, that is, may provide increased profits to a Brazilian national bourgeoisie and lead to increased conflict among the Brazilian state, its bourgeoisie, and the states of the metropoles, without ultimately leading to independent national industrialization.

Moreover, it is not clear that time is on the side of subimperialism or imperialism. This is the lesson of China. China, lacking the luxury of the autonomy of Japan, escaped satellite status through a socialist revolution that was led by a Communist party. China's revolution broke the ties that bound it to the capitalist world economy and has enabled it to move toward independent industrial development during the 1950s, 1960s, and 1970s.

As the multinational corporations have expanded their control over the globe since World War II, effective popular resistance, as contrasted to bourgeois resistance, has steadily grown. China's revolutionary path has been followed by Cuba, Vietnam, Cambodia, Laos, and others, and revolutionary Communist movements elsewhere are growing stronger. Chile has provided a tragic lesson: there may be no peaceful road to socialism.

Today, with revelations of the U.S. Central Intelligence Agency's interventionist activities around the world in support of the U.S. bourgeoisie's investments in the multinational corporations, it is becoming more and more difficult for scholars to interpret Third World underdevelopment in terms of the social, cultural, and personality characteristics of Third World peoples. It may be tempting for traditional society scholars to buttress their arguments by retreating into the cases of nineteenth-century China and Japan, but this study may cast some obstacles in their way.

Notes

Introduction

1 It is somewhat inaccurate to apply *Third World* to Japan inasmuch as the term implies a "Second World" of the socialist countries, which of course did not exist at the time Japan began to come under the influence of the "First World" of the advanced capitalist nations. See Irving Louis Horowitz, *Three Worlds of Development* (New York, 1966), pp. 3–46.

2 Cited by George C. Allen and Audrey G. Donnithorne in *Western Enterprise and Far Eastern Economic Development* (London, 1946), p. 225.

3 See Manning Nash's discussion of "diffusion" in "Approaches to the Study of Economic Growth," *Journal of Social Issues* 19 (1963): 1–6.

4 S. N. Eisenstadt, *Modernization: Protest and Change* (Englewood Cliffs, N.J., 1966), pp. 55ff.

5 W. W. Rostow, *The Process of Economic Growth* (New York, 1962), pp. 314–316.

6 On "Achievement motivation" see David McClelland, *The Achieving Society* (Princeton, 1961); on "empathy" see Daniel Lerner, *The Passing of Traditional Society* (Glencoe, Ill., 1958); on universalism," "achievement," etc., see Bert F. Hoselitz, "Social Stratification and Economic Development," *International Social Science Journal* 16(1964): 237–251.

7 On family loyalties see Marion J. Levy Jr., "Contrasting Factors in the Modernization of China and Japan," in Simon Kuznets, W. E. Moore, and J. J. Spengler, eds., *Economic Growth: Brazil, India, Japan* (Durham, N.C., 1955), pp. 496–536; on the effects of caste see Gunnar Myrdal, *Asian Drama* (New York, 1968), II: 741–798, 1093–1240. A classic analysis of the impact of bureaucracy is Albert Feuerwerker's *China's Early Industrialization* (Cambridge, Mass., 1958).

8 Rostow, *The Process of Economic Growth*, p, 284.

9 Introductions to the dependency perspective and essential bibliography may be found in Dale L. Johnson, *The Sociology of Change and Reaction in Latin America* (New York, 1973) and *Latin*

American Perspectives (New York, 1974), vol. 1: "Dependency Theory – A Reassessment"; James D. Cockroft, Andre Gunder Frank, and Dale L. Johnson, eds., Dependence and Underdevelopment (Garden City, N.Y., 1972); James Petras and Maurice Zeitlin, eds., Latin America: Reform or Revolution? (New York, 1968), Robert I. Rhodes, ed., Imperialism and Underdevelopment: A Reader (New York, 1970); Kathleen Gough and Hari Sharma, Imperialism and Revolution in South Asia (New York, 1972); and Walter Rodney, How Europe Underdeveloped Africa (London, 1972).

10 Ernest Mandel, Marxist Economic Theory (New York, 1969), II: 445–447.

11 Theotonio dos Santos, "The Structure of Dependence," in K. T. Fann and Donald C. Hodges, eds., Readings in U.S. Imperialism (Boston, 1971), pp. 225–236.

12 A good discussion of the function of the "infrastructure" in British India may be found in Helen Lamb, "The 'State' and Economic Development in India," in Kuznets, Moore, and Spengler, eds., Economic Growth: Brazil, India, Japan, pp. 464–495.

13 Dos Santos, "The Structure of Dependence," pp. 229–233.

14 Andre Gunder Frank, "Sociology of Development or Underdevelopment of Sociology," Catalyst (Summer 1967): 20–73.

15 Johnson, The Sociology of Change and Reaction in Latin America, p. 46.

16 Kathleen Gough, "The South Asian Revolutionary Potential," Bulletin of Concerned Asian Scholars 4 (1972): 78–81.

17 Levy, "Contrasting Factors in the Modernization of China and Japan," p. 496.

18 Paul A. Baran, The Political Economy of Growth (New York, 1957), pp. 150–151.

19 In the "traditional society" perspective see Levy, "Contrasting Factors in the Modernization of China and Japan," and Marion J. Levy Jr., "Some Aspects of 'Individualism' and the Problem of Modernization in China and Japan," Economic Development and Cultural Change 10 (1962): 225–240; Robert T. Holt and John E. Turner, The Political Basis of Economic Development (Princeton, 1966) (a comparison of Japan, China, England, and France); Norman Jacobs, The Origin of Modern Capitalism and Eastern Asia (Hong Kong, 1958); Edwin O. Reischauer and John K. Fairbank, East Asia: The Great Tradition (Boston, 1958); John K. Fairbank, Edwin O. Reischauer, and Albert M. Craig, East Asia: The Modern Transformation (Boston, 1965); Charles David Sheldon, "Some Economic Reasons for the Marked Contrast in Japanese and Chinese Modernization," Kyoto University Economic Review 23(1953): 30–60; Barrington Moore Jr., Social Origins of Dictatorship and Democracy (Boston, 1967); William W. Lockwood, "Japan's Response to the West: The Contrast with China," World

Politics 9(1956): 37–54; Joseph R. Levenson, ed., *European Expansion and the Counter-example of Asia, 1300–1600* (Englewood Cliffs, N.J., 1967); and Allen and Donnithorne, *Western Enterprise and Far Eastern Economic Development.*
In the "world economy" perspective see Baran, *The Political Economy of Growth*, pp. 134–162; Shigekei Toyama, "Politics, Economics and the International Environment in the Meiji and Taisho Periods," *Developing Economies* 4(1966): 419–446; and Huang I-feng and Chiang To, "Chung-kuo Yang-wu Yün-tung yü Jih-pen Mei-chih Wei-hsin Tsai Ching-chi Fa-chan Sang ti Pi-chiao" [A comparison of economic development in China's industrialization movement and in the Japanese Meiji Restoration], *Ching-chi Yen-chiu* 1(1963): 27–47. The latter is summarized at lengh in Alber Feuerwerker, ed., *History in Communist China* (Cambridge, Mass., 1968), pp. 235–236.
Beyond these explicitly comparative studies, comparative references abound in the monographic literature, especially works on China written in the traditional society vein. They are so many (and the apearance of comparative references to *other* societies is so rare) that one might imagine that the authors are fulfilling some obscure professional requirement. The following are only a few of the many works containing such references: Rhoads Murphey, *The Treaty Ports and China's Modernization: What Went Wrong?* Michigan Papers in Chinese Studies, no. 7 (1970); John K. Fairbank, Alexander Eckstein, and L. S. Yang, "Economic Change in Early Modern China: An Analytic Framework," in Joseph R. Levenson, ed., *Modern China: An Interpretive Anthology* (New York, 1971), pp. 155–186; Feuerwerker, *China's Early Industrialization;* S. N. Eisenstadt, "Tradition, Change and Modernity: Reflections on the Chinese Experience," in Ping-ti Ho and Tang Tsou, eds., *China in Crisis* (Chicago, 1968), 1, pt. 1: 753–774; Chi-ming Hou, *Foreign Investment and Economic Development in China, 1840–1937* (Cambridge, Mass., 1965); Victor Purcell, "The Rise of Modern China" (pamphlet of The Historical Association, London, 1962); and E. H. Norman, *Japan's Emergence as a Modern State* (New York, 1940).
It should be noted that, prior to the 1950s, China and Japan were rarely *compared* by scholars, although they were often treated in *parallel* fashion; see, for example, Colin Clark, *The Conditions of Economic Progress* (London, 1940) and H. B. Morse and H. F. MacNair, *Far Eastern International Relations* (Boston, 1931). An exception is John E. Orchard, "Contrasts in the Progress of Industrialization in China and Japan," *Political Science Quarterly* (1937), pp. 18–50. Today, the theme of the relationship of Chinese and Japanese traditional societies to their nineteenth-century development is increasingly superseded in popularity by another: the relationship of China's traditionally "autocratic" po-

litical system to the rise or structure of the contemporary "Communist political system." This is the theme of the articles collected in Ho and Tsou, eds., *China in Crisis* (cited above).

20 See pp. 144ff.

21 In "Contrasting Factors in the Modernization of China and Japan," p. 498.

22 Reischauer and Fairbank, *East Asia: The Great Tradition*, p. 670 (italics mine).

23 Fairbank, Reischauer, and Craig, *East Asia: The Modern Transformation*, p. 180.

24 "Japan's Transition: A Socio-Economic Interpretation," *Kobe University Economic Review* 9(1963): 1–2.

25 This is an *analytic* classification; not all authors stay consistently in one category or another.

26 Koya Azumi, "Japanese Society: A Sociological View," in Arthur Tiedemann, ed., *An Introduction to Japanese Civilization* (New York, 1974), pp. 515–535.

27 Fairbank, Reischauer, and Craig, *East Asia: The Modern Transformation*, pp. 179ff.

28 Jacobs, *The Origin of Modern Capitalism and Eastern Asia.*

29 Fairbank, Reischauer, and Craig, *East Asia: The Modern Transformation*, pp. 100ff, 193ff.

30 The ideal-type conception of decentralized Japanese feudalism versus Chinese bureaucracy, discussed here, is a synthesis of themes appearing in many of the "traditional society" comparative studies listed above in n. 19. It also fairly reflects, I believe, the imagery prevailing in numerous textbooks and popular works on Japanese and Chinese history. It should, however, be emphasized that this conception is by no means accepted by all students of Japanese and Chinese history. Many Japanese historians, for example, speak of the "centralized" character of Japanese feudalism. See John Whitney Hall, "Feudalism in Japan – A Reassessment," in John Whitney Hall and Marius B. Jansen, eds., *Studies in the Institutional History of Early Modern Japan* (Princeton, 1968), pp. 45ff. Japan scholars have also questioned the interpretation of the contribuion of a rising burgeoisie of the Meiji restoration and industrialization; see, for example, Albert M. Craig, *Choshu in the Meiji Restoration* (Cambridge, Mass., 1967). China scholars have also challenged the view that Chinese bureaucracy was decisive in China's underdevelopment; see, for example, Frank H. H. King, *Money and Monetary Policy in China, 1845–1895* (Cambridge, Mass., 1965) and Mark Elvin, *The Pattern of the Chinese Past* (Stanford, 1973).

31 On earlier conceptions of China see L. A. Maverick, *China – A Model for Europe* (San Antonio, 1946) and Donald F. Lach, *China in the Eyes of Europe* (Chicago, 1968).

32 Shlŏmŏ Avineri, ed., *Karl Marx on Colonialism and Modernization* (New York, 1968), p. 85.

33 Eric Hobsbawm, ed., *Pre-capitalist Economic Formations* (New York, 1965), pp. 69–70. (This is a translation of sections of *Grundrisse*.)

34 Avineri, ed., *Karl Marx on Colonialism and Modernization*, p. 88.

35 Karl Marx, *Capital* (New York, n.d.), I: 392–394.

36 Avineri, ed., *Karl Marx on Colonialism and Modernization*, p. 88.

37 Ibid.

38 Ibid.

39 Max Weber, *The Religion of China* (New York, 1964), pp. 13–21, 94, 147. See also Max Weber, *The City* (New York, 1966), pp. 80–89.

40 Weber, *The Religion of China*, p. 100.

41 Ibid., p. 103.

42 Ibid., p. 121.

43 Ibid., p. 247.

44 See "China as a Permanently Bureaucratic Society," in his *Chinese Civilization and Bureaucracy* (New Haven, 1964).

45 See Karl A. Wittfogel, *Oriental Despotism* (New Haven, 1957), pp. 50ff. See also idem, *Wirtschaft und Gesellschaft Chinas* (Leipzig, 1931); "Die theorie der orientalischen Gesellschaft," *Zeitschrift fuer Sozialforschung* 7(1938): 90–120; and "The Foundation and Stages of Chinese Economic History," *Zeitschrift fuer Sozialforschung* 4(1935): 26–58.

46 George Lichtheim, *Imperialism* (New York, 1971), p. 44.

47 Ibid., p. 59, n. 1 (italics mine).

48 Weber, *The Religion of China*, p. 248.

49 For example, see Marx's remarks in an 1850 article for the *Neue Rheinische Zeitung* (cited in Avineri, ed., *Karl Marx on Colonialism and Modernization*, pp. 44–45.): "Thousands of English and American vessels have been sailing to China, and the country has been immediately swamped with cheap British and American machine-made goods. Chinese industry, based on handicraft, succumbed to the competition of the machine. The unshattered Middle Kingdom was plunged into a major crisis. Taxes stopped flowing into the Exchequer, the state reached the brink of bankruptcy, the population sank massively into pauperism, rebelled. . . . The country came to the verge of perdition, and is clearly menaced by a violent revolution. But even worse, among the rebelling plebs, there have emerged people who point to the poverty of some and the richness of others, who demanded and demand a redistribution of property, even the total abolition of private property. . . . The oldest and most unshattered Empire on this earth has been pushed, in eight years, by the cotton ball of the English bourgeois toward the brink of a social upheaval that must have most pro-

found consequences for civilization. When our European reactionaries, on their next flight through Asia, will have finally reached the Chinese Wall, the gates that lead to the seat of primeval reaction and conservatism – who knows, perhaps they will read the following inscription on the Wall: *République Chinoise; Liberté, Égalité, Fraternité!"*

50 Ernest Mandel, *The Formation of the Economic Thought of Karl Marx* (New York, 1971), pp. 127, 128, 124. Certain contemporary Marxist scholars who disagree with Mandel's interpretation have suggested that the asiatic mode of production be regarded as a general intermediary or transitional stage between primitive communism and class society. My disagreement with Mandel does not imply acceptance of this latter position. For an overview of the recent revival of scholarship on the asiatic mode of production see Jean Chesneaux, "Ou En Est La Discussion Sur le Mode de Production Asiatique," *La Pensee*, vol. 114 (April 1964); vol. 122 (July–August 1965); vol. 129 (October 1966); vol. 138 (April 1968). See also George Lichtheim, "Marx and the Asiatic Mode of Production," *St. Anthony's Papers* 14(1963): 86–112, and Benjamin I. Schwartz, "A Marxist Controversy on China," *Far Eastern Quarterly* 13(1954): 143–153.
51 Hobsbawm, ed., *Pre-capitalist Economic Formations*, pp. 11, 36–37.
52 Ibid., pp. 21–22.
53 Marx, *Capital* (New York, n.d.) I: 392–394 (New York, 1967) III: 616–617.
54 Ibid., I: 784ff.
55 Immanuel Wallerstein, "Three Paths of National Development in Sixteenth-Century Europe," *Studies in Comparative International Development*, vol. 7, no. 2 (Summer 1972).
56 Daniel Chirot, "Commerce, Integration and Closures" (unpublished ms., Columbia University, 1968).
57 Johannes Hirschmeier, *The Origins of Entrepreneurship in Meiji Japan* (Cambridge, Mass., 1964), pp. 37–43, 89, 137–139.
58 Louis M. Hacker, *The Triumph of American Capitalism* (New York, 1965), p. 232–234.
59 See August Heckscher, *Mercantilism* (2 vols.; London, 1955). See also Werner Sombart, *Krieg und Kapitalismus* (Leipzig, 1913).

Chapter 1: Economy and social classes in Ch'ing China and Tokugawa Japan

1 Gilbert Rozman, *Urban Networks in Ch'ing China and Tokugawa Japan* (Princeton, 1973), p. 86. See also Benjamin Higgins, "The Political Basis of Economic Development" (M.A. thesis, McGill University, 1971), pp. 20–21. Higgins' thesis contains an excellent critique of the comparative studies of Levy, and Holt and Turner. His view of the similarities between Ch'ing China and Tokugawa Japan coincides with my own.

2 Rozman, *Urban Networks in Ch'ing China and Tokugawa Japan,* p. 83.

3 The rate of growth of per capita income in Japan prior to 1868 was probably less than 1.2 to 1.5 percent a year. Henry Rosovsky, "Japan's Transition to Modern Economic Growth, 1868–1885," in Henry Rosovsky, ed., *Industrialization in Two Systems* (New York, 1966), p. 95.

4 Thomas C. Smith, *The Agrarian Origins of Modern Japan* (Stanford, 1959), p. 72.

5 Ibid., p. 102; Dwight Perkins, *Agricultural Development in China, 1368–1968* (Chicago, 1969), pp. 56–58.

6 See Joseph Needham, "Commentary on Lynn White, Jr., 'What Accelerated Technological Change in the Western Middle Ages?'" in A. C. Crombie, ed., *Scientific Change* (New York, 1963), p. 32. Knowledge of Western technology may have been greater in Japan than in China. For example, some of the large *han* had schools of "Dutch Studies" that included such subjects as physics, metallurgy, and astronomy. Some of the schools established laboratories that built models of telegraphs, steamships, etc., and engaged in experiments with cotton spinning, photography, and the manufacture of glass and other items. However, knowledge does not amount to practice on an important scale. Rosovsky remarks of such endeavors: "Our inclination would be to discount these developments rather heavily as far as their relation to modern economic growth is concerned. The examples are isolated, and while they may testify to considerable intellectual ferment within an extremely restricted sphere of society, this is not the stuff of which industrial revolutions are made. It would be almost like saying that Leonardo da Vinci's experiments were the sign of the beginning of the industrial revolution!" Rosovsky, "Japan's Transition to Modern Economic Growth," pp. 104–105.

7 Elvin, *The Pattern of the Chinese Past.*

8 Rozman, *Urban Networks in Ch'ing China and Tokugawa Japan,* pp. 13ff.

9 Perkins, *Agricultural Development in China,* p. 16.

10 John Whitney Hall, *Japan* (New York, 1971), p. 202.

11 Rozman, *Urban Networks in Ch'ing China and Tokugawa Japan,* p. 76.

12 Hall, *Japan,* p. 201.

13 Susan B. Hanley and Kozo Yamamura, "Population Trends and Economic Growth in Pre-Industrial Japan," in D. V. Glass and Roger Revelle, eds., *Population and Social Change* (London, 1973), table 8, app. B, pp. 496–497. Hanley and Yamamura present data on total rice output and the average annual growth rate of rice output for the sixty-eight *kuni* (provinces) of Japan for the years 1645–1697, 1697–1829, and 1839–1873. The data are taken from bakufu surveys the authors consider to be fairly

reliable and from the 1873 Meiji survey. According to my calculations, (a) in forty of the sixty-eight kuni (or 58.8%) the average annual growth rate in the 1697–1829 period was *lower* than in the 1645–1697 period, and in forty-five of the sixty-eight kuni (or 66.1%) the average annual growth rate in the 1839–1873 period was *lower* than in the 1697–1829 period; (b) in only twenty-two of the sixty-eight kuni was the rate *higher* in the 1697–1829 period than in the 1645–1697 period; in only nineteen kuni was it *higher* in the 1839–1873 period than in the 1697–1829 period. According to my calculations, the kuni in which the average annual growth rate increased from 1645–1697 accounted for only about 23 percent of the total output in 1829; those in which the rate increased from 1697–1829 to 1839–1873 accounted for only about 27 percent in 1873. If the size of their output had been more highly substantial relative to the total, the generalization that the average annual rate of growth of output slowed down would, of course, be unwarranted.

14 Perkins, *Agricultural Development in China*, pp. 13–36. See Higgins attempt to estimate per capita grain output in The Political Basis of Economic Development," p. 24.

15 Perkins, *Agriculture Development in China*, pp. 24–29, 185–186; Hanley and Yamamura, "Population Trends and Economic Growth in Pre-Industrial Japan," p. 473.

16 Perkins, *Agricultural Development in China*, pp. 37–38; Smith, *The Agrarian Origins of Modern Japan*, p. 97. Higgins estimates that rice yields were roughly similar in mid-nineteenth century China and Japan. See "The Political Basis of Economic Development," pp. 22–23.

17 Perkins, *Agricultural Development in China*, pp. 70–76; Elvin, *The Pattern of the Chinese Past*, pp. 118ff.

18 Elvin, *The Pattern of the Chinese Past*, pp. 133ff.

19 Ibid., p. 139.

20 Ibid., pp. 305–306.

21 Rozman, *Urban Networks in Ch'ing China and Tokugawa Japan*, p. 63.

22 In Marx's terminology there is a change from an emphasis on production of *use* value to production of *exchange* value.

23 On the distinction between market and marketplace see W. C. Neale, "The Market in Theory and History," in Karl Polanyi, C. M. Arensberg, and H. W. Pearson, eds., *Trade and Market in the Early Empires* (Glencoe, Ill., 1957), pp. 357–372.

24 Cited in Herbert Heaton, *Economic History of Europe* (New York, 1948), pp. 343–344.

25 *Capital*, I: 820–821.

26 See G. William Skinner, "Marketing and Social Structure in Rural China," pt. I, *Journal of Asian Studies* 24 (November 1964): 3–44; pt. II, 24 (February 1965): 195–228; pt. III, 24 (May 1965):

363–400, and Rozman, *Urban Networks in Ch'ing China and Tokugawa Japan*, pp. 112ff.

27 Perkins, *Agricultural Development in China*, pp. 117, 119, 136.

28 Albert Feuerwerker, *The Chinese Economy ca. 1870–1911*, Michigan Papers in Chinese Studies, no. 5(1969), pp. 18–19.

29 Yeh-chien Wang, *Land Taxation in Imperial China, 1750–1911* (Cambridge, Mass., 1973), pp. 84–89.

30 Perkins, *Agricultural Development in China*, pp. 144–147.

31 Ping-ti Ho, *Studies on the Population of China, 1368–1953* (Cambridge, Mass., 1959), pp. 201–202.

32 Perkins, *Agricultural Development in China*, pp. 121–123.

33 Rozman, *Urban Networks in Ch'ing China and Tokugawa Japan*, pp. 128ff.

34 Smith, *The Agrarian Origins of Modern Japan*, pp. 67ff.

35 Rozman, *Urban Networks in Ch'ing China and Tokugawa Japan*, pp. 119–120.

36 Smith, *The Agrarian Origins of Modern Japan*, p. 69.

37 Ibid., pp. 68–69.

38 Sydney Crawcour, "The Japanese Economy on the Eve of Modernization," *Journal of the Oriental Society of Australia* 2(1963): 35.

39 Smith, *The Agrarian Origins of Modern Japan*, p. 72.

40 Crawcour, "The Japanese Economy on the Eve of Modernization," p. 35.

41 Rozman, *Urban Networks in Ch'ing China and Tokugawa Japan*, pp. 133–135. A similar view on levels of commercialization in China may be found in Higgins, "The Political Basis of Economic Development," pp. 24–27. Higgins concludes: "The percent of agricultural produce sold on the market (directly or indirectly through government agency) was similar in both China and Japan in the 1850's" (pp. 26–27).

42 Hall, *Japan*, p. 208.

43 See Elvin, *The Pattern of the Chinese Past*, pp. 216ff.

44 See Robert K. Sakai, "The Ryukyu (Liu Ch'iu) Islands as a Fief of Satsuma," in John K. Fairbank, ed., *The Chinese World Order* (Cambridge, Mass., 1968), pp. 112–124.

45 Eric R. Wolf, *Peasants* (Englewood Cliffs, N.J., 1966), pp. 50–54.

46 Immanuel C. Y. Hsü, *The Rise of Modern China* (New York, 1970), p. 57. The nobility consisted of three groups: "imperial clansmen," about 700 direct male descendants of the dynasty's founder; "titular nobility," divided into the grades of duke (*kung*), marquis (*hou*), earl (*po*), viscount (*tzu*), and baron (*nan*); and the 200,000 troops or "bannermen," who included Mongols and Chinese as well as Manchus.

47 The Chinese degree holders, whether officials or not, are usually referred to as the "gentry." According to Chung-li Chang's estimates, there were 1,100,000 men who were degree holders in the early nineteenth century. Of these, 120,000, or 11 percent, were

what he calls "higher gentry," eligible to compete for the available official positions. The remaining 980,000 "lower gentry" were ineligible for office. Chung-li Chang, *The Chinese Gentry* (Seattle, 1967), pp. 137–139. On the activities of the gentry see Chung-li Chang, *The Income of the Chinese Gentry* (Seattle, 1962), pp. 43ff.

48 See Elvin, *The Pattern of the Chinese Past,* pp. 234ff. On bursars see Yuji Muramatsu, "A Documentary Study of Chinese Landlordism in the Late Ch'ing and Early Republican Kiangnan," *Bulletin* of the London University School of Oriental and African Studies. 29(1966): 566–599.

49 Chang, *The Income of the Chinese Gentry,* pp. 127ff. Gentry landlords may have controlled a disproportionate amount of the land held by landlords. This is because the gentry enjoyed easier acess to the officials and were better able to have their taxes reduced. Thus, for example, in times of tenant desertion or refusal to pay rent, bad harvest, etc., a nongentry landlord might have to sell part of his land to pay taxes but a gentry landlord might not. Gentry landlords were also better able to utilize the state apparatus to force tenants to pay rent. See Chang, *The Income of the Chinese Gentry,* pp. 130–136.

50 Rozman, *Urban Networks in Ch'ing China and Tokugawa Japan,* p. 81. Kay Trimberger argues· that the daimyo and samurai were an *"elite,"* not a "ruling *class,"* because "they derived their income from . . . political power and not from economic activity." I believe it is mistaken not to think of the controllers and beneficiaries of the state in precapitalist societies as an upper or ruling class. An upper class is a stratum of people who do not engage in production and who maintain themselves in a living standard different from the rest of society through control over the surplus produced by others. Control may be exercised by means of a state apparatus or by means of private ownership; in either case a class situation exists. See Trimberger, "A Theory of Elite Revolutions," *Studies in Comparative International Development* 7(1972): 193.

51 Smith, *The Agrarian Origins of Modern Japan,* pp. 157ff.

52 See Fang-chung Liang, *The Single Whip Methods of Taxation in China* (Cambridge, Mass., 1956). See also Ho, *Studies on the Population of China,* pp. 20, 30, 34.

53 Conrad D. Totman, *Politics in the Tokugawa Bakufu, 1600–1843* (Cambridge, Mass., 1967), pp. 78–80.

54 This account is based on Elvin, *The Pattern of the Chinese Past,* pp. 234ff.

55 The following discussion is based on the account in Smith, *The Agrarian Origins of Modern Japan;* see esp. chaps. 1–3, pp. 58ff., and chaps. 8–12.

56 Ping-ti Ho, "The Significance of the Ch'ing Period in Chinese History," in Joseph R. Levenson, ed., *Modern China: An Interpre-*

tive Anthology (New York, 1971), p. 23. See also Ping-ti Ho, *Chung-kuo hui-kuan shih-lun* [A historical survey of the Chinese hui-kuan] (Taipei, 1966).

57 Ping-ti Ho, *The Ladder of Success in Imperial China* (New York, 1962), p. 42.

Chapter 2: State and economy in Ch'ing China

1 I am indebted to John T. Moffett for his interpretation of the relationship between bureaucratic organization and social control in "Bureaucracy and Social Control" (unpublished Ph.D. thesis, Columbia University, 1972). Martin Albrow's *Bureaucracy* (London, 1970) contains a useful introduction to the history and various formulations of the concept of bureaucracy.

2 Totman notes that the costs of collection of modern governments are under 10 percent of total revenues. In contrast, Louis XIV's collection system cost 20 percent of the total and eighteenth-century Egypt's 25 percent. *Politics in the Tokugawa Bakufu,* p. 285, n. 23.

3 See Moffet's account in "Bureaucracy and Social Control."

4 Gaetano Mosca, *The Ruling Class* (New York, 1939), p. 81.

5 Heckscher, *Mercantilism.*

6 Hsü, *The Rise of Modern China,* p. 38.

7 Ibid., p. 39.

8 The Grand Council was a Ch'ing innovation. It usurped the functions of the Ming institution of the Grand Secretariat, which had lasted for a time after the founding of the Ch'ing. See Silas H. L. Wu, *Communication and Imperial Control in China* (Cambridge, Mass., 1970), pp. 84ff.

9 Clear and brief descriptions of the Ch'ing administrative structure may be found in Sybille van der Sprenkel, *Legal Institutions in Manchu China* (London, 1962), pp. 37ff., and Hsü, *The Rise of Modern China,* pp. 59ff.

10 Most provinces had both a governor and a governor general (sometimes translated "viceroy"). The governor general usually related to the affairs of two, sometimes three provinces, the governor to only one.

11 Hsü, *The Rise of Modern China,* pp. 70–72; van der Sprenkel, *Legal Institutions in Manchu China,* pp. 39–40.

12 In addition to the regular land tax, which was generally commuted, was the "grain tribute," which was less generally commuted, except during times of crop failure or war. Shipped from eight Southern provinces to Peking via the Grand Canal, the grain tribute may have accounted for as much as 22 percent of total central government revenues and 30 percent of the revenues from land taxes in the eighteenth century, according to Wang, *Land Taxation in Imperial China,* table 4.2, p. 72. On the general char-

acter of the grain tribute system see Harold C. Hinton, *The Grain Tribute System of China (1845–1911)* (Cambridge, Mass., 1956).

13 E-tu Zen Sun, "The Board of Revenue in Nineteenth-Century China," *Harvard Journal of Asiatic Studies* 24(1962–1963): 195.

14 On the district magistrate see the excellent study by T'ung-tsu Ch'ü, *Local Government in China under the Ch'ing* (Cambridge, Mass., 1962).

15 Hsü, *The Rise of Modern China*, p. 63.

16 Lawrence D. Kessler, "Ethnic Composition of Provincial Leadership during the Ch'ing Dynasty," *Journal of Asian Studies* 28(1969): 496–500.

17 The only categories of the population of Ming and Ch'ing China that were not permitted to take the examinations were certain groups of "degraded" people such as the *yüeh-hu*, entertainers in Shansi and Shensi; *kai-hu*, beggars of Kiangsu and Anhwei; *tan-hu*, or boat people in Kwangtung; *shih-p'u*, or hereditary servants of southern Anhwei; and such people as prostitutes, entertainers, certain types of government runners, and bonded servants around the country. These groups amounted to less than 1 percent of the population. Prior to the Ch'ing period, these people had been denied the rights normally granted the rest of the population and intermarriage between them and others was prohibited. The Yungcheng emperor (1723–1735) emancipated them, and granted them the right to take the official examinations three generations after emancipation. Ho, *The Ladder of Success in Imperial China*, pp. 18–19. On the purchase of degrees and offices see Chang, *The Chinese Gentry*, pp. 8–12, 29–30.

18 Ho, *The Ladder of Success in Imperial China*, pp. 184–190, 194–209, 168–174.

19 Ibid., p. 42.

20 See Weber's analysis of the control structure in *The Religion of China*, pp. 46ff.

21 Peng Chang, "The Distribution and Relative Strength of the Provincial Merchant Groups in China, 1842–1911" (unpublished Ph.D. thesis, University of Washington, 1957), pp. 183ff.

22 Charles O. Hucker, *The Traditional Chinese State in Ming Times (1368–1644)* (Tucson, 1961), p. 31.

23 *Gentry* in this work will follow Chang's usage: the group of people who obtained an academic title by passing the civil service examinations or by purchase or any other method.

24 Chang, *The Income of the Chinese gentry*, pp. 152–154.

25 Ho, *Chung-kuo hui-kuan shih-lun*, pp. 1–3.

26 Chang, *The Income of the Chinese Gentry* (pp. 123–195), discusses the gentry's income obtained from land and commercial activity.

27 The following account is based on Wang, *Land Taxation in Imperial China*, pp. 49ff., 12–19.

28 E-tu Zen Sun, "The Board of Revenue in Nineteenth-century China," pp. 205–214; Wang, *Land Taxation in Imperial China*, pp. 18–19.

29 Wang, *Land Taxation in Imperial China*, pp. 69–72, 73–74.

30 Ch'ü *Local Government in China under the Ch'ing*, pp. 110–111.

31 Ibid., pp. 42–43.

32 Ibid., p. 55.

33 Ibid., p. 33.

34 See Hsin-pao Chang, *Commissioner Lin and the Opium War* (New York, 1970), pp. 219–221.

35 Ch'ü, *Local Government in China under the Ch'ing*, pp. 33–35.

36 Ibid., p. 22, 215, n. 36.

37 Ibid., p. 219, n. 68.

38 Ibid., p. 199.

39 Owen Lattimore, "The Industrial Impact on China, 1800–1950," *First International Conference on Economic History* (Paris, 1960), pp. 103–113.

40 In *Agricultural Development in China*, pp. 176–177.

41 Wang, *Land Taxation in Imperial China*, pp. 26–31. According to Wang, "at least a third of the newly cultivated land in the first century of the Ch'ing dynasty and about four fifths in the next one and a half centuries went unregistered" (pp. 26–27).

42 See Wolfram Eberhard, *Conquerors and Rulers: Social Forces in Medieval China* (Leiden, 1952). Eberhard argues (pp. 122–123): "Any understanding of the 'gentry' is possible only when one conceives of the 'gentry' as families. Gentry families are usually large, extended families with at least one family center, which is often kept for more than a thousand years. This center of the family usually lies somewhere in the province. . . . Here the family may have, and often has, large property holdings which are rented out to tenants. The family may also have economic interests in activities of temples, such as pawnshops, and in financial or commercial transactions of monasteries. The family may lose its property through mismanagement, bandits, war, etc. but the prestige of the gentry family in its home is so great that any such losses can be restored fairly easily by an energetic member of the family in the same or another generation. Therefore a process of oscillation . . . undoubtedly occurs but does not change the status of the family in the long run."

43 On rural uprisings during the Ch'ing period see Kung-chuan Hsiao, *Rural China* (Seattle, 1960), pp. 433ff.

44 *Oriental Despotism*, p. 328.

45 Perkins, *Agricultural Development in China*, p. 177.

46 Thomas Metzger, "Ch'ing Commercial Policy," *Ch'ing-shih wen-t'i* 1(1966): 4–10. See also Dwight Perkins, "Government as an Obstacle to Industrialization: The Case of Nineteenth Century China," *Journal of Economic History* 27(1967): 478–492.

47 Ho, *The Ladder of Success in Imperial China*, p. 46.

48 Hsü, *The Rise of Modern China*, pp. 79–80, 169.

49 Lien-sheng Yang, *Money and Credit in China* (Cambridge, Mass., 1952), p. 99.

50 Hucker, *The Traditional Chinese State in Ming Times*, p. 31.

51 Perkins, *Agricultural Development in China*, pp. 164–166.

52 Michael Greenberg, *British Trade and the Opening of China, 1800–1842* (Cambridge, 1951), p. 64.

53 Ping-ti Ho, "The Salt Merchants of Yang-chou: A Study of Commercial Capitalism in Eighteenth-Century China," *Harvard Journal of Asiatic Studies* 17(1954): 131, 137–141. See also Thomas A. Metzger, "The Organizational Capabilities of the Ch'ing State in the Field of Commerce: The Liang-huai Salt Monopoly, 1740–1840," in W. E. Willmott, ed., *Economic Organization in Chinese Society* (Stanford, 1972), pp. 9–45.

54 John K. Fairbank, *Trade and Diplomacy on the China Coast* (Stanford, 1969), p. 51. They were called the *shih-san hong* or "thirteen firms," but the number fluctuated.

55 Chang, "The Distribution and Relative Strength of the Provincial Merchant Groups," pp. 183–189.

56 Eric R. Wolf, *Peasant Wars of the Twentieth Century* (New York, 1969), p. 111.

57 Cited in Hsiao, *Rural China*, p. 472.

58 On the market town as the largest focus of peasant community, see Skinner, "Marketing and Social Structure in Rural China," pt. I, and Martin Yang, *A Chinese Village* (New York, 1945), pp. 190ff. On the loyalty of classmates, examination mates, and students and teachers see Kenneth E. Folsom, *Friends, Guests and Colleagues* (Berkeley, 1968), pp. 18ff.

59 See Yü-chüan Wang, "The Rise of Land Tax and the Fall of Dynasties in Chinese History," in Levenson, ed., *Modern China: An Interpretive Anthology*, pp. 130–154.

60 See Philip A. Kuhn's fascinating account of the "strategic hamlet" policy used by the government in suppressing the rebellion in *Rebellion and Its Enemies in Late Imperial China* (Cambridge, Mass., 1970), pp. 37ff.

61 Wang, "The Rise of Land Tax and the Fall of Dynasties," p. 130.

62 Ibid., p. 132.

Chapter 3: State and economy in Tokugawa Japan

1 The same Japanese characters are used for this term as for the Chinese Warring States Period that preceded the first unification under the Ch'in dynasty.

2 See Hall, *Japan*, chaps. 4–7. This is an excellent concise history of Japan from the beginnings to the present. See also Peter Duus, *Feudalism in Japan* (New York, 1969).

3 Hall, *Japan,* p. 170.
4 *Bakufu* means "tent government," that is, the government of a military commander in the field.
5 Craig, *Choshu in the Meiji Restoration,* pp. 10–12; Hall, *Japan,* pp. 166–167.
6 Totman, *Politics in the Tokugawa Bakufu,* pp. 65ff.
7 Ibid., pp. 110ff.
8 Ibid., pp. 156–157, 163, 167–168, 131.
9 Ibid., pp. 177–178.
10 The major work on the *sankin kotai* system is T. C. Tsukahira, *Feudal Control in Tokugawa Japan* (Cambridge, Mass., 1966).
11 Craig, *Choshu in the Meiji Restoration,* p. 15.
12 Harold Bolitho, *Treasures among Men: The Fudai Daimyo in Tokugawa Japan* (New Haven, 1974), pp. 18–19. This work has a comprehensive description of the bakufu's failure to attempt a further centralization of power.
13 Heckscher, *Mercantilism,* I:78.
14 Totman, *Politics in the Tokugawa Bakufu,* pp. 65–66.
15 Ibid., p. 69.
16 Ibid., pp. 74, 285, n. 23.
17 W. G. Beasley, *The Modern History of Japan* (New York, 1963), p. 13.
18 Totman, *Politics in the Tokugawa Bakufu,* pp. 87–88.
19 On the domain economies see Yasuzo Horie, "Clan Monopoly Policy in the Tokugawa Period," *Kyoto University Economic Review* 17(1942): 31–52, and "The Encouragement of *Kokusan* or Native Products in the Tokugawa Period," *Kyoto University Economic Review* 15(1941): 44–63. See also Craig, *Choshu in the Meiji Restoration,* pp. 26ff.
20 George Sansom, *A History of Japan 1615–1867* (Stanford, 1963), pp. 143–144.
21 Craig, *Choshu in the Meiji Restoration,* pp. 38–39.
22 Ibid., p. 99; Chang, *The Chinese Gentry,* p. 139.
23 Totman, *Politics in the Tokugawa Bakufu,* pp. 295, 149–152, and chap. 7 generally.
24 Craig, *Choshu in the Meiji Restoration,* pp. 40–41; Earl J. Hamilton, "Origin and Growth of the National Debt in Western Europe," *American Economic Review* 37(1947): 121, 125, 127, 128.
25 Takei Yazaki, *Social Change and the City in Japan* (Tokyo, 1968), pp. 133–134.
26 Daniel L. Spencer, "Japan's Pre-Perry Preparation for Economic Growth," *American Journal of Economics and Sociology* 17(1958): 199–200.
27 Evelyn S. Rawski, *Agricultural Change and the Peasant Economy of South China* (Cambridge, Mass., 1972), pp. 57ff.
28 Rawski, *Agricultural Change and the Peasant Economy of South China,* p. 97.

29 Robert Hartwell, "A Cycle of Economic Change in Imperial China: Coal and Iron in Northeast China, 750–1350," *Journal of the Economic and Social History of the Orient* 10(1967): pp. 102–159.

30 Hanley and Yamamura, "Population Trends and Economic Growth in Pre-Industrial Japan," pp. 482–485.

31 J. I. Nakamura and Matao Miyamoto, "Social Institutions, Population Change and Economic Growth: A Comparative Study of Tokugawa Japan and Ch'ing China," (unpublished paper, Columbia University, 1972); Rozman, *Urban Networks in Ch'ing China and Tokugawa Japan*, p. 120.

32 Weber, *The Religion of China*, pp. 103–104.

33 Moffet, "Bureaucracy and Social Control."

34 Immanuel Wallerstein, *The Modern World System* (New York, 1974), p. 57.

35 Ibid., pp. 58–60.

36 Hall, *Japan*, p. 202.

37 On Tokugawa peasant uprisings see Hugh Borton, *Peasant Uprisings in Japan of the Tokugawa Period* (New York, 1937).

38 Marius B. Jansen, *Sakamoto Ryoma and the Meiji Restoration* (Stanford, 1971), pp. 17, 19.

Part II: China and Japan in the nineteenth-century world economy

1 See Immanuel Wallerstein's analysis of the origins and development of the world economy in the sixteenth century in *The Modern World System*.

2 See Geoffrey Barraclough, *An Introduction to Contemporary History* (Baltimore, 1968), pp. 55ff. John Gallagher and Ronald Robinson, "The Imperialism of Free Trade," *Economic History Review*, 6(1953): 201–225.

3 Paul Reinsch, *Colonial Government* (New York, 1902), p. 43.

4 Benjamin Higgins argues, for example, that the "imperialist argument" for China's underdevelopment is invalid because foreign trade and investment were minimal on a per capita basis. See his "Political Basis of Economic Development," pp. 50ff.

5 Norman, *Japan's Emergence as a Modern State*, p. 46.

Chapter 4: China's incorporation into the world economy

1 Greenberg, *British Trade and the Opening of China*, pp. 2–3; E. J. Hobsbawm, *Industry and Empire* (Baltimore, 1969), p. 57.

2 Christopher Hill, *Reformation to Industrial Revolution* (Baltimore, 1969), p. 180.

3 Hobsbawm, *Industry and Empire*, p. 28.

4 Greenberg, *British Trade and the Opening of China*, p. 3.

5 Great Britain, Central Statistical Office, *Annual Abstract of Statistics*, no. 16, pp. 24–25; no. 31, pp. 44–45; no. 44, p. 67; no. 71, p. 315. British consumption of tea is declining today. In 1955, according to a Ministry of Agriculture survey, 9.3 pounds were consumed on the average but in 1972 the amount had dropped to eight. Coffee sales increased over the same period from 1.3 to 4.4 pounds. *New York Times*, September 2, 1973.

6 *Annual Abstract of Statistics*, no. 16, pp. 4, 7.

7 Greenberg, *British Trade and Opening of China*, p. 4.

8 This was because, as Emperor Ch'ien-lung put it in his famous statement to George III, China possessed "all things" and had no need of the manufactures of other nations. It was difficult to find a market for Western manufactures in China and silver had to be the major means of payment for whatever Western merchants took out of China. From 1721 to 1740, for example, the British exchanged about 95 percent specie and only 5 percent manufactures for Chinese products. Chang, *Commissioner Lin and the Opium War*, p. 41.

9 An interesting account of the smuggling in Britain is found in John Maurice Scott, *The Tea Story* (London, 1964), chap. 3.

10 Earl Pritchard, *The Crucial Years of Early Anglo-Chinese Relations 1750–1800*, Research Studies of the State College of Washington (1936), pp. 150–151.

11 David Edward Owen, *British Opium Policy in China and India* (New Haven, 1938), pp. 2ff.

12 Greenberg, *British Trade and the Opening of China*, pp. 9–17.

13 Ibid., p. 15.

14 Owen, *British Opium Policy in China and India*, p. 330.

15 Fairbank, Reischauer and Craig, *East Asia: The Modern Transformation*, p. 345; Greenberg, *British Trade and the Opening of China*, p. 221, table 2.

16 Chang, *Commissioner Lin and the Opium War*, p. 41.

17 Hobsbawm, *Industry and Empire*, p. 56.

18 Ibid., p. 58.

19 Romesh Dutt, *The Economic History of India under Early British Rule* (London, 1950), p. 261.

20 Ibid., p. 257.

21 Thomas J. McCormick, *China Market* (Chicago, 1967), p. 34. See chap. 1, "Exporting the Social Question," on the emergence of the theory in the United States in the 1890s. On the emergence of the theory on the Continent see William L. Langer, *European Alliances and Alignments, 1871–1890* (New York, 1950), chap. 9.

22 Nathan A. Pelcovits, *Old China Hands and the Foreign Office* (New York, 1948), pp. 11–12.

23 Feuerwerker, *The Chinese Economy ca. 1870–1911*, pp. 21–22, table 7. It was true in the East, as in Europe, that the first market

for textiles was for yarn rather than cloth; machine-made yarn "outcompeted" hand-spun yarn due to its cheapness and uniform quality but hand-loomed cloth, made from machine yarn, continued to be cheaper and more durable than machine-made cloth for a time.

24 Chang, *Commissioner Lin and the Opium War*, pp. 35–36.

25 Owen, *British Opium Policy in China and India*, pp. 117–118. Chang, *Commissioner Lin and the Opium War*, pp. 33–34; Ichisada Miyazaki, "The Nature of the Taiping Rebellion," *Acta Asiatica* 8(1965): 5–9.

26 See Chang, *Commissioner Lin and the Opium War*, pp. 85ff., and Fairbank, *Trade and Diplomacy on the China Coast*, p. 78, for accounts of the suppression of 1837–1839 and the debates within Chinese official circles on the best way to try to suppress the trade.

27 Hsü, *The Rise of Modern China*, pp. 231ff.

28 A summary of the treaties may be found in ibid., pp. 237–238.

29 Chi-ming Hou, *Foreign Investment and Economic Development in China, 1840–1937* (Cambridge, Mass., 1965), pp. 179–183.

30 Ibid., p. 167, table 35. On the situation in India see Morris D. Morris, "Towards a reinterpretation of 19th Century Indian Economic History," *Indian Economic and Social History Review* 5(1968): 1–15, and the rejoinders by Matsui, Chandra, and Raychaudhuri in the same issue.

31 On India see Dutt, *The Economic History of India*, pp. 258–260; on China, Pelcovits, *Old China Hands*, pp. 15–19, 4–5.

32 Hsü, *The Rise of Modern China*, pp. 265, 268.

33 For a summary of these agreements see Hsü, *The Rise of Modern China*, pp. 258–268, and Tyler Dennett, *Americans in Eastern Asia* (New York, 1922), p. 325.

34 Ibid., pp. 329–330. On the development of the foreign-controlled Imperial Maritime Customs see Stanley F. Wright, *Hart and the Chinese Customs* (Belfast, 1950).

35 Several times during the century treaties were not ratified, or almost not ratified, because British merchants complained that they were not adequately dealing with internal taxation. The Chefoo Convention of 1876 was not ratified until 1885 because of merchants' opposition; a convention revising the Tientsin Treaty (drawn up in 1869), was never ratified because merchants were opposed to it. On the latter see Mary C. Wright, *The Last Stand of Chinese Conservatism* (Stanford, 1966), chap. 11.

36 Morse and MacNair, *Far Eastern International Relations*, pp. 335–339.

37 Ibid., p. 344.

38 Ibid., pp. 335–339.

39 Ibid., p. 365.

40 Ibid., p. 407.

41 Fairbank, *Trade and Diplomacy on the China Coast*, p. 311.

42 Hou, *Foreign Investment and Economic Development in China,* p. 138.
43 Fairbank, *Trade and Diplomacy on the China Coast,* pp. 155–157.
44 Ibid., pp. 335–346.
45 Ibid., pp. 313–318.
46 Min-ch'ien T. Z. Tyau, *The Legal Obligations Arising Out of Treaty Relations between China and Other States* (Taipei, 1966 [1917]), p. 131; Stanley F. Wright, *China's Struggle for Tariff Autonomy: 1843–1938* (Shanghai, 1938), p. 193.
47 Hou, *Foreign Investment and Economic Development in China,* p. 59.
48 Ibid., p. 60. In 1970 a Japanese firm, strongly subsidized by the Japanese government, offered competition to the British firms; but as late as the 1930s Britain still dominated the Western sector of steam shipping in China. Total foreign tonnage was 810,000, according to Hou, of which 470,000 tons were British and 250,000 were Japanese (p. 61).
49 Tyau, *Legal Obligations,* p. 135.
50 Hou, *Foreign Investment and Economic Development in China,* p. 129.
51 Ibid., pp. 79, 81–83.
52 Allen and Donnithorne, *Western Enterprise and Far Eastern Economic Development,* pp. 55–57.
53 Hou, *Foreign Investment and Economic Development in China,* pp. 83–85.
54 Allen and Donnithorne,*Western Enterprise and Far Eastern Economic Development,* pp. 65–66.
55 Hou, *Foreign Investment and Economic Development in China,* p. 85.
56 Ibid., pp. 86, 130.
57 Ibid., pp. 87–88.
58 Ibid., pp. 89–90.
59 Wright, *The Last Stand of Chinese Conservatism,* pp. 263–268.
60 Knight Biggerstaff, "The Secret Correspondence of 1867–1868: Views of Leading Chinese Statesmen Regarding the Further Opening of China to Western Influence," *Journal of Modern History* 22(1950): 129–130.
61 Ibid., p. 130, and Stanley Spector, *Li Hung-chang and the Huai Army* (Seattle, 1964), p. 254.
62 Kia-Ngau Chang, *China's Struggle for Railway Development* (New York, 1943), pp. 23–24; Blair C. Currie, "The Woosung Railroad (1872–1877)", *Papers on China* 20(1966): 72–74.
63 Hou, *Foreign Investment and Economic Development in China,* p. 24.
64 Ibid., pp. 35–36.
65 Ibid., pp. 67ff.
66 Ibid., pp. 68, 70–71.

67 An excellent survey of such forms of control as "leased areas" and "spheres of influence," in comparative perspective, is found in Reinsch, *Colonial Government.*

68 Hou, *Foreign Investment and Economic Development in China,* pp. 23–31.

69 Ibid., pp. 31–33, 37–38.

70 Ibid., pp. 52–58.

71 Albert Feuerwerker, *The Chinese Economy, 1912–1949,* Michigan Papers in Chinese Studies, no. 1 (1968), pp. 56–59, 63–67.

72 Hsü, *The Rise of Modern China,* pp. 267–268.

73 Ibid., pp. 381–388.

74 Morse and MacNair, *Far Eastern International Relations,* pp. 565–567.

75 Hsü, *The Rise of Modern China,* pp. 389–394; Morse and Mac-Nair, *Far Eastern International Relations,* pp. 344–356.

76 Morse and MacNair, *Far Eastern International Relations,* pp. 362–364.

77 Ibid., pp. 560–562.

78 For an account of the course of the war see John L. Rawlinson, *China's Struggle for Naval Development, 1839–1895* (Cambridge, Mass., 1967), pp. 167ff.

79 On Korea see Hilary Conroy, *The Japanese Seizure of Korea: 1868–1910* (Philadelphia, 1960).

80 Kenneth S. Latourette, *A History of Christian Missions in China* (London, 1929), pp. 129, 195.

81 Ibid., pp. 158–184.

82 Ibid., pp. 183, 191, 194.

83 On Gutzlaff's career see Arthur Waley, *The Opium War through Chinese Eyes* (Stanford, 1958), pp. 222ff.

84 Latourette, *A History of Christian Missions,* p. 231.

85 Philip West, "The Tsinan Property Disputes (1887–1891): Gentry Loss and Missionary 'Victory,'" *Papers on China* 20(1966): 130, 141, n. 73.

86 Latourette, *A History of Christian Missions,* pp. 406, 479, 567.

87 Ibid., pp. 329, 563.

88 Ibid., pp. 741, 681.

89 Paul A. Cohen, *China and Christianity* (Cambridge, Mass., 1963), pp. 127–148, 170–185.

90 Payson Treat, *Diplomatic Relations between the United States and Japan* (Stanford, 1932), I:513.

91 Cohen, *China and Christianity,* pp. 275–276, 229ff.

92 Victor Purcell, *The Boxer Uprising* (Cambridge, 1963), chaps. 9 and 10, pp. 194ff. See also Edmund S. Wehrle, *Britain, China the Antimissionary Riots, 1891–1900* (Minneapolis, 1966), and Chester C. Tan, *The Boxer Catastrophe* (New York, 1967).

93 It should be noted that China did not repay the entire principal and interest on the Boxer indemnity. Many of the Western allies suspended their claims during World War I, German and Austrian

claims were canceled by the treaties of Versailles and St. Germain, and many nations later remitted the remainder of their claims. Nevertheless, of a total 982.2 million taels of principal and interest due by 1940, only 492.3 were remitted. See Hou, *Foreign Investment and Economic Development in China*, pp. 25–26.

94 Wehrle remarks: "Certain missionary groups declined to claim compensation; in fact, this was the regular policy of the China Inland Mission. But most missionaries considered that it was only just that they receive equitable compensation for their property losses. Some few tended to push their demand for compensation beyond reasonable limits. Such instances led the Chinese to regard all missionary claims with suspicion." *Britain, China and the Antimissionary Riots*, pp. 71–72. Cohen, *China and Christianity*, pp. 275–276.

Chapter 5: Japan's incorporation into the world economy

1 M. Paske-Smith, *Western Barbarians in Japan and Formosa in Tokugawa Days, 1603–1868* (Kobe, 1930), pp. 196–198; Y. Takekoshi, *The Economic Aspects of the History of Civilization of Japan* (London, 1930), II: 409–415.

2 Takekoshi, *Economic Aspects*, II: 411–412, 414–415. Cotton production did not begin in Japan until the sixteenth century and it was not until the seventeenth century that its cultivation and processing became widespread. Before the seventeenth century, only the upper classes could afford to wear cotton cloth, and the peasants dressed in rough linen. See William B. Hauser, *Economic Institutional Change in Tokugawa Japan: Osaka and the Kinai Cotton Trade* (London, 1974), p. 59. Similarly, before the seventeenth century, silk weaving was confined to urban artisans and the best yarn was imported from China. See Smith, *The Agrarian Origins of Modern Japan*, pp. 75–76.

3 Beasley, *Great Britain and the Opening of Japan*, pp. xiv–xix, 28–29, 45.

4 Cited by ibid., p. 4.

5 Morse and MacNair, *Far Eastern International Relations*, pp. 294–295.

6 Mary E. M. Harbert, "The Open Door Policy: The Means of Attaining Nineteenth Century American Objectives in Japan" (Ph.D. thesis, University of Oregon, 1967), pp. 12–48; Paske-Smith, *Western Barbarians*, pp. 135–136.

7 Harbert, "The Open Door Policy," pp. 72–79.

8 Ibid., p. 86.

9 Ibid., pp. 85–86.

10 Ibid., pp. 99–101.

11 Roy Hidemichi Akagi, *Japan's Foreign Relations* (Tokyo, 1936), pp. 29–30.

12 Good summaries of the American treaty and the Convention of

1866 may be found in Keishi Ohara and Tamotsu Okata, *Japanese Trade and Industry in the Meiji-Taisho Era* (Tokyo, 1957), pp. 69–79, 90–92.

13 Hikomatsu Kamikawa, ed., *Japan American Diplomatic Relations in the Meiji-Taisho Era* (Tokyo, 1958), p. 33.

14 Treat, *Diplomatic Relations between the United States and Japan,* I: 513–514.

15 Allen and Donnithorne, *Western Enterprise in Far Eastern Economic Development,* pp. 199–200.

16 Ibid., p. 200.

17 Ibid., p. 201.

18 Feuerwerker, *The Chinese Economy ca. 1870–1911,* p. 51.

19 Ibid., p. 52, table 17.

20 In *Americans in Eastern Asia,* p. 582.

21 U.S. Statistics Bureau, *Statements of Imports of Tea and Coffee into the U.S. Each Year from 1789 to 1882* (Washington, D.C., 1883).

22 Calculated from figures in Great Britain, Central Statistical Office, *Annual Abstract of Statistics,* no. 71.

23 D. R. Gadgil, *The Industrial Evolution of India* (London, 1934), p. 52.

24 Owen, *British Opium Policy in India and China,* pp. 311–312.

25 Hou, *Foreign Investment and Economic Development in China,* p. 201.

26 Allen and Donnithorne, *Western Enterprise in Far Eastern Economic Development,* pp. 218–220.

27 See, e.g., ibid., p. 218, or Lockwood, *The Economic Development of Japan,* pp. 545–549.

28 Allen and Donnithorne, *Western Enterprise in Far Eastern Economic Development,* p. 223.

29 In 1970, total foreign capital in Japan amounted to $7 billion. This represented about 2 percent of total Japanese corporate assets. In most sectors of the economy, foreign interests control only about 5 percent of the market. Jon Halliday and Gavan McCormack, *Japanese Imperialism Today* (New York, 1973), p. 5.

30 Paske-Smith, *Western Barbarians,* p. 225.

31 Allen and Donnithorne, *Western Enterprise in Far Eastern Economic Development,* p. 226.

32 John McMaster, "The Takashima Mine: British Capital and Japanese Industrialization," *Business History Review* 37(1963): 217–239.

33 Allen and Donnithorne, *Western Enterprise and Far Eastern Economic Development,* pp. 233–235. It was noted above that China had borrowed about £90 million by 1911. I have not found conversion tables for pounds and yen for 1911; however, if converted at the rate for the 1870s (as given in idem, *Western Enterprise in Far Eastern Economic Development,* p. 233); the amount bor-

rowed by Japan by 1914 comes to £416 million; if converted at the 1930s rate (as given in Lockwood, *The Economic Development of Japan*, p. 255), it comes to £200 million.

34 Lockwood, *The Economic Development of Japan*, pp. 254–258; Allen and Donnithorne, *Western Enterprise in Far Eastern Development*, pp. 233–235. "Viewing the Japanese case in retrospect," Lockwood writes, "one may conclude that it was a rather successful case of foreign borrowing in the sense that a large flow of private *rentier* capital from abroad was attracted, largely on government credit. It was utilized to tide the country over a difficult financial period, without introducing the political frictions or foreign controls which have often attended external borrowing elsewhere" (p. 258).

35 Allen and Donnithorne, *Western Enterprise in Far Eastern Economic Development*, p. 215.

36 Hou, *Foreign Investment and Economic Development in China*, p. 101.

37 George Sansom, *The Western World and Japan* (New York, 1950), p. 132.

38 Johannes Laures, *The Catholic Church in Japan* (Rutland, Vt., 1954), pp. 209–225; Joseph van Hecken, *The Catholic Church in Japan since 1859* (Tokyo, 1963), p. 32.

39 Van Hecken, *The Catholic Church in Japan*, p. 25.

40 Treat, *Diplomatic Relations between the United States and Japan*, I: 513.

41 Kamikawa, ed., *Japan-American Diplomatic Relations*, pp. 70–71.

42 Laures, *The Catholic Church in Japan*, pp. 209ff.; van Hecken, *The Catholic Church in Japan*, p. 32.

43 See Winburn T. Thomas, *Protestant Beginnings in Japan* (Rutland, Vt., 1959), pt. 3: "Rapid Growth, Then Retardation," pp. 161ff. Many Japanese had seen the adoption of Western legal institutions, school systems, philosophy, and religion as instruments in the attempt to abolish extraterritoriality because the Western powers repeatedly justified this principle in terms of the backwardness of Japanese civilization. However, when the British kept blocking Japan's efforts at treaty revision during the nineteenth century, despite its increasing Westernization, radical Westernizing of culture became less popular.

44 Thomas, *Protestant Beginnings*, pp. 197, 204.

45 The following account is based on Harbert, "Open Door Policy," pp. 282ff.

46 Ibid., pp. 338–339.

Part III: Incorporation, development, and underdevelopment

1 See Higgins, "The Political Basis of Economic Development," pp. 53–56. On Japan see also Hiroshi Shimbo, "An Aspect of Indus-

trialization in Japan in its Formative Stage," *Kobe University Economic Review* 13(1967): 19–42. On China see Feuerwerker, *The Chinese Economy ca. 1870–1911*, pp. 17ff.

2 Hou, *Foreign Investment and Economic Development in China*, p. 191.

3 Lockwood, *The Economic Development of Japan*, p. 357.

4 Perkins, *Agricultural Development in China*, p. 132.

5 Hou, *Foreign Investment and Economic Development in China*, p. 197.

6 Lockwood, *The Economic Development of Japan*, p. 317.

7 Hirschmeier, *The Origins of Enterpreneurship*, pp. 91–95.

8 Rosovsky, "Japan's Transition to Modern Economic Growth," p. 131.

9 Nobutaka Ike, *The Beginnings of Political Democracy in Japan* (Baltimore, 1950), pp. 138ff.

10 Kozo Yamamura, "The Founding of Mitsubishi: A Case Study in Japanese Business History," *Business History Review* 41(1967): 152–154. On other monopolies see Hirschmeier, *The Origins of Entrepreneurship*, p. 154.

11 Feuerwerker, *China's Early Industrialization*, pp. 183–186. Feuerwerker is actually writing of the firm's equally monopolistic successor, the Nippon Yusen Kaisha; see below, Chapter 7, "Capital accumulation."

Chapter 6: Transformation of the state

1 For a list of the revolts since the 1770s see Kwang-ching Liu, "Nineteenth Century China: The Disintegration of the Old Order and the Impact of the West," in Ho and Tsou, eds., *China in Crisis*, I, book 1: 95–98.

2 Others claim that the changing price ratio was the fault of the Chinese government. The government debased the copper coinage, then Gresham's law ("bad money drives out good") took effect: because copper was debased, people hoarded silver and thus the quantity in circulation declined and its price went up (see Fairbank, *Trade and Diplomacy on the China Coast*, pp. 75–76). That is, the opium trade had nothing to do with it.

It appears to me that both factors were involved but that the debasing of coinage was a *response* to the outflow of silver. As silver rose in value, the government increased the minting of copper and debased its value, because it was believed that if one form of money was in short supply, the problem could be rectified by increasing the supply of the other. Moreover, coins had been debased earlier without producing such a strong effect. See Jerome Chih-jang Ch'en, "The State Economic Policy of the Ch'ing Government" (Ph.D. diss., University of London, 1956), p. 44.

3 Chang, *Commissioner Lin and the Opium War,* pp. 39–40; Hsü, *The Rise of Modern China,* p. 218.
4 Hsü, *The Rise of Modern China,* p. 273.
5 Chang, *Commissioner Lin and the Opium War,* p. 45.
6 Wang, *Land Taxation in Imperial China,* p. 114; Ho, *Studies on the Population of China,* pp. 267–268.
7 Ramon H. Myers, *The Chinese Peasant Economy* (Cambridge, Mass., 1970), p. 277. The deflation also affected urban areas, causing a "conspicuous contraction of business activities and the concomitant decrease in employment and income." Wang, *Land Taxation in Imperial China,* p. 115.
8 Robert Hartwell, "Foreign Trade, Monetary Policy, and Chinese 'Mercantilism,'" paper presented at annual meeting of American Oriental Society, Cambridge, Mass., Apr. 6, 1971 (pp. 9–13).
9 Wang, *Land Taxation in Imperial China,* pp. 114–115.
10 Chang, *Commissioner Lin and the Opium War,* p. 37.
11 Pelcovits, *Old China Hands,* p. 13.
12 Robert Hartwell, "Classical Chinese Monetary Analysis and Economic Policy in T'ang – Northern Sung China," *Transactions of the International Conference of Orientalists in Japan,* vol. 13 (1968), and idem, "Foreign Trade, Monetary Policy and Chinese 'Mercantilism,'" pp. 9–13.
13 On the trade routes see Miyazaki, "The Nature of the Taiping Rebellion," pp. 5–9.
14 Ibid., p. 16.
15 The volume of the goods, other than opium, destined for export by way of Canton may not have declined *absolutely* until after the Taiping revolution had started. The revolt caused the disruption of southern trade routes and completed the decline of Canton that the Treaty of Nanking had begun. See Chang, *The Income of the Chinese Gentry,* pp. 167–168. On efforts of the Canton officialdom to preserve the importance of Canton after 1842 see Fairbank, *Trade and Diplomacy on the China Coast,* pp. 289, 292–293. For instance, they got the court to issue an edict preventing trade in Bohea tea at the open port of Foochow, even though it was adjacent to the main growing area. Until 1854, Bohea tea had to be shipped 600 miles to Canton for export.
16 Miyazaki, "The Nature of the Taiping Rebellion," p. 16.
17 On the feuding among peasant villages in Kwangtung see Wan Lo, "Communal Strife in Mid-Nineteenth Century Kwangtung: The Establishment of Ch'ih-ch'i," *Papers on China* 19(1965): 85–119.
18 Miyazaki, "The Nature of the Taiping Rebellion," p. 16. See also Frederic Wakeman Jr., *Strangers at the Gate* (Berkeley, 1966), pp. 126–131. On the British navy's efforts to suppress piracy along the coast after the 1830s see Grace Fox, *British Admirals and Chinese Pirates, 1832–1869* (London, 1940), pp. 85ff.
19 Lo, "Communal Strife," pp. 93–96. The following account of the

emergence of the Taipings and their program is based primarily on Hsü, *The Rise of Modern China*, pp. 275ff.

20 Miyazaki, "The Nature of the Taiping Rebellion," p. 9.

21 Ibid., p. 22.

22 James T. K. Wu, "The Impact of the Taiping Rebellion on the Manchu Fiscal System," *Pacific Historical Review* 19(1959): 273.

23 Hsü, *The Rise of Modern China*, p. 288.

24 Spector, *Li Hung-chang and the Huai Army*, pp. xl–xli, 13.

25 Hsü, *The Rise of Modern China*, pp. 303–306; Miyazaki, "The Nature of the Taiping Rebellion," pp. 24, 33, 35–36.

26 Hsü, *The Rise of Modern China*, pp. 320–321.

27 H. B. Morse, *The International Relations of the Chinese Empire* (London, 1910), II: 65.

28 Fairbank, Reischauer, and Craig, *East Asia: The Modern Transformation*, pp. 175–176; J. S. Gregory, *Great Britain and the Taipings* (New York, 1969), pp. 157–167.

29 Wang, *Land Taxation in Imperial China*, p. 80.

30 Ibid., pp. 71, 77, 80, table 4.8.

31 Ibid., p. 80.

32 Spector, *Li Hung-chang and the Huai Army*, pp. 178, 216.

33 See Wakeman, *Strangers at the Gate*, for an account of a landlords' reign of terror in Kwangtung after the Red Turban uprising of the 1850s had been suppressed.

34 On Li's position see Spector, *Li Hung-chang and the Huai Army*, pp. 171–172.

35 Hsü, *The Rise of Modern China*, pp. 348, 474–475.

36 Spector, *Li Hung-chang and the Huai Army*, pp. 196–233. Spector points out that it is better to speak of "regionalism" in nineteenth-century China than "provincialism" since the decentralization of power transcended provincial boundaries.

37 On Li's network of power see Folsom, *Friends, Guests and Colleagues*, esp. pp. 158ff., and Spector, *Li Hung-chang and the Huai Army*, pp. 152ff., 275ff.

38 On the pacification of the rebellions and the program of agrarian reconstruction see Wright, *The Last Stand of Chinese Conservatism*, pp. 96ff.

39 John McMaster, "The Japanese Gold Rush of 1859," *Journal of Asian Studies* 19(1960): 273–287.

40 That fear at that time was enormous can be ascertained by a brief examination of the British consular reports. See Great Britain, Parliament, House of Commons, *Sessional Papers*.

41 Yazaki, *Social Change and the City in Japan*, p. 278. The government had also undertaken inflationary monetary policies to counteract the effects of the outflow of gold, which contributed to the inflation's severity.

42 Miyazaki, "The Nature of the Taiping Rebellion," p. 16.

43 Grace Fox, *Britain and Japan, 1858–1883* (Oxford, 1969), pp. 331–334.

44 The following account is based on W. G. Beasley's introduction to his edited and translated *Select Documents on Japanese Foreign Policy 1853–1868* (London, 1955). This is an excellent survey of the complicated chain of events in the Meiji Restoration. See also idem, *The Meiji Restoration* (Stanford, 1972), Paul Akamatsu, *Meiji 1868* (New York, 1972), and Harry D. Harootvnian, *Towards Restoration* (Berkeley, 1970).

45 E. H. Norman, *Soldier and Peasant in Japan: The Origins of Conscription* (New York, 1943), pp. 3–40.

46 As far as I can ascertain, these are the only two cases in which sizable indemnities were imposed in Japan.

47 Fox, *Britain and Japan*, p. 95.

48 Ibid., pp. 179–181.

49 Akagi, *Japan's Foreign Relations*, p. 57.

50 Gordon Daniels, "The British Role in the Meiji Restoration: A Reinterpretive Note," *Modern Asian Studies* 2(1968): 291–313.

51 On the abolition of the bakufu-han system and the creation of a new state see W. G. Beasley, *The Modern History of Japan* (New York, 1963), pp. 98, 138; John W. Hall, "From Tokugawa to Meiji In Japanese Local Administration," in John Whitney Hall and Marius B. Jansen, eds., *Studies in Institutional History of Early Modern Japan* (Princeton, 1968), pp. 375–386; Masao Takahashi, *Modern Japanese Economy since 1868* (Tokyo, 1968), pp. 47–49; and Hyman Kublin, "The 'Modern' Army of Early Meiji Japan," *Far Eastern Quarterly* 9(1949): pp. 20–41.

52 Beasley, *The Modern History of Japan*, p. 127.

53 Ibid., p. 128.

54 On the following, see especially Takahashi, *Modern Japanese Economy*, pp. 50–66.

55 Kublin, "The 'Modern' Army." Kublin cautions that the often drawn contrast between the decrepit feudal samurai army of Satsuma and the modern bureaucratic conscript army of the Meiji government is somewhat of an exaggeration. The Meiji army of 1877 was not the strong and well-disciplined modern army it had become by the 1890s.

56 Beasley, *The Modern History of Japan*, p. 110; Takahashi, *Modern Japanese Economy*, pp. 60–62.

57 Thomas C. Smith, *Political Change and Industrial Development in Japan* (Stanford, 1955), p. 83.

58 The renewed inflation is not easily explained. It was associated with an increased government issue of inconvertible paper notes to pay for the costs of pacifying the Satsuma rebellion and in connection with the commutation of samurai stipends. Banks were established that were empowered to issue inconvertible notes

against the commutation bonds. However, the government had issued paper notes in the earlier years without the same result (and the net increases in earlier years had been larger). Tsuru has suggested that it was due to an increased maturity of the "capitalist milieu," so that the impact of such measures was less localized than before. See Rosovsky, "Japan's Transition to Modern Economic Growth," p. 130.

59 Rosovsky, "Japan's Transition to Modern Economic Growth," pp. 122, 139.
60 Beasley, *The Modern History of Japan*, pp. 124–126.
61 On the rise and decline of the Liberal party see Ike, *Political Democracy in Japan*.
62 Hall, "From Tokugawa to Meiji," pp. 381ff.
63 Ibid., p. 385.
64 Ibid., p. 386.

Chapter 7: The state and national industrialization

1 On the reluctance to invest see Hirschmeier, *The Origins of Entrepreneurship*, pp. 28–44 (on the bourgeoisie), pp. 58–59, 66–67 (on the samurai), pp. 97–100 (on the rural merchants). On the bourgeoisie, see also Smith, *Political Change and Industrial Development*, pp. 36–41.
2 Hirschmeier, *The Origins of Entrepeneurship*, p. 139.
3 Ibid., pp. 140–141.
4 Smith, *Political Change and Industrial Development*, pp. 46–47.
5 George C. Allen, *A Short Economic History of Modern Japan: 1867–1937* (London, 1946), pp. 74–75.
6 Smith, *Political Change and Industrial Development*, pp. 54–56.
7 Ibid., pp. 60–61.
8 Ibid., pp. 62–65.
9 Ibid., pp. 48, 50.
10 Hirschmeier, *The Origins of Entrepreneurship*, p. 144.
11 Allen, *A Short Economic History*, p. 76.
12 Ibid., pp. 84–86.
13 Ibid., pp. 85–86, and Hirschmeier, *The Origins of Entrepreneurship*, p. 146.
14 Smith, *Political Change and Industrial Development*, pp. 86–100.
15 Hirschmeier, *The Origins of Entrepreneurship*, p. 151.
16 Ibid., p. 36.
17 Allen, *A Short Economic History*, p. 38.
18 Hirschmeier, *The Origins of Entrepreneurship*, p. 58.
19 Ibid., p. 57.
20 Ibid., p. 59.
21 Allen, *A Short Economic History*, pp. 46–49.
22 Smith, *Political Change and Industrial Development*, pp. 67–85.

23 G. Ranis, "The Financing of Japanese Economic Development," *Economic History Review* 2(1959): 446, table 3.

24 Ibid., pp. 447–448, table 6.

25 Edwin P. Reubens, "Foreign Capital and Domestic Development in Japan," in Kuznets, Moore, and Spengler, eds., *Economic Growth*, p. 189.

26 Angus Maddison, *Economic Growth in Japan and the USSR* (New York, 1969), p. 15.

27 Albert Feuerwerker, "China's Early Industrialization – The Case of the Hanyehp'ing Coal and Iron Company, Ltd," in C. D. Cowan, ed., *The Economic Development of China and Japan* (New York, 1964), p. 102.

28 M. Shinohara, cited by Maddison in *Economic Growth*, p. 15.

29 Hirschmeier, *The Origins of Entrepreneurship*, p. 153.

30 Ibid., pp. 154–155.

31 Allen, *A Short Economic History*, p. 77.

32 Lockwood, *The Economic Development of Japan*, p. 381.

33 Yamamura, "The Founding of Mitsubishi," pp. 150ff.

34 McMaster, "The Takashima Mine," p. 218.

35 Ibid., p. 225.

36 Akagi, *Japan's Foreign Relations*, pp. 106–112; Lockwood, *The Economic Development of Japan*, p. 546. See also F. C. Jones, *Extraterritoriality in Japan and the Diplomatic Negotiations Resulting in Its Abolition* (New Haven, 1931).

37 Allen, *A Short Economic History*, pp. 121–123.

38 John E. Orchard, *Japan's Economic Position* (New York, 1930), pp. 432–444; Lockwood, *The Economic Development of Japan*, p. 339.

39 There were also enterprises called *kuan-shang ho-pan* ("joint government and merchant understakings") but they appear to have been very similar to the *kuan-tu shang-pan* variety.

40 Hsü, *The Rise of Modern China*, pp. 346–347.

41 In *The Rise of Modern China*, p. 345.

42 In *China's Early Industrialization*, p. 243.

43 Smith, *Political Change and Industrial Development*, pp. 70–71.

44 Hsü, *The Rise of Modern China*, p. 517.

45 Koichi Emi, *Government Fiscal Activity and Economic Growth in Japan, 1868–1960* (Tokyo, 1963), p. 88.

46 See Feuerwerker, "China's Early Industrialization," for the troubles of the Hanyang ironworks.

47 Kwang-ching Liu, "Steamship Enterprise in Nineteenth-Century China," *Journal of Asian Studies* 18(1959): 438–440, 448–450.

48 Immanuel C. Y. Hsü, *China's Entrance into the Family of Nations* (Cambridge, Mass., 1960), p. 143.

49 Liu, "Steamship Enterprise," p. 442.

50 Ibid., pp. 442–443.

51 Allen and Donnithorne, *Western Enterprise in Far Eastern Economic Development*, pp. 131–132.

52 Hou, *Foreign Investment and Economic Development in China*, pp. 68, 79.

53 Feuerwerker, "China's 19th Century Industrialization," p. 101.

54 Ibid.; E-tu Zen Sun, "The Pattern of Railway Development in China," *Far Eastern Quarterly* 14(1955): 184–185.

Summary and conclusions

1 Gustave V. Dans, "Brazil on the Offensive," *Latin America and Empire Report*, vol. 9 (1975): "Brazil: The Continental Strategy," p. 2.

Bibliography

Books and theses cited

Akagi, Roy Hidemichi. *Japan's Foreign Relations*. Tokyo: The Hokuseido Press, 1936.

Akamatsu, Paul. *Meiji 1868*. New York: Harper and Row, 1972.

Albrow, Martin. *Bureaucracy*. New York: Praeger, 1970.

Allen, George C. *A Short Economic History of Modern Japan: 1867–1937*. London: Allen and Unwin, 1946.

 and Audrey G. Donnithorne. *Western Enterprise in Far Eastern Economic Development*. London: Allen and Unwin, 1954.

Avineri, Shlomo, ed. *Karl Marx on Colonialism and Modernization*. New York: Doubleday, 1968.

Balasz, Etienne, *Chinese Civilization and Bureaucracy*. New Haven: Yale University Press, 1964.

Baran, Paul A. *The Political Economy of Growth*. New York: Monthly Review, 1957.

Beal, Edwin George, Jr. *The Origin of Likin (1853–1864)*. Cambridge, Mass.: Harvard University Press, 1958.

Beasley, W. G. *Great Britain and the Opening of Japan, 1834–1858*. London: Lazac, 1951.

 The Meiji Restoration. Stanford: Stanford University Press, 1972.

 The Modern History of Japan. New York: Praeger, 1963.

 Select Documents on Japanese Foreign Policy, 1853–1868. London: Oxford University Press, 1955.

Bolitho, Harold. *Treasures among Men: The Fudai Daimyo in Tokugawa Japan*. New Haven: Yale University Press, 1974.

Borton, Hugh. *Peasant Uprisings in Japan of the Tokugawa Period*. New York: Paragon, 1968 (1937).

Chang Chung-li. *The Chinese Gentry*. Seattle: University of Washington Press, 1955.

 The Income of the Chinese Gentry. Seattle: University of Washington Press, 1962.

Chang Hsin-pao. *Commissioner Lin and the Opium War*. New York: Norton, 1964.

Chang Kia-Ngau. *China's Struggle for Railway Development*. New York: Day, 1943.

236   Bibliography

Chang Peng. "The Distribution and Relative Strength of the Provincial Merchant Groups in China, 1842–1911." Ph.D. diss., University of Washington, 1957.

Ch'en, Jerome Chih-jang. "The State Economic Policy of the Ch'ing Government." Ph.D. diss., University of London, 1956.

Ch'ü, T'ung tsu. Local Government in China under the Ch'ing. Stanford: Stanford University Press, 1969 (1962).

Clark, Colin. The Conditions of Economic Progress. London: Macmillan, 1940.

Cockroft, James D., Andre Gunder Frank, and Dale L. Johnson, eds. Dependence and Underdevelopment. Garden City, N.Y.: Doubleday, 1972.

Cohen, Paul A. China and Christianity. Cambridge, Mass.: Harvard University Press, 1963.

Conroy, Hilary. The Japanese Seizure of Korea: 1868–1910. Philadelphia: University of Pennsylvania Press, 1960.

Craig, Albert M. Choshu in the Meiji Restoration. Cambridge, Mass.: Harvard University Press, 1967.

Crowley, James B., ed. Modern East Asia: Essays in Interpretation. New York: Harcourt Brace Jovanovich, 1970.

Dennett, Tyler. Americans in Eastern Asia. New York: Macmillan, 1922.

Dutt, Romesh. The Economic History of India under Early British Rule. London: Routledge and Kegan Paul, 1956.

Duus, Peter. Feudalism in Japan. New York: Knopf, 1969.

Eberhard, Wolfram. A History of China. Berkeley: University of California Press, 1969.

    Conquerors and Rulers: Social Forces in Medieval China. Leiden: Heinman, 1952.

Eisenstadt, S. N. Modernization: Protest and Change. Englewood Cliffs: Prentice-Hall, 1966.

Elvin, Mark. The Pattern of the Chinese Past. Stanford: Stanford University Press, 1973.

Emi, Koichi. Government Fiscal Activity and Economic Growth in Japan, 1868–1960. Tokyo: Kinokuniya Bookstore, 1963.

Fairbank, John K. Trade and Diplomacy on the China Coast. Stanford: Stanford University Press, 1969 (1953).

    ed. The Chinese World Order. Cambridge, Mass.: Harvard University Press, 1968.

    Edwin O. Reischauer, and Albert M. Craig. East Asia: The Modern Transformation. Boston: Houghton Mifflin, 1965.

Fann, K. T., and Donald C. Hodges, eds. Readings in U.S. Imperialism. Boston: Sargent, 1971.

Feuerwerker, Albert. China's Early Industrialization. New York: Atheneum, 1970 (1958).

    The Chinese Economy ca. 1870–1911. Ann Arbor: Michigan Papers in Chinese Studies (no. 5), 1969.

The Chinese Economy, 1912–1949. Ann Arbor: Michigan Papers in Chinese Studies (no. 1), 1968.

——— ed. *History in Communist China.* Cambridge, Mass.: MIT Press, 1968.

Folsom, Kenneth E. *Friends, Guests and Colleagues.* Berkeley: University of California Press, 1968.

Fox, Grace. *Britain and Japan, 1858–1883.* London: Oxford University Press, 1969.

——— *British Admirals and Chinese Pirates, 1832–1869.* London: K. Paul, Trench, Trubner, 1940.

Gadgil, D. R. *The Industrial Evolution of India.* London: Oxford University Press, 1934.

Glass, D. V., and Roger Revelle, eds. *Population and Social Change.* London: Crane-Russak, 1973.

Greenberg, Michael. *British Trade and the Opening of China, 1800–1842.* Cambridge: Cambridge University Press, 1969 (1951).

Gregory, J. S. *Great Britain and the Taipings.* New York: Praeger, 1969.

Hacker, Louis. *The Triumph of American Capitalism.* New York: McGraw-Hill, 1965.

Hall, John Whitney. *Japan.* New York: Dell, 1970.

——— and Marius B. Jansen, eds. *Studies in the Institutional History of Early Modern Japan.* Princeton: Princeton University Press, 1968.

Halliday, Jon, and Gavan McCormack. *Japanese Imperialism Today.* New York: Monthly Review, 1973.

Harbert, Mary E. M. "The Open Door Policy: The Means of Attaining Nineteenth Century American Objectives in Japan." Ph.D. diss., University of Oregon, 1967.

Harootunian, Harry D. *Towards Restoration.* Berkeley: University of California Press, 1970.

Hauser, William B. *Economic Institutional Change in Tokugawa Japan.* Cambridge: Cambridge University Press, 1974.

Heaton, Herbert. *Economic History of Europe.* New York: Harper and Row, 1948.

Heckscher, August. *Mercantilism.* 2 vols. London: Macmillan, 1955 (1935).

Higgins, Benjamin. "The Political Basis of Economic Development." M.A. thesis, McGill University, 1971.

Hill, Christopher. *Reformation to Industrial Revolution.* Baltimore: Penguin, 1969.

Hinton, Harold C. *The Grain Tribute System of China (1845–1911).* Cambridge, Mass.: Harvard University Press, 1956.

Hirschmeier, Johannes. *The Origins of Entrepreneurship in Meiji Japan.* Cambridge, Harvard University Press, 1964.

Ho Ping-ti. *Chung-kuo hui-kuan shih-lun* [A historical survey of the Chinese hui-kuan]. Taipei, 1966.

Studies on the Population of China, 1368–1953. Cambridge, Mass.: Harvard University Press, 1959.

The Ladder of Success in Imperial China. New York: John Wiley, 1962.

and Tang Tsou, eds. *China in Crisis.* Vol. 1, books 1 and 2. Chicago: University of Chicago Press, 1968.

Hobsbawm, Eric. *Industry and Empire.* Baltimore: Penguin, 1969.

——— ed. *Pre-Capitalist Economic Formations: Karl Marx.* New York: International Publishers, 1965.

Holt, Robert T., and John E. Turner. *The Political Basis of Economic Development.* Princeton: Van Nostrand, 1966.

Horowitz, Irving Louis. *Three Worlds of Development.* New York: Oxford University Press, 1966.

Hou Chi-ming. *Foreign Investment and Economic Development in China, 1840–1937.* Cambridge, Mass.: Harvard University Press, 1965.

Hsiao Kung-chuan. *Rural China.* Seattle: University of Washington Press, 1960.

Hsü, Immanuel C. Y. *China's Entrance into the Family of Nations.* Cambridge, Mass.: Harvard University Press, 1960.

——— *The Rise of Modern China.* New York: Oxford University Press, 1970.

Hucker, Charles O. *The Traditional Chinese State in Ming Times (1368–1644).* Tucson: University of Arizona Press, 1961.

Ike, Nobutaka. *The Beginnings of Political Democracy in Japan.* Baltimore: Johns Hopkins Press, 1951.

Jacobs, Norman. *The Origin of Modern Capitalism and Eastern Asia.* Hong Kong: Hong Kong University Press, 1958.

Jalee, Pierre. *The Pillage of the Third World.* New York: Monthly Review, 1968.

Jansen, Marius B. *Sakamoto Ryoma and the Meiji Restoration.* Stanford: Stanford University Press, 1971.

Johnson, Dale L. *The Sociology of Change and Reaction in Latin America.* New York: Bobbs-Merrill, 1973.

Jones, F. C. *Extraterritoriality in Japan and the Diplomatic Negotiations Resulting in Its Abolition.* New Haven: Yale University Press, 1931.

Kamikawa, Hikomatsu, ed. *Japan-American Diplomatic Relations in the Meiji-Taisho Era.* Tokyo: Pan-Pacific Press, 1958.

King, Frank H. H. *Money and Monetary Policy in China, 1845–1895.* Cambridge, Mass.: Harvard University Press, 1965.

Kuhn, Philip A. *Rebellion and Its Enemies in Late Imperial China.* Cambridge, Mass.: Harvard University Press, 1970.

Kuznets, S., W. E. Moore, and J. J. Spengler, eds. *Economic Growth: Brazil, India, Japan.* Durham: Duke University Press, 1955.

Lach, Donald F. *China in the Eyes of Europe.* Chicago: University of Chicago Press, 1968.

Japan in the Eyes of Europe. Chicago: University of Chicago Press, 1968.

Langer, William L. *European Alliances and Alignments, 1871–1890*. New York: Vintage Books, 1950.

Latourette, Kenneth S. *A History of Christian Missions in China*. Taipei: Ch'eng-Wen Publishing Co., n.d. (1929).

Laures, Johannes. *The Catholic Church in Japan*. Rutland, Vt.: Tuttle, 1954.

Lerner, Daniel. *The Passing of Traditional Society*. Glencoe, Ill.: Free Press, 1964 (1958).

Levenson, Joseph R., ed. *European Expansion and the Counter-Example of Asia, 1300–1600*. Englewood Cliffs: Prentice-Hall, 1967.

——. ed. *Modern China: An Interpretive Anthology*. New York: Macmillan, 1971.

Liang Fang-chung. *The Single Whip Method of Taxation in China*. Cambridge, Mass.: Harvard University Press, 1956.

Lichtheim, George. *Imperialism*. New York: Praeger, 1971.

Lockwood, William W. *The Economic Development of Japan*. Princeton: Princeton University Press, 1954.

McClelland, David. *The Achieving Society*. Princeton: Van Nostrand, 1961.

McCormick, Thomas J. *China Market*. Chicago: Quadrangle, 1967.

Maddison, Angus. *Economic Growth in Japan and the USSR*. New York: Norton, 1969.

Mandel, Ernest. *Marxist Economic Theory*, 2 vols. New York: Monthly Review, 1969.

——. *The Formation of The Economic Thought of Karl Marx*. New York: Monthly Review, 1971.

Martin, R. M. *Past and Present State of the Tea Trade of England and of the Continents of Europe and America*. London: Parbury, 1832.

Marx, Karl. *Capital*. Vol. 1. New York: Random House, n.d.

——. *Capital*. Vol. 3. New York: International Publishers, 1967.

Mason, Mary Gertrude, "Western Concepts of China and the Chinese, 1840–1876." Ph.D. diss., Columbia University, 1939.

Maverick, L. A. *China – A Model for Europe*. San Antonio: Paul Anderson, 1946.

Metzger, Thomas A. *The Internal Organization of Ch'ing Bureaucracy*. Cambridge, Mass.: Harvard University Press, 1973.

Moffett, John T., "Bureaucracy and Social Control." Ph.D. diss., Columbia University, 1972.

Moore, Barrington, Jr. *Social Origins of Dictatorship and Democracy*. Boston: Beacon Press, 1967.

Morse, H. B. *The International Relations of the Chinese Empire*. 3 vols. London: Longmans, 1910.

——. and H. F. MacNair. *Far Eastern International Relations*. Boston: Houghton Mifflin, 1931.

240 Bibliography

Mosca, Gaetano. *The Ruling Class*. New York: McGraw-Hill, 1939.
Murphey, Rhoads. *The Treaty Ports and China's Modernization – What Went Wrong?* Ann Arbor: Michigan Papers in Chinese Studies (no. 7), 1970.
Myers, Ramon H. *The Chinese Peasant Economy*. Cambridge, Mass.: Harvard University Press, 1970.
Myrdal, Gunnar. *Asian Drama*. 3 vols. New York: Pantheon, 1968.
Norman, E. H. *Japan's Emergence as a Modern State*. New York: Institute of Pacific Relations, 1940.
  Soldier and Peasant in Japan: The Origins of Conscription. New York: Institute of Pacific Relations, 1943.
Ohara, Keishi, and Tamotsu Okata. *Japanese Trade and Industry in the Meiji-Taisho Era*. Tokyo: Pan-Pacific Press, 1957.
Orchard, John E. *Japan's Economic Position*. New York: McGraw-Hill, 1930.
Owen, David Edward. *British Opium Policy in China and India*. New Haven: Archon, 1968 (1934).
Paske-Smith, M. *Western Barbarians in Japan and Formosa in Togugawa Days, 1603–1868*. New York: Paragon, n.d. (1930).
Pelcovits, Nathan A. *Old China Hands and the Foreign Office*. New York: Institute of Pacific Relations, 1948.
Perkins, Dwight H. *Agricultural Development in China, 1368–1968*. Chicago: Aldine, 1969.
Petras, James, and Maurice Zeitlin, eds. *Latin America – Reform or Revolution?* New York: Fawcett World Library, 1968.
Polanyi, Karl, Conrad M. Arensberg, and Harry W. Pearson, eds. *Trade and Market in the Early Empires*. Glencoe, Ill.: Free Press, 1957.
Pritchard, Earl. *The Crucial Years of Early Anglo-Chinese Relations, 1750–1800*. Pullman: State College of Washington, 1936.
Purcell, Victor. *The Boxer Uprising*. Cambridge: Cambridge University Press, 1963.
  The Rise of Modern China. London: Historical Association, 1962.
Rawlinson, John L. *China's Struggle for Naval Development, 1839–1895*. Cambridge, Mass.: Harvard University Press, 1967.
Rawski, Evelyn Sakakida. *Agricultural Change and the Peasant Economy of South China*. Cambridge, Mass.: Harvard University Press, 1972.
Reinsch, Paul. *Colonial Government*. New York: Macmillan, 1902.
Reischauer, Edwin O., and John K. Fairbank. *East Asia: The Great Tradition*. Boston: Houghton Mifflin, 1958.
Rhodes, Robert I., ed. *Imperialism and Underdevelopment: A Reader*. New York: Monthly Review, 1970.
Rodney, Walter. *How Europe Underdeveloped Africa*. London: Bogle L'Ouverture, 1972.
Rostow, W. W. *The Process of Economic Growth*. New York: Norton, 1962.

Rozman, Gilbert. *Urban Networks in Ch'ing China and Tokugawa Japan*. Princeton: Princeton University Press, 1973.

Sansom, George. *A History of Japan, 1615–1867*. Stanford: Stanford University Press, 1963.

———. *The Western World and Japan*. New York: Knopf, 1950.

Schurmann, H. F. *Ideology and Organization in Communist China*. Berkeley: University of California Press, 1966.

Scott, James Maurice. *The Tea Story*. London: Heinemann, 1964.

Smith, Thomas C. *Political Change and Industrial Development in Japan*. Stanford: Stanford University Press, 1955.

———. *The Agrarian Origins of Modern Japan*. Stanford: Stanford University Press, 1959.

Sombart, Werner. *Krieg und Kapitalismus*. Leipzig: Duncker and Humboldt, 1913.

Spector, Stanley. *Li Hung-chang and the Huai Army*. Seattle: University of Washington Press, 1964.

Takahashi, Masao. *Modern Japanese Economy since 1868*. Tokyo: Japan Cultural Society, 1968.

Takekoshi, Y. *The Economic Aspects of the History of Civilization of Japan*. 3 vols. London: Allen and Unwin, 1930.

Tan, Chester C. *The Boxer Catastrophe*. New York: Norton, 1967.

Thomas, Winburn T. *Protestant Beginnings in Japan*. Rutland, Vt.: Tuttle, 1959.

Totman, Conrad D. *Politics in the Tokugawa Bakufu, 1600–1843*. Cambridge, Mass.: Harvard University Press, 1967.

Treat, Payson. *Diplomatic Relations between the United States and Japan*. 3 vols. Stanford: Stanford University Press, 1932.

Tsukahira, T. G. *Feudal Control in Tokugawa Japan*. Cambridge, Mass.: Harvard University Press, 1966.

Tyau, Min-ch'ien T. Z. *The Legal Obligations Arising Out of Treaty Relations between China and Other States*. Taipei, 1966 (1917).

van der Sprenkel, Sybille. *Legal Institutions in Manchu China*. London: Athlone Press, 1962.

van Hecken, Joseph. *The Catholic Church in Japan since 1859*. Tokyo: n.p., 1963.

Wakeman, Frederic, Jr. *Strangers at the Gate*. Berkeley: University of California Press, 1966.

Waley, Arthur. *The Opium War through Chinese Eyes*. Stanford: Stanford University Press, 1958.

Wallerstein, Immanuel. *The Modern World System*. New York: Academic Press, 1974.

Wang Yeh-chien. *Land Taxation in Imperial China, 1750–1911*. Cambridge, Mass.: Harvard University Press, 1973.

Weber, Max. *The City*. New York: Free Press, 1966.

———. *The Religion of China*. New York: Macmillan, 1964.

Wehrle, Edmund S. *Britain, China and the Antimissionary Riots, 1891–1900*. Minneapolis: University of Minnesota Press, 1966.

Wittfogel, Karl A. *Oriental Despotism.* New Haven: Yale University Press, 1957.
Wirtschaft und Gesellschaft Chinas. Leipzig: Hirschfeld, 1931.
Wolf, Eric R. *Peasant Wars of the Twentieth Century.* New York: Harper and Row, 1969.
Peasants. Englewood Cliffs: Prentice-Hall, 1966.
Wright, Mary C. *The Last Stand of Chinese Conservatism.* New York: Atheneum, 1966 (1957).
Wright, Stanley F. *China's Struggle for Tariff Autonomy, 1843–1938.* Shanghai: Kelly and Walsh, 1938.
Hart and the Chinese Customs. Belfast: William Mullan, 1950.
Wu, Silas H. L. *Communication and Imperial Control in China.* Cambridge, Mass.: Harvard University Press, 1970.
Yang Lien-sheng. *Money and Credit in China.* Cambridge, Mass.: Harvard University Press, 1952.
Yang, Martin. *A Chinese Village.* New York: Columbia University Press, 1945.
Yazaki, Takeo. *Social Change and the City in Japan.* Tokyo: Japan Publications, 1968.

Articles cited

Azumi, Koya. "Japanese Society: A Sociological View," in Arthur Tiedemann, ed., *An Introduction to Japanese Civilization.* New York: Heath, 1974.
Biggerstaff, Knight. "The Secret Correspondence of 1867–1868: Views of Leading Chinese Statesmen Regarding the Further Opening of China to Western Influence." *Journal of Modern History* 22(1950): 122–136.
Chesneaux, Jean. "Ou En Est La Discussion sur Le Mode de Production Asiatique." *La Pensee,* vol. 114(1964), 122(1965), 129 (1966), 138(1968).
Chirot, Daniel. "Commerce, Integration and Closure." Unpublished ms., Columbia University, 1968.
Crawcour, E. S. "The Japanese Economy on the Eve of Modernization." *Journal of the Oriental Society of Australia* 2(1963): 34–41.
Currie, Blair C. "The Woosung Railroad (1872–1877)." *Papers on China* 20(1966): 49–85.
Daniels, Gordon. "The British Role in the Meiji Restoration – a Reinterpretive Note." *Modern Asian Studies* 2(1968): 291–313.
Dans, Gustavo V. "Brazil on the Offensive." *Latin America and Empire Report* 9(1975): 5–28.
dos Santos, Theontonio. "The Structure of Dependency" in K. T. Fann and Donald C. Hodges, eds., *Readings in U.S. Imperialism.* Boston: Sargent (1971), pp. 225–236.
Eisenstadt, S. N. "Tradition, Change and Modernity: Reflections on the Chinese Experience," in Ping-ti Ho and Tang Tsou, eds.,

China in Crisis, vol. 1, bk. 1. Chicago: University of Chicago Press (1968), pp. 753–774.

Fairbank, John K., Alexander Eckstein, and L. S. Yang. "Economic Change in Early Modern China: An Analytic Framework," in Joseph R. Levenson, ed., *Modern China: An Interpretive Anthology.* New York: Macmillan (1971), pp. 155–186.

Feuerwerker, Albert. "China's Early Industrialization: The Case of the Hanyehp'ing Coal and Iron Company, Ltd.," in C. D. Cowan, ed., *The Economic Development of China and Japan.* New York: Praeger, 1964.

"Industrial Enterprise in Twentieth Century China: The Chee Hsin Cement Company," in Albert Feuerwerker et al., eds., *Approaches to Modern Chinese History.* Berkeley: University of California Press (1966), pp. 304–342.

Frank, Andre Gunder. "Sociology of Development and Underdevelopment of Sociology." *Catalyst* 1(1967): 20–73.

Gallagher, John, and Ronald Robinson. "The Imperialism of Free Trade." *Economic History Review* 6(1953): 201–225.

Gough, Kathleen. "The South Asian Revolutionary Potential." *Bulletin of Concerned Asian Scholars* 4(1972): 77–97.

Hall, John Whitney. "From Tokugawa to Meiji in Japanese Local Administration" in John Whitney Hall and Marius B. Jansen, eds., *Studies in the Institutional History of Early Modern Japan.* Princeton: Princeton University Press (1968), pp. 375–386.

Hamilton, Earl J. "Origin and Growth of the National Debt in Western Europe." *American Economic Review* 37(1947): 118–129.

Hartwell, Robert. "A Cycle of Economic Change in Imperial China: Coal and Iron in Northeast China, 750–1350." *Journal of the Economic and Social History of the Orient* 10(1967): 102–159.

"Classical Chinese Monetary Analysis and Economic Policy in T'ang – Northern Sung China." *Transactions* of International Conference of Orientalists in Japan, vol. 13 (1968).

"Foreign Trade, Monetary Policy, and Chinese 'Mercantilism.'" Paper presented at annual meeting of American Oriental Society, Cambridge, Mass., Apr. 6, 1971.

Ho Ping-ti. "The Salt Merchants of Yang-chou: A Study of Commercial Capitalism in Eighteenth-Century China." *Harvard Journal of Asiatic Studies* 17(1954): 130–168.

Horie, Yasuzo. "Clan Monopoly Policy in the Tokugawa Period." *Kyoto University Economic Review* 17(1942): 31–52.

"The Encouragement of Kokusan or Native Products in the Tokugawa Period." *Kyoto University Economic Review* 15(1941): 44–63.

Hoselitz, Bert F. "Social Stratification and Economic Development." *International Social Science Journal* 16(1964): 237–251.

Kessler, Lawrence D. "Ethnic Composition of Provincial Leadership during the Ch'ing Dynasty." *Journal of Asian Studies* 28(1969): 489–511.

Kublin, Hyman. "The 'Modern' Army of Early Meiji Japan." *Far Eastern Quarterly* 9(1949): 20–41.

Lamb, Helen. "The 'State' and Economic Development in India" in S. Kuznets, W. E. Moore, and J. J. Spengler, eds., *Economic Growth: Brazil, India, Japan.* Durham: Duke University Press (1955), pp. 464–495.

Latin American Perspectives, vol. 1 (1974).

Lattimore, Owen. "The Industrial Impact on China, 1800–1950" in *First International Conference on Economic History* (Paris, 1960), pp. 103–113.

Levy, Marion. "Contrasting Factors in the Modernization of China and Japan" in S. Kuznets, W. E. Moore, and J. J. Spengler, eds., *Economic Growth: Brazil, India, Japan.* Durham: Duke University Press (1955), pp. 496–536.

"Some Aspects of 'Individualism' and the Problem of Modernization of China and Japan." *Economic Development and Cultural Change* 10(1962): 225–240.

Lichtheim, George. "Marx and the Asiatic Mode of Production." *St. Anthony's Papers* 14(1963): 86–112.

Liu Kwang-ching. "Nineteenth-Century China: The Disintegration of the Old Order and the Impact of the West" in Ping-ti Ho and Tang Tsou, eds., *China in Crisis,* vol. 1, bk. 1. Chicago: University of Chicago Press (1968), pp. 93–202.

"Steamship Enterprise in Nineteenth-Century China." *Journal of Asian Studies* 19(1959): 435–456.

Lo Wan. "Communal Strife in Mid-Nineteenth Century Kwangtung: The Establishment of Ch'ih-ch'i." *Papers on China* 19(1965): 85–119.

Lockwood, William W. "Japan's Response to the West: The Contrast with China." *World Politics* 9(1956): 37–54.

McMaster, John. "The Japanese Gold Rush of 1859." *Journal of Asian Studies* 19(1960): 273–287.

Metzger, Thomas. "Ch'ing Commercial Policy." *Ch'ing-shih wen-t'i* 1(1966): 4–10.

"The Organizational Capabilities of the Ch'ing State in the Field of Commerce: The Liang-huai Salt Monopoly, 1740–1840" in W. E. Willmott, ed., *Economic Organization in Chinese Society.* Stanford: Stanford University Press (1972), pp. 9–45.

Miyazaki, Ichisada. "The Nature of the Taiping Rebellion." *Acta Asiatica* 8(1965): 1–39.

Morris, Morris D. "Towards a Reinterpretation of Nineteenth-Century Indian Economic History." *Indian Economic and Social History Review* 5(1968): 1–15.

Muramatsu, Yuji. "A Documentary Study of Chinese Landlordism in Late Ch'ing and Early Republican Kiangnan." *Bulletin of the London University School of Oriental and African Studies* 29 1966): 566–599.

Nash, Manning. "Approaches to the Study of Economic Growth." *Journal of Social Issues* 19(1963): 1–6.

Needham, Joseph. "Commentary on Lynn White, Jr., 'What Accelerated Technological Change in the Western Middle Ages?'" in A. C. Crombie, ed., *Scientific Change*. New York: Basic Books, 1963.

Obelsky, Alvan. "Japan's Transition: A Socio-Economic Interpretation." *Kobe University Economic Review* 9(1963): 1–12.

Orchard, John E. "Contrasts in the Progress of Industrialization in China and Japan." *Political Science Quarterly* (1937), pp. 18–50.

Perkins, Dwight H. "Government as an Obstacle to Industrialization: The Case of Nineteenth-Century China." *Journal of Economic History* 27(1967): 478–492.

Ranis, G. "The Financing of Japanese Economic Development." *Economic History Review* 2(1959): 440–454.

Reubens, Edwin P. "Foreign Capital and Domestic Development in Japan" in S. Kuznets, W. E. Moore and J. J. Spengler, eds., *Economic Growth: Brazil, India, Japan*. Durham: Duke University Press (1955), pp. 179–228.

Rosovsky, Henry. "Japan's Transition to Modern Economic Growth, 1868–1885" in Henry Rosovsky, ed., *Industrialization in Two Systems*. New York: Wiley (1966), pp. 91–137.

Sakai, Robert K. "The Satsuma–Ryukyu Trade and the Tokugawa Seclusion Policy." *Journal of Asian Studies* 23(1964): 391–403.

Sheldon, Charles David. "Some Economic Reasons for the Marked Contrast in Japanese and Chinese Modernization." *Kyoto University Economic Review* 23(1953): 30–60.

Shimbo, Hiroshi. "An Aspect of Industrialization in Japan in Its Formative Stage." *Kobe University Economic Review* 13(1967): 19–42.

Skinner, G. William. "Marketing and Social Structure in Rural China" (3 parts). *Journal of Asian Studies* 24(1964–1965): 3–44, 195–228, 363–400.

Spencer, Daniel L. "Japan's Pre-Perry Preparation for Economic Growth." *American Journal of Economics and Sociology* 17 (1958): 195–216.

Sun, E-tu Zen. "The Board of Revenue in Nineteenth-Century China." *Harvard Journal of Asiatic Studies* 24(1962–1963): 175–228.

"The Pattern of Railway Development in China." *Far Eastern Quarterly* 14(1955): 179–199.

Toyama, Shigekei. "Politics, Economics and the International Environment in the Meiji and Taisho Periods." *Developing Economies* 4(1966): 419–446.

Trimberger, Kay. "A Theory of Elite Revolutions." *Studies in Comparative International Development* 7(1972): 191–207.

Wang Yü-chüan. "The Rise of Land Tax and the Fall of Dynasties in Chinese History" in Joseph R. Levenson, ed., *Modern China: An*

Interpretive Anthology. New York: Macmillan (1971), pp. 130–154.

West, Philip. "The Tsinan Property Disputes (1887–1891): Gentry Loss and Missionary 'Victory.'" *Papers on China* 20(1966): 119–143.

Wittfogel, Karl A. "Die theorie der orientalischen Gesellschaft." *Zeitschrift fuer Sozialforschung* 7(1938): 90–120.

"The Foundations and Stages of Chinese Economic History." *Zeitschrift fuer Sozialforschung* 4(1935): 26–58.

Wu, James T. K. "The Impact of the Taiping Rebellion on the Manchu Fiscal System." *Pacific Historical Review* 19(1959): 265–275.

Yamamura, Kozo. "The Founding of Mitsubishi: A Case Study in Japanese Business History." *Business History Review* 41(1967): 141–160.

Documents cited

Great Britain, Board of Trade. *Annual Abstract of Statistics.*

Great Britain, Board of Trade. *British and Foreign Trade and Industry, 1854–1908.* London, 1908.

Great Britain, Parliament, House of Commons. *Sessional Papers* (consular reports).

United States, Bureau of the Census. *Historical Statistics of the United States, Colonial Times to 1957.* Washington, D.C., 1960.

United States, Statistics Bureau. *Statements of Imports of Tea and Coffee into the United States Each Year from 1789 to 1882.* Washington, D.C., 1883.

Index